BELOVED OF THE SKY

TURNING POINT SERIES

BELOVED OF THE SKY

Edited by

John Ellison

Photographs by

Christopher Harris

Broken Moon Press • Seattle

Some of the essays in this collection were written especially for this book. Others first appeared in periodicals or books; to their editors and publishers, thanks are due. The essays appear by special permission of the authors and of the publishers of the following publications:

"The Crooked Wood," copyright © 1977 by Edward Abbey. From *The Journey Home* by Edward Abbey. Used by permission of the publisher, Dutton, an imprint of New American Library, a division of Penguin Books USA, Inc.

"Losing Balance: Just How Multiple Is Our Multiple Use?" copyright © 1986 by Michael Frome. Reprinted by permission of the author. This essay originally appeared in *Wilderness*, The Wilderness Society, Summer 1983.

"Who Cares for Forests," copyright © 1990 by W. S. Merwin. Reprinted by permission of the author. This essay originally appeared in *Organica*, Summer 1990.

"Ancient Forests of the Far West," copyright © 1990 by Gary Snyder. From *The Practice of the Wild*, published by North Point Press and reprinted by permission of Farrar, Straus & Giroux, Inc.

"The Ancient Forest," copyright © 1990 by Catherine Caufield. Reprinted by special permission. This essay originally appeared in *The New Yorker*.

"From Indian Country" excerpt copyright © 1979, 1980, 1981, and 1984 by Peter Matthiessen. From *Indian Country* by Peter Matthiessen. Used by permission of Viking Penguin, a division of Penguin Books USA, Inc.

"The Forest of Eyes," copyright © 1989 by Richard Nelson. From *The Island Within*, Vintage Books, a division of Random House, Inc., New York. Originally published by North Point Press, 1989. Reprinted by permission of Susan Bergholz Literary Services, New York.

Printed in the United States of America.

ISBN 0-913089-38-9
Library of Congress Catalog Card Number 92-72432

Cover image, *Scorned as Timber, Beloved of the Sky*, (detail) by Emily Carr. Collection: Vancouver Art Gallery, Emily Carr Trust. Used by special permission of the Vancouver Art Gallery, Vancouver, British Columbia, Canada.

Text preparation: Bonnie Mackay
Copyeditor: Audrey M. Thompson
Proofreader: Paula Ladenburg

Broken Moon Press
Post Office Box 24585
Seattle, Washington 98124-0585 USA

CONTENTS

PREFACE

While estimates vary, it is commonly believed that the remaining old-growth forests in North America will be completely cut down within the next twenty years, or sooner. In the last few years, controversy about the ancient forest has raged in legislatures, in small towns, on college campuses, all over the United States and Canada, turning communities against themselves. Lines have been drawn. Generational livelihoods have been threatened. Tempers have flared—sometimes out of control. Difficult questions have emerged: Can we as a society live without the forest? How do we live without the products we need from the timber industry? Should we sell these forests to customers around the world? How do we live without the spiritual gifts an old-growth forest provides? How do we move from the emotional, over-simplified "jobs versus owls" rhetoric to a real discussion of the issues? How do we find a way to talk about this issue in a way that allows everyone a voice?

We first envisioned this project a few years ago while on a vacation drive through what is left of the Olympic National Forest, a drive that I remember from childhood as being along one of the most beautiful stretches of highway in Washington State. We drove south, with memories of thousands of acres of uncut old-growth forest. A place where one could imagine industrialized society being halted in favor of the land, in favor of the forest. We expected to see the same forested lands, the same calming forest I expected always to be there. But what we found was a shocking contrast and the shattering of the myth that the forest would go on forever. We encountered clearcuts for mile after mile. No effort had been made to leave even a buffer of trees along the road, a common practice to "hide" particularly ugly cuts from passing motorists. I realized how much I had wrongly accepted the idea that the old-growth forest would exist forever.

I happened to have a copy of Gary Snyder's *The Practice of the Wild* (North Point Press, 1990) with me on that trip. Being an admirer of Snyder's writing, I simply intended to read his essays while on my vacation. Instead, his writing caused me to think back on the scene of the logging destruction along the highway. I found myself reflecting on when I had learned my limited thoughts about the forest, when I had been taught that the forest is "renewable."

Although we are all affected by the destruction of the ancient forest, many of the writers in this collection see and feel that destruction on a daily basis. Many of them live and work in areas hardest hit by the practice of clearcutting. They have made protection and preservation of the forest a part of their life's work. In coming to realize how personal an issue this is, I have attempted to put together a *personal* book, with writings by environmentalists, journalists, poets, and some who simply love the forest. For me, the unifying thread in this "reader" is heartfelt concern and the emphasis on the stake *everyone* has in the ancient forest. We now live in a new "global community," so it follows that we need a new model upon which to build and grow this community. The old model is no longer appropriate. The writers in this collection challenge us to change our thinking about the forest as we face the turn of the twenty-first century.

Finally, a note of thanks. This collection would not have happened without the generous support of many people who gave freely of their time and advice. These friends include Scott McIntyre, Willard Holmes, and Rosemary Emery in Vancouver, B.C., who helped us obtain permission to use a detail of Emily Carr's painting *Scorned as Timber, Beloved of the Sky* on the cover of this book. This image perfectly captures the notion that there is more to an old-growth forest than simply trees as "timber." I also thank Susan Bergholz; Florence Eichin at Penguin USA; Michael Frome; Gregory McNamee, who provided leads to some of the contributors; Gary Snyder, whose writings and correspondence inspired this collection; and Joy Weiner at *The New Yorker,* who assisted me in obtaining Catherine Caufield's essay. Thanks also to Lesley Link, my co-publisher and partner, who supported this book from its beginning and also provided many suggestions on shaping its contents; and to Charlie Golder, without whose vision none of this work would have been done.

—John Ellison, Seattle

BELOVED OF THE SKY

Edward Abbey

The Crooked Wood

For four seasons I worked as a fire lookout on the North Rim of the Grand Canyon. To get to my job I walked for a mile and a half each morning up a trail through a dense grove of quaking aspens. I called this grove "the crooked wood" because the trees there, nearly all of them, have been curiously deformed. The trunks are bent in shapes that seem more whimsical than natural: dog legs, S-curves, elbows, knees. The deformity is always found in the lower part of the trunk, four or five feet above the ground. Above that level the trunks assume the vertical attitude normal to aspens, supporting the usual symmetric umbrella of graceful, delicately suspended, dancing leaves which gives this tree its specific name, *tremuloides*.

Why the deformation? The explanation is simple. On the North Rim, at an elevation of 8,000 to 9,000 feet above sea level, winter snows are heavy. In well-shaded places, such as the ridge where my crooked grove is found, massive drifts of snow survive through May and into June, overlapping part of the growing season. Under the creeping weight and pressure of these snowdrifts the young aspens—seedling and sapling—grow as best they can, in whatever direction they must, through spring after spring, seeking the sunlight that is their elixir, until they reach a height where their growth is not affected by the snow.

The life of trees. We know so little about this strange planet we live on, this haunted world where all answers lead only to more mystery. The character of trees, for example, their feelings, emotions, personalities—Shelley was not the first to speak of "the sensitive plant." The mandrake, they believed, screams when uprooted. Contemporary researchers suggest that plants respond to music (preferring Mozart to the Rolling Stones, I'm not surprised to hear) and to human emotions. I'm inclined to believe it. And I'm the type inclined to doubt. But four seasons of solitary walking under those aspen trees, through the green translucence of summer and the golden radiance of autumn, alone in the stillness of the forest, can do queer things to a man's common sense.

We think we perceive character or "personality" in the shape, face, eyes of our fellow humans; why not find something similar in the appearance of plants—especially trees? How avoid it? Obvious analogies come at once to mind: the solemnity of the dark, heavy, brooding spruce; the honest, hopeful nobility of the yellow pine; the anxiety of white fir; the remote grandeur of the bristlecone pine; the brightness, the gaiety, the charm, the feminine sensitivity, the aspiring joyousness of *Populus tremuloides*. (Our name; what the aspen calls itself we may never know.)

I can hear the laughter down in the pit and up in the peanut gallery as I write these vulnerable words. (I'm a hardnosed empiricist myself, one who believes only in what he can hear, see, smell, grab, bite into, so I understand.) But—I repeat—if you could spend as I did the sweeter part of four good years in that forest, scanning a sea of treetops for a twist of smoke, walking beneath that canopy of leaves in the chill clear mornings and again in the evenings—evenings sometimes full of golden peace and sometimes charged with storm and lightning—you too might begin to wonder, not only about yourself but also about those *beings,* alive, sentient, transpiring, which surround you. Especially the aspens, the quaking aspens, always so vibrant with light and motion, forever restless, always whispering, in tune like ballerinas to the music of the air. Walking there day after day, among those slim trim trees, so innocent (it seems) in their white and green or white and gold, you become aware after a while not only of the trees but of the trees' awareness of you. What they felt I had no notion of; I never got to know them well as individuals. But their conscious presence was unmistakable. I was not alone.

My father has been a logger, sawyer, and woodsman for most of his life. I myself have put in a fair share of time with ax, crosscut saw, chain saw, sledge, and wedge at the reduction of trees into fuel, post, and lumber. I understand and sympathize with the reasonable needs of a reasonable number of people on a finite continent. All men and women require shelter. All life depends upon other life. But what is happening today, in North America, is not rational use but irrational massacre. Man the Pest, multiplied to the swarming stage, is attacking the remaining forests like a plague of locusts on a field of grain. Knowing now what we have learned, unless the need were urgent, I could no more sink the blade of an ax into the tissues of a living tree than I could drive it into the flesh of a fellow human.

Howie Wolke

The Great Myth of Clearcut Forestry

The great myth of modern forestry is that clearcutting and related logging techniques (shelterwood, seed trees, overstory removal) emulate natural processes such as wildfire, insect infestations, windstorms, and avalanches. Mostly, though, and especially in the West, clearcutting is supposed to emulate wildfire. According to the myth, since nature periodically levels forests, we might as well do the same and obtain wood fiber for people, too. How convenient!

Many myths are born in a grain of truth. Selective applications of knowledge can create mythical Saharas of non-existent dunes. In this case, the grain of truth is that with both clearcutting and natural disturbances, living trees die and fall. And there the similarity ends. So let's get one thing straight: a clearcut does *not* mimic a natural disturbance. It's time to debunk the great myth.

For one thing, the mosaic of biotic communities formed by clearcutting and wildfire are strikingly different. A flight over Oregon's heavily clearcut Willamette National Forest, for instance, will at best reveal a horrifying checkerboard landscape of clearcuts interspersed with standing forest. At worst, the flight will occasionally reveal entire mountainsides and watersheds denuded and eroding, virtually devoid of living or dead trees.

By contrast, a visit to Yellowstone, which burned extensively in 1988, will reveal a dramatically different mosaic of standing forest burned to varying degrees interspersed with lightly or unburned green woods and lush meadows. (It's important to realize that in the burned forests of Yellowstone, unlike in clearcuts, standing trees still cover most of the land.) In places, the burn mosaic is a pattern of elongated roughly parallel strips of alternately scorched and green forest, generally running in a southwest-northeast direction, attesting to the strong prevailing winds that fanned the flames.

The fires created a habitat mosaic of incredible complexity due to a number of variable factors. Differences in wind speed and direction, slope aspect, woody fuel accumulation, and the location of natural fire barriers such as lakes, streams, and marshes are among them. Also, pre-fire species and age composition, weather, and even the time of day at which the flames reached a given location all resulted in different burn intensities at different times and locations. Depending upon the various ways in which these factors interacted at any given place, either few, many, or all of the trees were killed by the flames. The bottom line is that nature isn't neat; she abhors uniformity and consistency. There's no way that we can emulate the inconsistent and complex patterns created by these factors.

Perhaps the most profound contrast between a clearcut and a natural cataclysm is the kind of forest that follows. A major goal of clearcut forestry is to replace a biologically diverse natural forest of considerable structural complexity with a simplified tree farm of one or two economically desirable species. The goal of clearcutting is uniform simplicity; nature's "goal" is increasing complexity. And that complexity begins during the fire, with the tangled interplay of the various factors already mentioned. Moreover, burned forests often mature, sometimes to a classic old-growth condition, before they burn again. By contrast, the goal of clearcutting is to produce a "crop" that can be "harvested" again long before the forest matures, usually less than a century after the clearcut.

Compared with a natural forest—even a recently burned one—clearcuts and the tree farms that follow are biological deserts. I mentioned standing trees. Ironically, they usually characterize recent burns, like those of Yellowstone, 1988. In fact, literally *millions upon millions* of standing dead trees cover Yellowstone's burned forests. The snags will remain standing, some for many decades. Contrast that with a clearcut. There, virtually all of the standing trees are removed or piled as slash to be burned.

The ecological functions of fire-killed snags are many. Snags are habitat for beetles and other insects, which feed woodpeckers and other birds, which in turn feed hawks, owls, and other predators both furred and feathered. Many species of birds and mammals nest and roost in snags. Standing snags shade the forest floor, reducing evaporation and therefore encouraging tree reproduction. This is especially important in the central and northern Rockies, where summer drought is common and sunlight is intense. It's also important in the Pacific Northwest, where dry summers also prevail. As the snags gradually fall, they check erosion. When they fall upon stream banks they stabilize the stream bank, particularly during periods of high water.

Fallen logs also provide habitat for many critters. Grouse drum on them. Winter wrens glean insects and spiders from them. The boreal redback vole utilizes the shelter of big fallen logs. This little critter is not only primary sustenance for the American marten, but like its Pacific cousin, the California redback vole, it probably injests and spreads the spores of fungi that form mycorrhizae associations with tree roots. Without these attached fungi, tree growth is dramatically impaired. Snags (and live trees) also fall into streams where they create habitat (pools and cover) for trout and other aquatic organisms.

Snags and deadfall are important in other ways, too. Fallen trees rot: slowly in the cold arid Rockies, and more rapidly in the soggy Northwest and the humid East. Thus, in a natural forest a constant supply of nutrients is released by microorganisms into the soil. In a clearcut, though, because so much of the big woody material is removed, nutrient cycling is often impaired. Some scientists, like forest ecologist Chris Maser, now believe that the dying forests of Germany and other parts of Europe are primarily due to soil depletion stemming from many centuries of intensive logging and firewood removal. Fallen trees also nourish aquatic ecosystems. They decompose slowly in cold water, and over many decades or centuries they release nutrients basic to the aquatic food web. Again, in contrast to clearcut forests, the recent Yellowstone burns remain tree-covered. The dead trees are not at the mill; they're still in the forest. Over the next century or two, they'll nourish the soils and waters that support the plethora of life that we call the Yellowstone Ecosystem. In short, while clearcutting removes most woody material, either via log truck or by slash burning, natural lightning-ignited wildfire usually allows much of the wood to remain within the system, interacting and encouraging organic diversity in too many ways to quantify. In other words, in profound contrast to clearcutting, in the wake of fire there remains a forest ecosystem.

It is important to note that many wildfires simply aren't hot enough to really scorch the forest. Often, few live trees are killed, or only the younger trees and saplings die, leaving a park-like old-growth forest with a grassy floor and little undergrowth. Such a burn pattern characterizes many of our western Douglas fir, ponderosa pine and giant sequoia forests, which tend to burn lightly at frequent intervals. These forests remain tree-covered and green, even during and right after fire.

Conveniently and consistently excluded from the clearcut forester's argument are the roads associated with all kinds of industrial forestry, not just clearcutting. In many ways, the impact of roads upon wildland ecosystems is far worse than the actual logging. Roadcuts on steep slopes not only are horrible eyesores, but are constant sources of erosion. They frequently create mass slope failure, which results in the destruction of aquatic ecosystems of adjacent streams. Roads fragment habitat: many species simply won't cross them, so populations become isolated and vulnerable to genetic deterioration. Other species, such as elk and grizzly, show a dramatic decline in their utilization of habitat as road densities increase. Roads also kill; therefore we have the term "roadkill." Roads destroy wilderness values, eliminating vast public wildlands from formal Wilderness consideration, thus opening them to a multitude of destructive activities, not just logging. Roads provide access for poachers, off-road vehicles, miners, and subdividers. They also create avenues of disturbed ground for the spread of noxious weeds, like the Eurasian spotted knapweed in the northern Rockies. And the average Forest Service logging road completely obliterates about five acres of habitat per mile. Clearcut forests are laced with roads; wild forests, burns and all, are not.

America's national forests are already laced with about 375,000 road miles. Nearly all have been built for logging. That's about equal to one and a half times the distance from the Earth to the moon. Over 110 million acres of our 191-million-acre national forest system are already densely roaded. Another 80 million acres of national forest are still roadless and wild, but only about 33 million of these acres have been formally protected by Congress as Wilderness. Unfortunately, most of the protected lands consist primarily of high-altitude rock and ice. Almost 50 million acres, though, are still undeveloped, vulnerable de facto wilderness. Assaulting these dwindling enclaves is the ever-expanding tangled spider web network of unending forest road. The logging roads sprawl over a matrix of obvious devastation. But clearcuts and roads also cause the more subtle but very real demise of wilderness-dependent and deep forest species. The northern spotted owl, flamulated owl, northern goshawk, pileated woodpecker, American marten, grizzly, elk, and black bear are all endangered or seriously declining in parts of their ranges due to modern industrial forestry. In fact, though clothed in euphemisms ("harvest," "even-aged management," "commercial timber," "to access," etc.), legitimized by land grant universities, and sanitized by selective science, clearcutting is nothing more than old-fashioned cut-and-run, rape-and-ruin logging. At best, it transforms a forest into a farm; at worst, it leaves in its wake total long-term devastation (many clearcuts continue to fail to regenerate). So let's step beyond the myth and into reality; a typical clearcut and road-laced industrial forest, be it on private or public land, is the antithesis of a native forest with all of its natural cataclysms like wildfire. There's simply no comparison.

Some foresters advocate individual-tree and group-selection logging as a sound alternative to clearcutting. Certainly, these techniques are usually superior, creating far less ecological damage. (A good definition for group selection is the creation of a clearing no wider than the height of the surrounding forest trees. When the clearing is bigger, most responsible foresters call it a clearcut.) But it's important to realize that even selective logging requires extensive road building, skidding, use of heavy equipment and a drastic reduction in snags and deadfall. Selection forestry should be utilized where timber cutting is appropriate: private woodlots and industry-owned lands, for instance. But it's no panacea.

Many government and industry foresters are now advocating a variation on clearcutting called "New Forestry." Well, remember the "New Nixon" of 1968? That was proven to be nothing but a new image. Like the "New Nixon," the New Forestry is more image than substance. It works like this: you leave a few snags, maybe even a few live trees in the clearcut. Instead of piling all of the non-merchantible logs into slashpiles for burning, you leave some of them scattered across the ground, to encourage biodiversity. And maybe you vary the shape and reduce the size of the clearcut, too. That's better than the old 40-acre-square bare patch of total devastation, yes, but the differences are minor, not profound. Even the New Forestry fails to mimic the natural disturbances that occur in a natural forest. Most of the woody material is still removed from the ecosystem. Most of the soil is still exposed to the sun, to storms, and to heavy machinery. Log skidding still destroys the topsoil. Toxic herbicides are still used to kill vegetation that competes with the new "crop" of conifers. Cavity nesters are still deprived of habitat. And then there are the roads. . . .

American Indian activist Russell Means once declared, "Rationality is a curse, since it can cause humans to forget the natural order of things." Since we two-legged apes pretend to know far more than is remotely possible, we rationalize. But nature isn't rational; she's functional. And her functions don't always mesh with our expectations.

One could discuss the technical differences between natural wildfire and clearcutting ad nauseum. But because nature is infinitely complex, such analyses are bound to leave us groping. There's always more and our knowlege is never complete, can never be complete. Means is right: rationality often *is* a curse; it implies a level of understanding that is impossible to achieve.

Over the years, I've explored forested wildlands from Maine to Arizona and from British Columbia to Tennessee. I've also seen my share of forest wastelands. Although I consider myself relatively knowledgeable about wildland ecosystems, I'm more of a naturalist than a scientist; more of an outdoorsman than a researcher. My observations come primarily from living in and exploring forests and other wildlands. Thus, many of my observations are subjective. And that's OK. We live on the dying planet Earth, rational age, A.D. (After Dinosaurs). In the midst of the greatest extinction event since the big lizards' demise, I think it appropriate to suggest that we begin to go beyond rational thinking. Beyond it, that is, to our recent past. Back to our guts and to our emotional bond with the land. Back to the elemental observation of simple right versus wrong, survival versus death.

One needn't be a rocket scientist to see that clearcutting is wrong. Look at a landscape of clearcuts and you *know* it. One needn't have a Ph.D. to realize that a "forest" laced with roads, poisoned with chemicals, and devoid of native species isn't a forest at all. And one needn't conduct years of research to see the profound differences between a natural forest with its fires, blowdowns, and avalanches and the simplified even-aged roaded tree farms created by clearcut forestry. We need only be animals, with big brains and pretty good eyes, and most important, with heart, to see that clearcut forestry—in all of its minor variations—is patently and utterly *insane.*

I don't know if the following suggestion is rational or not, and I don't much care. What I'm about to suggest is probably politically unrealistic, too. And I hope it's grievously offensive both to clearcut foresters and to so-called "reasonable" conservationists (the ones who avoid, at all costs, making enemies). Let's save America's remaining unplundered native forests, *all* of them: not in tiny museum patches but in chunks big enough for evolution. Big enough to incorporate a shifting mosaic of disturbance-driven habitats. Big enough to protect complete native ecosystems with viable populations of all indigenous species. Let's restore big forest wilderness on abused public lands. Let's ban industrial forestry on public lands, and let's outlaw habitat destruction everywhere, period, no qualifier. That includes clearcutting. In 1987 only 13 percent of America's timber production came from the national forests. Let's learn to live with 13 percent less wood. And let's have less junk mail, less packaging, less waste.

By the same token, let's have sustainable, careful, sensitive selection forestry on private lands. It may be legal but it isn't moral to allow Weyerhaeuser, Plum Creek, Champion International, Scott Paper, and Maxam to completely denude vast forestlands to pay off junk bonds. It may be legal but it's also crazy to sacrifice virgin redwoods, old-growth rainforest, and big wilderness in the Rockies in order to supply logs to Japanese mills, to build condos in Vail or Fort Lauderdale, or to make hot tubs for enlightened liberals in Eugene. Let's kick the timber barons off the public lands and force them to do it right, on their land.

It's been noted that civilizations have decayed with the demise of the soil and the forest. In the rational age, the demise of native forests threatens the survival of all known life, not just isolated societies. It's time that we begin to treat our forests as though life on Earth is worth saving.

Edward C. Fritz

They Can Log Without Clearcutting

In our federal forests, from coast to coast, the almost universal system of logging is clearcutting and its two-stage variations, seed tree, shelterwood, and huge group cuts. They call them the "even-age system." This is the most devastating system of continuous logging ever devised.

There are two ways to end even-age devastation in federal forests. We need them both. One way is to ban all logging there. Congress has shown no inclination to do that except in old-growth forests and some other wooded areas, including wildernesses, that are rich in native biodiversity.

Forest reformers are urging Congress to preserve several million more acres. That leaves 80 million acres of federal timberland unprotected from even-age ravishment.

The second way is to shift to selection management on all unprotected timberlands, with special provisions to spare native ecosystems. This is a system that produces wood without destroying biodiversity.

Selection involves the growing of trees of several ages and species in each stand, cutting a small minority of various sizes every five to twenty years, and leaving the rest, including the most promising specimens, for future harvests. It is classic silviculture, but most industrial timber companies and government agencies have avoided it.

On June 4, 1990, Dale F. Robertson, Chief of the Forest Service, directed a 70 percent reduction in clearcutting. He called for "ecosystem management." The trouble is, he proposed that his agency replace clearcutting with two-stage clearcuts. That is essentially more of the same. The Chief also mentioned selection as an option, but that is like telling a whiskey drinker to shift to vodka, gin, or milk.

Dr. Jerry Franklin, veteran Forest Service researcher, while decrying the brutalities of clearcutting and advocating a "new forestry," does not call for selection management. He recommends patching up and re-motivating even-age forests, including by clearcutting and shelterwood cutting.

There are those who say selection cannot be done in Douglas fir, or on the slopes greater than 70 percent, or in the Cascades, but I have seen selection management thriving in these sites.

In the Pacific Northwest, for example, for twenty-seven years the Malcolm McIntosh family has been maintaining and harvesting a selection forest of about five hundred acres ten miles south of Olympia, Washington. Big Douglas fir, western red cedar, Oregon ash, red alder, big leaf maple, and western hemlock thrive there in beautiful majesty. Beneath them, little disturbed by periodic logging of a tree here and another there, the naturally regenerated seedlings, saplings, and middle-canopy progeny of the big trees grow on, along with colorful vine maple, red huckleberry, Oregon grape, and diverse other species. The leaf litter and soil are rich with small to microscopic plants, animals, and fungi that are vital to the health of larger species. And almost every kind of animal known to that place since the arrival of European man probably survives there.

You can log and maintain diversity. Jack Winn, Olympia forester, does it for the McIntosh family.

In Oregon, Portland forester Scott Ferguson and others have been managing predominantly Douglas fir, alder, Oregon white oak, and grand fir on rugged slopes under the selection system since 1923, with ever-improving quantity and yields.

Around Dunsmuir, California, Hal Bowman operates several forests under selection. Near Redding, W.M. Beaty, selection-manages 465,000 acres. Their forests include Douglas fir, incense cedar, ponderosa pine, sugar pine, and California black oak.

Still further south, adjoining Yosemite National Park, forester James E. Greig, of Lake Havasu City, Arizona, manages an imposing forest of white fir, sugar pine, incense cedar, and other species under single-tree selection. On the coastal range, north of Santa Cruz, he manages an eye-pleasing forest dominated by huge redwoods, and including Pacific dogwood, tan oak, coast live oak, and most of the plants and animals of the old Redwood groves.

In places, these forests have steep slopes, but the operators move the logs under selection without a hint of harm to the ecosystem. Moreover, under selection, the roads are narrow and hug the contours, in contrast to the broad, straight highways of the Forest Service that cause erosion and fragmentize the forest.

In 1989, I conducted a nationwide mail survey of three hundred foresters. The sixty respondents estimated that, state by state, a mean of 46 percent of private non-industrial forests are selection-managed. In Washington, foresters estimated only 1 percent, the lowest in the nation. The commercially available timber in national forests in Washington is totally under even-age management, except some experimental plots. It is not surprising that few Washington citizens mention selection as a solution to the crisis. They simply don't know enough about it.

The Oregon tally was only 5 percent selection. California registered close to 98 percent selection. California regulates private logging fairly strictly.

Those who use even-age logging exclusively, like the U.S. Forest Service in most regions, claim that selection management is less profitable. However, the only in-depth economic comparison indicates that selection is more economical on a cost/benefit basis and also on a cost efficiency standard. The Forest Service made that study at its experimental station at Crossett, Arkansas, but scarcely mentions it.

Selection management relies upon natural regeneration, thereby avoiding the heavy costs of site preparation (usually by bulldozer or herbicides) and planting incurred after clearcutting, and its two-stage variants, seed-tree and shelterwood cutting.

In the last seven years, I have observed and photographed private selection forests from coast to coast. Some look almost as rich as old-growth forests. Others concentrate on commercial trees. But all of them have far richer diversity than the even-age stands of the U.S. Forest Service, Bureau of Land Management, Bureau of Indian Affairs, or state agencies.

To save native diversity at its fullest, we need to stop logging altogether in a wider variety of old-growth communities. Without human intervention, Nature has done an incomparable job of transforming native diversity into an infinitesimal maze, rich with gene pools from which some elements are likely to survive everything from ice ages to global warming—everything, that is, except massive human exploitation.

But it is politically unlikely that we can stop logging in all our remaining old-growth federal forests. Wherever Congress chooses not to save Nature from logging, we must insist, at least, on saving her from even-age logging.

Citizens have failed for two decades to convince federal agencies to shift from even-age to selection management. Under an outdated 1930 law, called Knutson-Vandenberg, the Forest Service can and does allocate almost three hundred million dollars per year to its own budget from even-age sales even though most of those sales lose money. The KV law does not allow nearly so large an allocation from selection sales. With this budget-padding incentive, the bureaucrats fervently cling to even-age logging.

Many citizens have concluded that the only road to reform is legislative. In response, Congressman John R. Bryant, of Dallas, Texas (three hours from the national forests of East Texas), filed the Forest Biodiversity and Clearcutting Prohibition Act to restrain even-age logging in all national forests. Sixty-nine congressmen of both parties and sexes, from Florida to California, co-sponsored the bill. On June 16, 1992, the House Agriculture Committee gave the bill a hearing, but declined to approve it. Bryant is expected to file a stronger bill in 1993. Senator David L. Boren of Oklahoma has filed a bill by the same name in the Senate.

These bills also require the maintenance of native diversity to the extent possible under whatever exploitation (logging, mining, grazing, pond-building, etc.) may continue in the national forests.

Most supporters of clearcutting restraint also want to preserve all remaining patches of old-growth timber in the national forests. Regardless of how much old-growth Congress may prevent from logging, the old-growth patches cannot long retain their complete native diversity in a vacuum. Under modern principles of biogeographical fragmentation, native diversity cannot maintain itself in small "islands." The vast "seas" in between, where logging proceeds, must also maintain some native diversity, or the entire gene pool will decline. That is why clearcutting-restraint legislation is essential to the long-range well-being of the earth, including that of human beings.

One of the best ways to get a grip on the clearcutting issue is to analyze why federal agencies avoid individual-tree-selection, also known as all-age, all-tree-species selection management. My book *Clearcutting: A Crime Against Nature* (Eakin Press, 1989) presents such an analysis, including the following:

Why Do the Bureaucrats Avoid Individual Tree Selection?

In answer to this big question, let us first analyze some reasons that they give:

1. They say they have to clearcut to grow their chosen species.

The Forest Service insists that the various pines and hardwoods that bring the best market returns are too shade-intolerant to regenerate in the selection system. They say that, without radical clearing, loblolly pines in the Gulf Coastal Plain, nuttall oaks in moist sites of the Deep South, black cherry on some Appalachian Mountain sites, ponderosa and sugar pine in the Rockies, lodgepole pine further west, and Douglas fir on the West Coast, cannot get started as seedlings and saplings in adequate numbers to grow into well-stocked stands.

Selection foresters prove this to be false. Over and over, they have demonstrated excellent natural regeneration in individual-tree-selection forests. Gordon Robinson did it with Douglas fir and ponderosa pine on a million acres of Southern Pacific Transportation Company lands in California and Oregon. Individual Tree Selection Management does it in Oregon. Leo Drey regenerates southern red oak, white oak and shortleaf pine on 173,000 acres in Missouri. Chuck Stoddard regenerates red pine and other species naturally in Wisconsin. Leon Tolliver does it with northern red oak and tulip poplar on his weekend four hundred acres near Bedford, Indiana. Leon Neal regenerates longleaf pine and various hardwoods that way in Southern Georgia, and Wilmon Timberlands regenerates a wide diversity on varying sites in Alabama. Hundreds of others raise many forest types productively on many kinds of sites, for a profit.

I have observed saplings coming up by the hundreds around my feet in most of these forests. It can be done. It is being done on millions of acres.

2. They say selection harvesting is a lost art.

The Forest Service argues that a timber owner can no longer find foresters who know how and when to select the trees that should be removed and chain-saw operators who can fell trees without excessively damaging the "save" trees.

The timber industry makes grants to forestry schools, including research grants and chair endowments. Schools that depend most heavily on timber industry grants tend to emphasize even-age management. This does create a growing shortage of all-around foresters. Nevertheless, you can still find some in every region and selection harvesting skills will revive rapidly if we curtail clearcutting.

As to operators, numerous loggers in every region can still aim the drop so that the unharvested trees in a selection stand are not damaged. They do so for the landowners who selectively harvest. They also aim the drop when thinning even-age stands.

When he went into the selection system, Paul Shaffner, of Fordyce, Arkansas, had to train his chain-saw contractors how to fell marked trees more cleanly. The initial training cost him some dollars, but he soon made up for it in increased vigor of the trees saved.

Shaffner obtained his forestry degree at Yale University, where they still teach selection management, as well as clearcutting.

3. They say that selection management requires more roads than even-age.

In the Monongahela National Forest Plan and EIS (July 1986), the Forest Service wooed some citizen groups away from a selection alternative by claiming that selection required more roads. Agency planners pulled this trick by arbitrarily allowing more public use of the roads in the selection than in the even-age alternative, and by claiming that uneven-age requires more frequent entries (although this system requires no site preparation, and no burning, and no thinning other than at regular harvest time). The EIS ignored the fact that selection forestry can be practiced all the way to the edge of existing roads where clearcutting is not allowed for aesthetic reasons.

In actual practice, selection forests require no greater road mileage nor higher standards than even-age management. In fact, the roads that I've seen in selection forests were narrower than most Forest Service roads, and were often closed canopy, yet quite passable in all seasons.

I have also observed numerous wash-outs on Forest Service roads.

4. They say clearcutting brings bigger dollars.

When you argue with clearcutters down to the bottom line, their main reason for insisting on clearcutting becomes just that, the bottom line.

In the 1976 Texas clearcutting case under the Monongahela case precedent of 1974, Forest Service and timber company witnesses testified that selective harvesting was not profitable. They swore that nobody could stay in business doing it. The environmentalists found Paul Shaffner, a timber operator from Arkansas, who took the stand against the Forest Service and proved that he was making a satisfactory profit at selection harvesting. Obviously, he was not buying any timber from the Forest Service.

Many Texas timber owners are making a profit on individual-tree selection stands.

Louisiana Pacific's Southern Division practices individual-tree selection on its own lands and many other lands throughout the South that it manages for smaller owners.

Here is a passage from LP's 1987 slick-paper color brochure:

> Louisiana-Pacific's motto, "Helping the forest work for people," starts with LP Forestry's environmentally sound forest management policy of single tree selection, which allows the forest to grow and reproduce naturally. The excessive costs and detrimental environmental impacts associated with clear-cutting are avoided.

When the Forest Service offers a clearcut sale, it gives no choice to LP or anyone else to use selection harvesting. So LP-Southern clearcuts on Forest Service land, a genuine tragedy.

Temple-Eastex, Inc., the largest timber owner in Texas, used selection harvesting until it merged with Time, Inc. Arthur Temple, Jr., who then headed the combined company, told me that the financial experts in New York showed him figures indicating that clearcutting was more profitable, so he permitted the change to clearcutting. Even after spinning back to a separate company, Temple continued to clearcut.

5. They don't tell you how expensive clearcutting is.

The Forest Service does not acknowledge the biggest expense of clearcutting—interest charges. They invest a lot of money for site preparation and planting and do not receive most of their returns until the timber sale some forty to one hundred twenty years later. This involves a heavy charge for the use of money, realistically at least 7.5 percent, cumulative. The Forest Service should include that interest in its sale price to the company that buys the timber. But the Service uses a much lower figure, 4 percent. On some items, it omits the interest cost altogether.

When we apply a realistic interest rate (under sound economic procedures reversed into a "discount" rate), the costs of clearcutting exceed the returns in almost all national forests, according to forest economist Randal O'Toole in *Citizen's Guide to Economics.*

Selection harvesting is different. It does not involve site preparation and planting (a major saving in itself). Each stand involves a harvest every five to twenty years. Pre-commercial thinning is done at the same time, reducing that cost. Once sustained yield is established in a stand, the expenses forever after are mostly in the same year as the harvest, and altogether in the same decade or so. The interest charges are minimal.

Using sound accounting methods, some forest economists have shown that 109 national forests out of 122 making timber sales are losing money. Randal O'Toole, of Portland, Oregon, calculates the overall total loss on timber sales for FY 1991 at $314,456,000.00. The Forest Service used its own highly convoluted accounting system that counts certain road-building and other costs as revenues. It claims overall net revenues every year, although it concedes that a majority of national forests are receiving less revenues than their costs.

Dr. James B. Baker, director of the Forest Service Experiment Station at Monticello, Arkansas, compared the economics of selection and even-age over a fifty-year period. He reported a cost efficiency of "conventional" selection at 143.2 board feet of sawlogs produced per dollar of costs, compared to 55.2 for an even-aged plantation, a two-and-a-half to one advantage. Adding pulp and poles to the picture, the advantage decreased to about 20 percent. But our national forests are mainly in the sawlog business.

Using a discount rate of 7 percent, Baker also calculated net present value at 341 for selection and 444 for plantation, but he later wrote:

> The high NPV for even-aged plantation management is misleading in that it resulted more from the relatively large investment required by the system than from its efficiency. The results of this comparison indicate that a landowner should select this system only if he desires one of the non-economic benefits associated with it—such as maximum total output or production, the opportunity to plant superior seedlings, or ease of management.

In a commentary on the Baker paper, Texas forester Bill Carroll wrote:

> Under the multiple use and other concepts in our national forests, "maximum total output," "superior seedlings" and "ease of management" should give way to public benefit. Furthermore, the Forest Service's use of "superior seedlings" on a grand scale is reducing our native diversity and is saddling our timber stock with strains that are more susceptible to insects and diseases.

A private company might be able to justify to its stockholders the use of drastic surgery on its lands in order to produce a larger profit in the short run. To damage the public lands for such a slender increase in returns would be unconscionable. The government is not supposed to be driven by the profit motive in running the public lands, especially not at the expense of native diversity, wildlife, recreation, soil, and other benefits to present and future generations. Of course, the Forest Service says it has all those other benefits in mind as well as profits, but that answer is contrived, as we shall discuss.

In many regions, there is probably some labor saving in the logging stage of clearcutting because, with larger openings and with operators intending to knock down all the vegetation anyhow, loggers can use heavier skidders and can operate them at a higher speed. The Forest Service claims that intensive logging, even during market slumps, is necessary to provide employment. If that is true, then the selection system would be preferable, since it requires more employees.

Furthermore, the Forest Service is in no position to insist on maximum profits from its sales. It sells its timber in all but two regions at a loss to the American taxpayer. When there is a market glut and offerings fail to attract bidders, the Forest Service reoffers its timber at lower minimum prices, suffering even greater losses.

Since raising most species of trees is something the Forest Service cannot do under even-age management without selling below cost, there is no sense in ripping up our national forests under this method. We would do better to let private timberlands supply that portion of our timber demand.

In short, the Forest Service's economic defense of even-age management is skewed.

6. They don't count the intangible losses.

The Forest Service does not take into account many of the costs of cutting timber that make timber harvesting in the national forests even more of a waste of money than economists indicate. Among these costs are losses of soil, water quality, wildlife habitat, native diversity, and natural open space recreation. They are left out of benefit/cost analyses because they are not readily quantified.

Although the Forest Service refuses to assign dollars to decreases in acreages for wildlife and recreation, John White, assistant director of the Forest Service in Washington, in an interview with the *Knoxville News-Sentinel* published May 10, 1987, showed how the Forest Service takes advantage of wildlife and recreation benefits. Admitting that "some" national forests lose money on timber sales, White added that some timber sales are designed to achieve some wildlife objective, and concluded "...we do receive some benefits in wildlife protection, as well as some recreational uses."

In Monongahela National Forest, staffers showed us several

clearcuts that they had the nerve to claim were designed for black bear and varying hare (snowshoe rabbit), although there were already numerous other clearcuts available for whatever tendencies black bear might have to leave the deep forests to which they are well adapted, and for the varying hare, as well.

The Forest Service also fails to include the cost of fertilizers that would be necessary because of losses of soil nutrients resulting from repeated clearcuts.

7. They claim that selection cannot be done on a grand scale.

In its recent forest plans, the Forest Service has included an ever-evolving appendix delineating the arguments against selection management. Always adept at defenses, the bureaucrats claim that the selection system is too complex, variable, and tree-specific to fill the need for forest-wide production predictions and planning ("forest-level timber regulation," they call it). They say that stable annual production is necessary for a big agency and the economy that it serves.

The bureaucrats fail to note that several private companies are successfully regulating timber under the selection system on acreages comparable to national forests. These include Louisiana-Pacific, on one million acres in the South, Leo Drey on 153,000 acres in Missouri, and Collins Pine on 87,000 acres in California. The Forest Service, itself, was able to inventory and to regulate the national forest timber on the selection basis until 1964, when it switched to clearcutting.

With all of its defenses exposed, even-age logging is hanging on like tobacco manufacturing. A dedicated Congress or President can end it on federal lands. Before that is likely to happen, hundreds of thousands of citizens will have to express their views.

C. L. Rawlins

On Spread Creek

"Why do all the meadows have stumps in them?" I looked at the woman, her silver hair bobbing slightly with the stride of her easy old horse. At her back was an opening in the forest, hemmed by lodgepole, bare ground filling in with fireweed and blueberry elder. It was 1973. I was taking dudes on a ride in the upper forks of Spread Creek. The only reason for the road being there was to haul logs. The dudes were incidental.

"It's a timber cut. It was thick woods before. See how square the margins are? The natural openings all have grass and sedge in them, not this shrubby stuff."

"How long ago did they cut it?" Her straw hat cast a shadow over her eyes.

I looked at the stumps just starting to go silver from the weather, at the thick patches of fireweed and a few raspberries starting to come in. "Eight, ten years. We passed some newer ones coming in. You can still see the Cat tracks."

"Cat?"

"Caterpillar tractor, what they use to pile the slash to burn it."

"Slash?"

"The leftovers, scrap. Tops, limbs, the wood that's too small to truck out. They pile it up and torch it. See that bare hump with the thick bushes around it?" I reined into the cut-block and she followed, the hooves of the horses quieter than on the hardpacked road. Burnt stubs fingered out of a low mound. Getting off my horse, I kicked at the chalky dirt, turning up charcoal. "This was a big slashpile. The ash fertilized around it, so the bushes come in thick, but the heat sterilized the dirt where the pile burned. It won't grow much for a while."

She ran out of questions. But at least she asked. Not many people did. I never knew whether they saw the clearcuts as necessary subtractions from the landscape, or whether they noticed them at all. The line of dudes and horses went out of sight ahead, but I saw the flash of sunglasses, her husband looking back. "We'd better catch up." I mounted and reined toward the dirt road.

From the east, following the thin crescents of horse tracks, came the wagons. The bishop's pair of white Shires led the train. Hooped canvas thumped like sails in the noon breeze. The bishop waved and his draft team tossed their heads. It looked like something out of a movie, or a dream. The woman fumbled for her camera. Under the plank wagonboxes, I could see the fat, black rubber tires.

The people on the wagon trips wanted it easy: they could ride gentle horses or loll on the foam-padded benches in the wagons, which made down into beds. They paid a hundred or so a day, per head, to be dragged over logging roads in the north end of the Gros Ventre Range and feel like—what?—pioneers, I guess.

We pulled into camp about three. The canvas flies of the chuckwagon were spread like sooty wings, and the iron fireboxes were staked in place. The trucks were hidden behind some thick spruce, but I could see the glint of a bumper. After the horses were hobbled and turned out, I got a double-bit axe and a two-handed crosscut—the Misery Whip—and started to get wood for camp. There was a dead lodgepole nearby, and the ring of the axe brought the dudes with their cameras.

When the tree came down, Uncle Marvin limped out to grab the helm of the crosscut, and we bucked the tree into three-foot lengths, cameras clicking like hail around us. "Keep it old-timey," the boss said, "because that's what they pay for." We were expected to wear cowboy hats, western shirts, and boots. "No ski-resort T-shirts or baseball caps or stuff like that."

I felt like I was cheating the dudes with all this Western shuck-and-jive, while something else was being overlooked. It wasn't the horse lore or the woods-craft that nagged. It was the deception we practiced, the rubber-tired haywagons tricked up with planks and white canvas. We were actors in a thoroughly American drama. Manifest Destiny: a Passion Play. We revived the frontier illusion, one week at a shot.

If people had asked, we might have talked about the clearcuts and the roads, which seemed to me to be linked with our wagon-train of tourists, part of the same strange fabric, whether of history or misunderstanding. I might have taught them to recognize a few plants—mule-ear sunflower, lupine, larkspur—but most of them were impatient with such things. They wanted to learn how to saddle a horse, how to swing a double-bit, how to hinge-cut a dead pine so that it would fall, just so. I would scuff two marks, shoulderwidth, on the ground with my cowboy boot and take bets that the firewood tree would fall between them.

The dudes had time and money to spend. We drew a lot of doctors and lawyers and midwestern retirees. I liked most of the people I guided, but I also liked to disillusion them. Something about them scared me: their eagerness to believe. At times, when the cameras clicked at one of our *tableaux*, I felt like those hired characters at Disneyland, with the white gloves and the rubber heads. Around the night fire, when my guitar was supposed to ring with "Goodbye, Old Paint" and "The Old Chisholm Trail," I'd throw in a heartbreaker by Buffy Sainte-Marie, "Now That the Buffalo's Gone." History. Conscience. In the quiet that followed, it seemed the night grew eyes.

Each day there were a few uncomfortable questions. Q: Where does this road go? A: To clearcuts. Q: What's all this rusty junk—this cable? A: Junk. The loggers left it. Q: When will the trees grow back? A: Who knows?

Faced with clearcuts, the illusion wavered. For them, I guess, it was like heading for the beach and ending up in a fish cannery. But they wanted to believe, despite the graded roads and other evidence, that they were in some way first. Where they recognized damage, they wanted to believe it was an exception, that the West was still fresh and empty. I shared that regret, because I shared their hunger, for Shining Mountains, for virgin ground, for a paradise always on the edge of what was known.

My family came to the Great Basin and the Rockies in the late 1840s and lived as farmers, ranchers, teachers, teamsters, quarriers, and mining engineers. We wintered out, proved up, and got by, but there was a longing for something besides what we had, a restless desire.

My grandad set me on a horse before I could walk. The year before the wagons, 1972, I spent three months south of the Tetons, in the drainage of Grey's River, herding and wrangling, without seeing an electric light or riding in a car. I lived on horseback, slept in a tent without mosquito net, and got a sense of how-it-all-was. I saw bears almost every day, and was bugled and charged by elk. After cooking, I stared into the fire each night, trying to gaze into the heart of the world.

But I saw other things that I didn't want to see: steep roads bleeding silt, rusty snakes of cable half-buried, and little streams blown out into collapsing gulleys, taking twelve-foot drops where the snowmelt hit raw, track-chewed soil.

Clearcuts. While Teton National Park had grown and Jackson Hole had become a profitable fantasy-preserve, the Grey's River country had been mined for quick timber. Logging roads, chopped into steep slopes, were crumbling into the creeks. Half-burnt slash-piles looked like funeral pyres. Hedges of blowdown were jack-strawed at the edge of the woods. Riding down from the roadless upper canyons into the logged-out zone was like coming on the aftermath of a battle.

I wheeled my horse and rode away, but something whispered after. As much as I loved the mountains, I had begun to know that consequences lived there, too. I had begun to sense how all events, all changes, all effects communicated to every part of the land.

My guiding didn't begin with the wagon train. I started with pack trips into the southern Absaroka Range, over trails into the forks of Pacific Creek and the Buffalo River. "What's that over there?" they'd say. A bear in the berries, a moose in the willows, an eagle tipping broad wings, catching light at the edge of the sky. One night I took out my guitar and sang for the boss's daughter: a mistake. A week later, I was stuck on the wagons where she was head cook, to wrangle, run camps, and yodel at each night's fire.

But I would have done anything to be in the mountains that year. Scrubbed tin plates. Dug toilet holes. Between wrangling and guiding and driving, I walked away from camp, trying to get the feel of the place. I remember the names in that country: *Togwotee Pass, Grizzly Creek, Buff Creek, Grouse Creek, Kettle Creek, Grouse Mountain.* "What's over that ridge?" they'd ask: *Bearpaw Fork, Skull Creek, Hidden Lake, Aspen Creek, Lily Lake, Mount Leidy.*

After the first snow, the dude business trickled to nothing. The boss told me I was a hell-of-a-hand and offered me a big raise and a hunting camp to run. I pictured a wall-tent full of drunks, each boasting that he, the first goddamn thing in the morning, would bag the biggest son-of-a-bitching elk ever seen in Wyoming and You Bastards Will Be Kissing My Ass. "Sorry," I muttered. On the wagon train, my working hours had been from 5 A.M. to 11 P.M. I was worn out. And I had to get away from the boil of the fantasy.

When I hear, as one often hears in the West, that tourists are our only future, that we are to become innkeepers and dude wranglers and waitresses, I feel grim. It's not the travelers themselves so much as the dumb pressure of their belief, the lurching burden of our Western myth.

I'd rather drink with loggers, who at least know the smell and touch of woods, who may at times feel the power of the trees they cut, who have been afraid, hanging a big one on the stump and wondering which way to run. I'd rather drink with cowboys, who have endured animal perversity and bad weather, who see the basic link between grass and flesh, between livelihood and the land. Even in our disagreement, there's a common knowledge. My notions might lean toward a different future than theirs, but we share a reference in the land. In our arguments, the land, and not desire, is the axiom.

I have a friend, Shelley, who fiddles in a swing band. She also waits tables. We met in Utah, two musicians in a Mormon town. She was a violinist, city-bred, gently trained, but she learned to fiddle while she got a forestry degree. She wanted to live in Wyoming and work in the woods. So she became a forester, laying out timber sales in the north end of the Gros Ventre Range.

In the late seventies, we met sometimes on the Union Pass Road when I hauled water from a spring. She wasn't happy. She would shake her head and sigh. "It isn't like I hoped," she'd say. "We're cutting too much, too fast. It's pretty sad."

I was a range foreman, camped out on Pinion Ridge with a Shoshoni crew, spiking log fence up to keep the Fish Creek cows from dropping south into the Upper Green with the first snows. I lived there for three summers in a tent, building buck-and-pole fence, and watched clearcuts march over ridgetops and along the little creeks, notching the horizon. We learned to pull off the narrow roads, shut down the pickup, and listen for logging trucks. You could hear the drivers, miles away, gunning around the long curves. Loaded, going off the hill, they were careful. Coming back empty, they were dangerous.

The next year, I didn't find Shelley in the mountains anymore. She'd quit her timber job and joined a band. The guitar player, now her husband, was an ex-wildlife biologist. It can be hard to reconcile your need to be in the woods with what you'll do to stay there. Jackson Hole absorbs a lot of refugees from those quiet wars.

I recall, from a college anthropology text, that it's hard to analyze personality apart from culture. Culture—all those shared assumptions about *what is*—provides a structure to which our identities can cling. We learn early to fit our perceptions into this deeper sense of order.

It's strange, looking back, how I lived out the whole frontier dance, step by step, as if there were a pattern etched in my bones. How I learned to stalk deer and swing a double-bit. How I rode horseback, leading the wagons. How I built log fences and herded stock. How I was drawn to cabins at the road's far end. How I tried to know my place, my heritage, my forebears, by doing precisely what had been done, by stumbling in the ruts. How clearcuts were a part of what I was, as much as the horses, or the wagons, or the songs.

You go so far, and then the way is lost. The sun, that beacon in the west, goes down and the clouds open on expressionless dark. And the stars, that night, don't seem to be scattered diamonds, or distant campfires, or witnessing eyes. You see the dark for what it is, and look straight through your dreams. And the stars blur and prism through tears. And you turn to where the sun might rise again, and in the cold, you wait.

~~~

Things don't make more sense now, but my feelings do. I work in the mountains still, collecting rain and snow, monitoring long-range air pollution in a wilderness. But I spend more time at home. In our garden, the peas grow, dreaming in their pods, rounding in the late June rain, and I know them, long before I taste and see. In August the smell of sage accompanies thunder, and the eastern clouds trail rainbows down the lanes of mountain after-
~~~

noon. The garden fills out and our baskets fill up. I like to turn the egg-sized red potatoes up with just my hands and feel the moist cling of the earth around their skins.

At first, the trees were like ore, a wealth simply to be taken. You couldn't put fly ash back into the earth and grow more coal. So we cut the trees, sowing fire and flood. Out of that disillusionment came the National Parks and Forest Reserves.

Then, wearing science like an ammunition belt, we decided we could grow pines as straightforwardly as peas, or red potatoes. That we could go into the mountains of the west and blade roads, hack out the harvest, skid it down, haul it to the mill, dozer-pile the slash, torch it off, and zang: new trees for old. If trees grew here before, they damn well would again, and again, and again.

And then we had to start seedling farms for conifers, and try to replant on the cuts that didn't come back green. And then we replanted the bad plantations, once, twice, and fenced out the cows, and sent minimum-wage crews in to poison the ground squirrels in their holes, so they wouldn't gnaw the planted seedlings.

And then we found out how much sheer, cellular effort was tied up in those trees, and about nutrient losses, surface temperatures, and soil compaction. We found out that burning slashpiles didn't work like natural groundfire. Phrases like "cumulative effects" and words like "biodiversity" began to show up. And those bald spots on the aerial photos began to look more and more like a fatal disease.

I can grasp the thrill of a brand-new, yellow, articulated highwheel loader that can juggle four-foot-thick logs; the thrill of a metallic-blue Peterbilt with chrome stacks as big around as your head, and of hearing the diesel rap back from the ranks of pine; the gleam of new, oiled sawchain spinning around a forty-eight-inch bar, the spew of fragrant chips, and the condensed whump of a big fir hitting the dirt; the rush of banking big checks that seem to come straight from Almighty God.

And you can see the results, as I've seen them in the Gros Ventres, the Absarokas, the Salt Rivers, the Wyoming Range, the Hoback, the Snake River Range, the Bighorns, the Bear Rivers, the Uintas, the Wasatch, the Sawtooth, and the Medicine Bow. You can see the scraped ground, the tangled slash, the rusty chokers, the slumping banks, the gashed streams, the silted gravel, the rutted roads, and you can feel the sadness that hovers over every ill-used place.

In our minds, we still hold that forested archetype, cherishing the grand scale of this continent. *It will come back,* we say, closing our eyes both to the stumps and to the asphalt battlegrounds. *It will come back.* And there is, too, a corresponding kind of squint-eyed, tight-fisted, broad-shouldered insistence in the American mind, an anger that strains against the massive guilt we have incurred.

Why do all the meadows have stumps in them? It's strange, how that question repeats itself. How, after twenty years, it acts like a lens to focus so much in so few words. Yet I can't picture the woman's face. I see her white straw hat, and the way its arc of shadow hid her eyes, and her hair, a gentle silver in the sun. And the way she held her shoulders back, waiting to hear what I'd say.

I thought I was a guide. How many questions was I asked that year? *Where does this road go? Is the trail good? What's over that ridge? What's that in the willows? What did the Indians call this place?* How many questions was I asked and how many did I think I'd answered? Yet hers is the only one that still carries a voice, even if the face and name are gone.

Michael Frome

Losing Balance: Just How Multiple Is Our Multiple Use?

Almost twenty-five years ago the director of information of the U.S. Forest Service, Clint Davis, an intrepid public relations man if ever there was one, invited me to join him on a pack trip in the Bridger Wilderness of western Wyoming. In those days I knew little about "multiple use" or "sustained yield" or any of those other goodies from the forestry lexicon. I was captivated, however, by what I discovered on the trail—a thousand clear lakes, massive rock formations almost as large as those in Yosemite, living glaciers, flowering alpine meadows, and snowy starkness high above timberline. If this was part of the multiple use and scientific management, I was all for them. I wanted to join the front line of advocates and supporters of these principles.

In the quarter century since then I daresay that I have seen more of the national forests, out in the field with all kinds of folks from rangers to strangers, than anyone not directly associated with the Forest Service, and probably more than most people who work for the agency. Even after all this time, I continue to feel the same way: I believe in multiple use, forestry, and the role of the national forests in the American scheme of things.

Multiple use is a valid and sound concept, a design to protect and perpetuate public forests in the interests of all people. Whether it is properly applied in practice, or applied at all, is another matter.

Origin of Multiple Use Concept

To trace its historic roots, multiple use begins with Theodore Roosevelt and Gifford Pinchot. While president early in the century, Roosevelt declared, "If there is any duty which more than another we owe to our children and our children's children to perform at once, it is to save the forests of this country, for they constitute the first and most important element in the conservation of natural resources of the country."

That was the foundation on which the national forest system as we know it today came into being. Pinchot, chief forester of the United States under Roosevelt and his close ally, saw forestry not as a technical end in itself, but as a democratic force: "The rightful use and purpose of our natural resources is to make the people strong and well, able and wise, well-taught, well-fed, well-clothed, well-housed, full of knowledge and initiative, with equal opportunity for all and special privilege for none."

Pinchot sparked a cadre of social and land-use reformers. Of the eight men of vision who joined to found The Wilderness Society in 1935, four—Bernard Frank, Aldo Leopold, Benton MacKaye, and Robert Marshall—were trained in the Forest Service ranks. Marshall, in a classic little book, *The People's Forests,* which has too long been forgotten, discussed forest values and uses: "As sources of greatly needed raw material [the forests] play a vital part in raising the physical standards of American life. As conservers of soil and water they are absolutely necessary if we are not willing to have our country become as denuded and flood-swept as the Chinese hillsides and valleys. As environment for the highest type of recreational and aesthetic enjoyment, they are essential to the happiness of millions of human beings. Economic, physical, and social considerations all demand that we maintain a bountiful forest resource."

Marshall wrote this book in 1933. Six years later, when he was in charge of recreation and lands for the Forest Service, his friend, Chief Forester Ferdinand A. Silcox, put it all together and called it multiple use. In his 1939 annual report, Silcox explained that national forests were to be "administered on a multiple-use basis." He went on to elaborate that Forest Service stewardship involved more than mere protection of national forests from fire, insects, and disease but included the development and administration of all aspects of the forest—land, water, timber, forage, wildlife, and recreation—for the public welfare.

From the very beginning of the Forest Service through World War II, multiple use—or at least conservative use—remained in force. National forests generally were administered with restraint in order to ensure their future. The two exceptions were grazing, often abusive and destructive regardless of regulation, and mining, spurred and sanctioned by the generous Mining Law of 1872 and sustained by the political influence of the industry. Pressures for federal timber were light, however, and logging was in scale with other uses.

The record since the end of World War II differs sharply. The 1960 Multiple Use-Sustained Yield Act endeavored to keep things on track, defining national forest purposes as based on "the most judicious use of the land for some or all of these resources," referring to outdoor recreation, soil, timber, watershed, wildlife, and fish. But it has not functioned effectively.

Does Multiple Use Work? "Management always implies use, but 'use' does not necessarily require the harvesting of a crop," wrote Samuel T. Dana and Evert W. Johnson in *Forestry Education Today and Tomorrow,* published in 1963. "It can also provide for recreational activities, conservation of water supplies, scientific studies in natural areas, and the enjoyment of scenic wonders." That lofty concept indicates that good forestry embraces management of wooded lands for a variety of goods and services required by society. Unfortunately, this concept has not been well applied either.

By way of direct illustration, I quote from a letter written by John Turner, of Jackson, Wyoming, to Reid Jackson, supervisor of the Bridger–Teton National Forest in 1981: "I generally support the multiple-use philosophy and yet we have witnessed timber programs render many areas in this region of Wyoming into almost single-use land units. We have seen scenic values decline, recreational opportunities whittled away, resident wildlife populations pushed out, big game migration routes destroyed, watersheds impacted, and opportunities for small timber operators decline. Considering that this region possesses some of the finest outdoor resources left in North America, such management programs must change or these unsurpassed values will be lost forever."

As a Wyoming state senator, and a Republican at that, John Turner spoke for a conservative constituency rooted to the land. Not only he, but the commissioners of Sublette County, the Wyoming Game and Fish Department, and even the Wyoming congressional delegation interceded with the Forest Service in order to halt projected timber sales on the flanks of the Wind River Range. Through it all, Forest Supervisor Jackson continued to insist that he was the doctor who knew best.

Over the years I have looked for change, hopefully and prayerfully, in attitudes and actions. There is some, but not much, certainly not enough to hail multiple use as a principle proven in practice.

In 1955, Richard E. McArdle, chief of the Forest Service, warned in his annual report: "The needs for water, timber, and forage, for recreation, for wilderness areas, and for hunting and fishing, mount constantly. This places our multiple-use principle of management under severe strain and tests our skill in both resource management and human relations."

In 1967, however, William E. Towell, then executive vice-president of the American Forestry Association, indicated that his fellow professionals were flunking the course on both counts. At a symposium on forestry education, he warned of the failure of some foresters "to give proper consideration to their environmental responsibilities." Towell cited floods and erosion resulting from the clear-cutting of steep slopes; the diminution of fish and game populations in whole watersheds from indiscriminate spraying to control forest pests; and the destruction of roadside vistas and the beauty of the landscape through careless harvest methods. "Most foresters seem particularly weak in aesthetic appreciation," he concluded.

In 1979, Roy Feuchter, Forest Service director of recreation management, commented, "Foresters are generally timber-oriented, not people-oriented." Since timber paid the freight in most wildland management activities, and since there existed a lack of recognition of recreational values within the Forest Service, Feuchter added, "I think our biggest training job is to convince the wildland managers, not the public, of the values of outdoor recreation."

And in 1980, Dr. Carl Reidel, who left the Forest Service to pursue a career in education as a professor of forestry and director of the Environmental Program at the University of Vermont, raised these challenging questions: "How can foresters be trusted to manage a natural preserve when they can't identify the birds or wildflowers in the area, much less understand their special environmental requirements? How can foresters even be trusted to mark timber for intermediate cutting if they are insensitive to the practical problems of felling a tree or locating a skid trail on a rocky side hill?"

These criticisms come from within the forestry establishment, not from sentimental tree-huggers who just do not understand. Such expressions raise my optimism. They also make it clear that if multiple use is not functioning, national forest administrators and decision makers must bear responsibility.

They like to cite directives from the White House and Office of Management and Budget, the influence of the Department of Agriculture, congressional legislation, and the political clout of the industry. These defenses are valid, but only up to a point.

By emphasizing funding for road construction, timber sales, and other commodity production, Congress in fact has sanctioned short-term consumption at the expense of long-term protection. The Reagan administration, however, has directed the Forest Service to show increased receipts by selling more timber and accelerating the leasing of mineral, oil, and gas resources. Dollar values plainly prevail over non-market values, and certainly over biosystems. Assistant Secretary of Agriculture for Natural Resources and Environment John B. Crowell, Jr., has set a course designed to "operate the Forest Service like a corporation and show a profit," although such a public agency operates on different principles and answers to a different kind of board of directors than does a private profit-making corporation.

These influences are real. But I hear them cited when it proves convenient, not when management plans are being prepared, nor when land is being allocated, the best of it for commodity production. What I do hear is that performance standards, the key to promotion and pay grades, are based on "hard outputs," or quantifiables, such as volumes of timber logged, heads of livestock grazed, tons of minerals extracted, and volumes of visitors received.

Do Recreation and Wildlife Matter?

Among the multiple uses, watershed protection, recreation, and wildlife hold low priority. Foresters and engineers dominate in personnel numbers, pay grades, and influence in decision making.

There is no civil service classification for recreation management—it is not considered worth recognizing as a profession. Alas, when wilderness is measured in "recreation visitor days," it fares poorly, subject to a standard that scarcely treats its broader values. I have met concerned and committed people involved in wilderness activity, but they are out of the mainstream; most of their colleagues feel wilderness lacks the challenge of management, though it may demand more skill (if not reward) than any other use.

In 1969, Edward C. Crafts, a former assistant chief of the Forest Service, testified before a congressional hearing on the imbalance of uses. He said his old outfit had committed a grave error by permitting the term "allowable cut" to be substituted for "sustained yield." Between 1950 and 1969, the annual allowable cut of sawtimber had risen from 5.6 billion to 12.8 billion board feet. "Allowable cut used to be the ceiling above which the cut would not be allowed to go," Crafts testified. "Then it became the floor below which the cut would not be allowed to fall."

Resource Quotas The post-war building boom, depletion of resources on private land, and low cost of federal timber all contributed to the logging upsurge. Individual national forests and ranger districts were assigned tough quotas. A few administrators balked, but generally they fell in line. It became convenient to cite logging as a multiple-use tool rather than an end in itself, asserting that timber sales made possible the beginning of road systems. Maybe so, but logging and road building were sanctioned on various ill-suited sites: where tree species were at the limits of their range; where there were infertile, shallow soils and rough terrain; and where intensive operations proved costly and damaging to watershed, wildlife, mountain scenery, and recreation.

The Bitterroot Mountains of western Montana became symbolic of the most devastating clear-cutting practices on steep slopes, including a costly method of mechanical terracing. Led by a retired forest supervisor, Guy M. Brandborg, citizens protested with vehemence. Dale Burk, outdoor editor of *The Missoulian* (Montana), prepared a sizzling series of illustrated articles that attracted nationwide attention. Regional Forester Neal Rahm failed to call a halt to the logging, but later substantiated the public's criticism by listing the unprofessional blunders of his own personnel: wrong silviculture system choice, poor choice of site preparation measures, and the allowance of logging and road equipment and logging debris in stream courses.

In neighboring Wyoming, sportsmen, dude ranchers, stockmen, and others objected to timber sales at high elevations on the western flanks of the Wind River Range adjacent to the Bridger Wilderness. They argued that the Forest Service was subsidizing, with public funds and public multiple-use lands, a lumber mill operated by an out-of-state firm. A six-member Forest Service team came to investigate this and other Wyoming logging activities. In 1970, the team reported: "The criticism we heard is that the Forest Service has given priority to timber production, whereas it should have given priority to watershed, wildlife, recreation, and scenic values; that is, to preserving the quality of the environment. Public confidence in the ability of the Forest Service to manage forests has suffered."

Edward P. Cliff, then chief of the Forest Service, refused to give ground. He stonewalled the public and his own people who advocated a return to multiple use. Before the 1966 Pacific Logging Congress, Cliff declared: "For the young, 'citified,' articulate part of our citizenry, it is especially easy and natural to get stirred up about outdoor beauty, recreation, wilderness, vanishing wildlife species, and environmental pollution. It is not likely that very many know or even particularly care much about how timber is grown, harvested, and used to meet their needs."

Chief Cliff in December 1971 was a busy letter writer, dispatching correspondence to the editors of esteemed periodicals. He wrote to *The Atlantic, Reader's Digest,* and *The Washington Monthly* about derisive articles (written, incidentally, by Paul Brooks, James Nathan Miller, and James Risser, all considered journalists of distinction). He lectured *The New York Times,* in response to a critical editorial, on the Forest Service's interpretation of multiple-use planning, concluding that, as a result of these practices, "the national forests are producing more goods and services for the use and enjoyment of the American people, and in greater variety, than ever before."

Loss of Wilderness Lands It all depends, however, on how "goods and services" are measured. If they refer to watershed, wildlife, recreation, scenic, aesthetic, and cultural values, Cliff's statement was miles—nay, light years—off the mark. The same, I fear, would be true of any such statement today. "Each year I see land that once was wilderness receive the blessings of what they call multiple use," Ted Trueblood, my friend and old colleague at *Field and Stream* magazine wrote before his death in 1982. "First come the bulldozers, then the loggers and logging trucks. Then come the ORV riders, riding just to be riding, or perhaps trying to shoot a deer without the honest sweat that should be part of any hunt. Idaho has already lost some of its choicest wild country and even now the Forest Service proposes to open still more roadless areas to development. So we're not looking at how much more wilderness we're going to have, but how much less of it there will be."

Idaho is called the Gem State, but it holds no finer jewel than the River of No Return, an area of rugged peaks, forests, and lakes, with portions of the wild Salmon River and its tributaries flowing through deep granite gorges. The wilderness is larger than Yellowstone, and in some places wilder, with a greater variety of plants, fish, and wildlife.

The land is lovely to view but difficult to exploit. Logging and road construction along a small portion of the South Fork of the Salmon River during the sixties resulted in catastrophic erosion and siltation, virtually wiping out critical salmon spawning grounds. It will now take either a hundred years to recover naturally or the investment of heavy federal expenditures (which may or may not work anyway).

Multiple use tells me the best thing to do is to leave it alone. The very qualities that make the region unsuitable for development make it valuable for enjoyment. Protecting the watershed protects the streams for Chinook salmon, cutthroat, steelhead, and rainbow trout. The same is true of protecting the forests for game. You do not have to do *anything* to enhance natural beauty; on the other hand, it is all but impossible to re-create it once you have reduced a forest to stumps.

For me, every part of the national forest system is filled with wonder; it is a reservoir of the original America. Its parts are like life museums, considering their vast array of trees, plants, geological forms, and wildlife. They are designed by law for use—protecting watersheds and wildlife habitats, and furnishing timber, rangeland, minerals, and various types of recreation—and I am for all those uses so long as they do not preclude future use.

A lot of good things have been done—like protecting the northern Minnesota timber wolf and the Puerto Rican parrot—thanks to conscientious personnel in the ranks. Yet these incidents have been isolated rather than integral parts of the Forest Service's multiple-use planning. Sure, there is a plan for the grizzly bear, but it is mostly on paper. When it comes to priorities, grazing, logging, and mineral exploration come before the bear.

What Should the Public Expect?

The public has a right to expect better balance and a more professional performance. "To a large extent private timberland outside the national forests is still being thoughtlessly exploited with little regard for the future," editorialized the Asheville, N.C., *Citizen Times* on August 23, 1970. "The U.S. Forest Service is the agency that must set the example for the future." The example was not being set then and is hardly being set today.

That editorial was written in the midst of a period of abundant public discontent, which throughout the 1970s sparked congressional inquiries and reform legislation. The National Forest Management Act (NFMA) of 1976 was intended to make multiple use work at last. That law called for equal consideration for, and protection of, all renewable resources in an optimal mix. It challenged forest administrators to "recognize the interrelationships between, and interdependence within, the renewable resources," and the "fundamental need to protect and, where appropriate, improve air, water, and soil quality."

That is exactly how a public forest should be run in pursuit of the concepts of Theodore Roosevelt and Gifford Pinchot. "To the broad vision of Pinchot we owe much in the development of attitudes that now make possible the preservation of natural areas, at a time when the need is so deeply realized," declared Howard Zahniser, executive director of The Wilderness Society, during the tough crusade that led to the passage of the Wilderness Act of 1964. "The best apparent hope for success in the preservation of wilderness is actually in the application of the multiple-use principle."

But when will that principle be applied? In 1979 a committee of scientists, appointed by the Secretary of Agriculture, issued a set of regulations to implement the purpose of NFMA. The regulations were clearly based on multiple use and forest science. The committee directed: "The interdisciplinary team shall be guided by the fact that the forests and rangelands are ecosystems and, hence, that the management of goods and services requires an awareness of the interdependencies among plants, animals, soil, and other factors that occur within such ecosystems."

The Reagan Heritage The Reagan administration through one device and another has sought to undo these regulations and the intent of NFMA, and it has not encountered much resistance from within the Forest Service. Production quotas, now called "targets," are handed down and willingly accepted by forest supervisors, who generously impose the burden of fulfillment on district rangers. Of course, there is a planning process, which makes for jobs and busy computers, yet it seems to be distinct from the apparent commitment to single-use production.

Mineral development keeps people busy, too. Officials are too ready to issue exploration leases covering entire national forests without weighing the environmental feasibility or impact on other uses. Where administrators should be heard speaking out, it is left instead to the public to defend the resource. As stated, for example, in this editorial which appeared in the Hendersonville, N.C., *Times News* on October 6, 1980: "The key is the ability of the forest to handle another exploitation and survive. If Pisgah is damaged by fire, oil spill, erosion, or logging, it can unbalance the entire ecology and environment downstream. The entire effort isn't worth it, no matter the benefit to our nation's industrial economy, if the forest and, subsequently, the downstream country are damaged. No matter the assurance that it is safe, there should be no exploration for oil in Pisgah National Forest. The risk is too great because of Pisgah's role in providing water to a regional civilization."

Why shouldn't the essence of that statement come from the supervisor of the Pisgah National Forest, or from the regional forester, or from the chief of the Forest Service? It would be in keeping with the vision enunciated by Dana and Johnson in their book on forestry education who see the professional forester of the future as "a man who is well-grounded in the principles of forest land management, together with the underlying arts and sciences on which such management is based. At the same time he must have the breadth of view and the understanding of the economic, social, and political world in which he lives to enhance his competence not only as a professional man but as a citizen and an individual." From my long association with the agency and its personnel, as both supporter and critic, I feel the desire is there, deep within the ranks, to live this role.

Stewardship of the Land Often the words are there, but they get lost in the shuffle of expediency. I do not think anyone could ask for a firmer declaration than the one by F. Dale Robertson in 1974, when he was supervisor of the Siuslaw National Forest, following a period of logging abuse and resource degradation: "Responsible land stewardship includes the protection of soil, water quality, and fish and wildlife habitat." Robertson's vision of an acceptable timber sale was one that would be harvested within acceptable environmental constraints and would not leave its mark on the land or degrade watershed values or require correction with appropriated funds. "Short-run economics," he asserted, "will not override long-term needs of high quality land management."

Or the statement by Don Boyer, director of watershed management of the Pacific Northwest Region in 1979, when he spoke of the need to elevate the job of erosion control—one that does not easily lend itself to a "production measuring stick"—to a higher level of recognition. Boyer emphasized that a "successful stabilization program is the reflection of our organizational concern for the soil and water resources . . . [and] in a sense, our land ethic. . . ."

Or the assertion by Carl R. Puuri and Raymond G. Weinman in 1981, when they noted that the silviculturist, once primarily oriented to timber, now "must be concerned with management objectives that also include regulation of water yields, enhancement of wildlife habitat, and improvement of recreational values."

One of the most important lessons foresters have yet to learn is how to listen, or perhaps I should say, how to open their eyes, ears, and minds to the aspects of multiple use their technical training overlooked. In 1981, Tom Costen, regional forester of the Northern

Region, eloquently expressed how the Forest Service could begin to do this: "Some administrators in the past have felt public involvement was cumbersome and a stumbling block in the way of efficient management. That I don't accept. It has proven a great benefit to the national forests of the Northern Region. Participating individuals and groups help Forest Service personnel make better decisions and confirm the democratic approach to public land management. National forests don't belong to just those working in the Forest Service—they are part of our national heritage."

The truth is that I have not said anything that people in the agency have not said, or felt, themselves. The Forest Service appears, understandably, like a paramilitary organization, but I like to think it is not monolithic, and no more static than multiple use. This leads me to conclude that, while laws and regulations have their place, in the final analysis only people can make things work. Perhaps the open, democratic approach may yet fulfill the promise of multiple-use management of our public forests.

Gregory McNamee

Mountain Under Heavens

From the flat roof of my adobe house in downtown Tucson, whenever the dust and automobile exhaust are down, a clear-eyed observer can see four astronomical observatories in as many directions. The oldest, on the campus of the University of Arizona, has been in use since the first years of the twentieth century, before the discovery of Pluto. The others are of more recent vintage: the Mount Lemmon complex north of the city and the Kitt Peak National Observatory, in the sacred Baboquívari Mountains to the west, date to the 1960s, while the Mount Hopkins Multiple-Mirror Telescope complex, on the road south to Mexico, opened in 1973, in the days when southern Arizona's night sky blazed with stars now hidden by evidence of our progress.

Beyond the city lie many other observations. Of southeastern Arizona's major mountain ranges, only three—the Chiricahuas, Huachucas, and Pinaleños—are free of astronomical facilities. For years astronomers from around the world have traveled to Tucson to take their turn at one or another of these observatories, so many that home-grown junior scholars often have difficulty booking time to complete their research projects; the demand for more and more scopes is consequently high. Used to having their way, the astronomers were not prepared to take seriously Arizona congressman Morris Udall's warning, at the dedication of the Mount Hopkins complex, that they allot their resources conservatively. For this, he said, would be the last southern Arizona mountaintop to be shaved off in the name of science.

Rather than reduce the number of observers and make do with what was already an embarrassment of riches, the administration of the University of Arizona, determined to safeguard the school's reputation as "the Wall Street of astronomy," turned to the last of the unscarred mountains. It set its sights on the Pinaleño range a hundred miles east of Tucson, the summit of which, 10,700-foot Mount Graham, seemed an ideal spot for a new observatory, with no city lights to obscure the faint glow of faraway galaxies, few turbulent windstreams, and little humidity in the desert air. Lying within the Coronado National Forest, the range had been hunted, logged, mined, and grazed—for such is the fate of land entrusted to the United States Forest Service—and a network of roads led nearly to its top. The job of subduing the mountain had been under way for years, and it would be a simple enough matter to divert a few million dollars of the university's operating budget in order to build a modern highway, clearcut the old-growth spruce and fir forest, and wrest away the secrets of the firmament.

But, the university learned, matters were more complicated than that. In the early 1980s, Representative Udall, chairman of the House Interior Committee, saw to it that the Pinaleños were included in the Arizona Wilderness Bill, which would have protected vast tracts of the public domain from the Forest Service's disastrous multiple-use doctrine. The university protested that it had other ideas for the mountains' future, and, by way of compromise, the committee filed the high peaks of the range away in a proposed wilderness-study area. A delighted university administration turned to its blueprints and refined its plans to clear away three thousand acres of forest along the range's two highest points, Mount Graham and Emerald Peak, for an astronomical complex that would house eighteen giant telescopes, among them the nascent 11.3-meter Columbus. But then another complication kept the university from immediately razing the area.

Ecologists call the mountains of the basin-and-range provinces of the Greater Southwest "mountain islands," for they stand in roughly the same relation to the surrounding desert as an island does to the sea. Isolated from like ecological zones, the mountains harbor animal and plant populations that in time differentiate themselves from their kin, so that a cougar in the Animas Range of New Mexico will bear slightly different markings from one in the Chiricahua Mountains of Arizona, thirty miles away. For wide-ranging animals like the mountain lion and the black bear (both now almost extinct), who travel among the ranges through the net of riparian corridors connecting them, these differences will be small, but for more sedentary populations, they will become more and more pronounced as time passes. Atop Mount Graham, one such population held the space scientists at bay.

This was *Tamiasciurus hudsonicus grahamensis,* a subspecies of the common red squirrel, a denizen of the spruce-fir forests of the mountain islands. Long a target of hunters who presumably prized the animal more for its coat than its scant meat, the Mount Graham red squirrel population had declined by the early 1980s to only thirty or so mating pairs, no more than a hundred individuals in all, a count small enough to warrant its being entered on the federal roster of endangered species. Although in times of want the squirrel descends into the lower mixed-conifer zone, its preferred habitat is the highest peaks of the Pinaleños—exactly where the University of Arizona wanted to build its astronomical complex, now in partnership with the Smithsonian Institution, the Vatican Observatory, the University of Chicago, and the Max Planck Institute of West Germany.

Owing to the endangered status of *Tamiasciurus hudsonicus grahamensis,* the United States Fish and Wildlife Service ordered that the telescope complex not be built until it conducted a thoroughgoing environmental-impact study, as mandated by the National Environmental Policy Act of 1970. Fearing that Fish and Wildlife would eventually determine (as some of its officers were then arguing) that the red-squirrel habitat be closed to any development whatever and that the Pinaleños be readmitted into the Arizona Wilderness Bill, the University of Arizona went to war. Its administration hired the Washington law firm of Patton, Biggs and Blow, which had engineered the multibillion-dollar Chrysler Corporation bailout of the early 1980s, to lobby Arizona's congressional delegation and members of the House Interior Committee to hold Mount Graham exempt from a constellation of environmental-protection laws and the provisions of the Endangered Species Act. Millions of dollars later, the university had its way. Although Arizonans were overwhelmingly opposed to the scopes, Morris Udall (the best representative Alaska ever had, people around here are fond of saying) and his colleagues endorsed a rider to the Arizona–Idaho Conservation Bill of 1988 that left the high Pinaleños open to construction. Top University of Arizona administrators and astronomers celebrated this legislative end-run by throwing a party, the centerpiece of which was a papier-maché piñata in the shape of a Mount Graham red squirrel.

The lobbying worked both ways, however. Thanks to the efforts of the Sierra Club Legal Defense Fund and agitation from Earth First!, Greenpeace, and other environmental groups, Congress whittled down the university's original demands to an 8.6-acre site that would house eight telescopes. In the ensuing chain of injunctions and counterinjunctions, the Fish and Wildlife Service demanded that an environmental-impact study be conducted despite the congressional ruling, and even the Forest Service agreed that the law must be obeyed. Environmental organizations nationwide joined the cause, and the University of Arizona administration building became the site of frequent demonstrations of the sort Tucson had not seen since the early 1970s. The leaders of the San Carlos Apache nation, whose domain once included the Pinaleño Mountains, reminded the university that mountaintops are properly sacred in Apache belief and suggested that enough summits had already been sacrificed in the interest of science. The presiding judges of the Ninth Federal Circuit Court ruled in favor of the protesters one day, the astronomical coalition the next, adding to the mounting tangle of legal claims on both sides. And so it went for the next two years, with construction delays costing the University of Arizona—or rather the taxpayers of Arizona—$25,000 a day, the equivalent of an assistant professor's annual salary.

Having demonstrated its regard for due process, the university eventually took the initiative. During a lull in the legal combat during the summer of 1990, the judges having momentarily rested in its favor, the university ordered its crew of sawyers to clearcut the Mount Graham site. In a few hours' time some two hundred and fifty old-growth spruce and fir trees fell before a battery of chainsaws, and another three hundred saplings were removed and replanted down the slope. Red-squirrel middens were bulldozed, a construction road was hurriedly scraped into the rocky forest floor, and the issue of Mount Graham descended from abstraction into bitter reality.

As I write, in the early spring of 1991, with the winter's accumulation of snow fast melting from Mount Graham and new legal arguments against the scopes having been turned away from the bench, it appears that concrete foundations will be poured within weeks. The astronomers—no, not the astronomers, for many joined in opposition to the scopes, at the risk of their jobs and professional futures—the scientific-industrial complex carried the day.

And what has it won? Half a century ago Aldo Leopold observed, "A thing is right when it tends to preserve the integrity, stability, and beauty of the biotic community. It is wrong when it tends otherwise." The astronomical complex atop Mount Graham can be of no possible benefit to any biotic community other than *Homo Sapiens bureaucratensis,* whose lives are measured in federal grants. The administration's actions have made many new enemies for the University of Arizona, especially among those who are expected to pony up its operating budget year after year, and alienated thousands of alumni. And, ironically, the scopes will be of marginal value to the international community of astronomers and space scientists, for direct observation of the heavens yields little important data these days, as the recent Hubble Telescope debacle made clear. Instead, radio telescopy, which can be conducted from the plains of Kansas or the suburbs of Florida as profitably as it can from the top of a southern Arizona mountain, has become the mainstay of contemporary astronomical research. Mount Graham, it is now abundantly clear, was sacrificed not for knowledge but mere power.

Who loses? The Mount Graham red squirrel, for one, so seemingly insignificant, another of the thousands of species marched off to extinction in the twentieth century at the hands of humankind. It may be that *Tamiasciurus hudsonicus grahamensis* will find a new habitat in the mixed-conifer zone below the high peaks, but its survival is improbable in the extreme. No one can yet foresee the effects of its absence, but it will surely be felt on the mountain, for small creatures are invariably more important to a habitat than its megafauna; a honeybee shapes an environment far more profoundly than does an elk. The owls and hawks and eagles that feed on the red squirrel must find new prey or move on, the pine cones that sustained the Mount Graham red squirrel will go ungathered, and the *grahamensis* subspecies itself will perhaps be remembered only through a piñata and a few stuffed specimens gathered surreptitiously by University of Arizona biologists.

In the end, despite the arrogant claims of humanism, all of us will lose. The heart of the issue is not the red squirrel, for its population had dwindled to the point where recovery may not have been possible in any event; extinction is not the exception but the norm in life, and extinction may have been the squirrel's only future. The issue is the mountain itself. Mount Graham stands as a small example of the rapacity of modern corporatism, of which the modern university and scientific community are an integral part. A tract of 8.6 acres seems scarcely worth noticing in the face of corporatism's recent accomplishments: since 1970, after all, more than a million acres of virgin old-growth forest have been clearcut in the United States alone, and today more than 53 acres of rainforest are felled globally every minute. The 8.6 acres of ancient forest atop the Pinaleño Mountains were clearcut by the colluding first-world powers of science, government, and academia, an unholy trinity responsible for the earth's larger losses. The disappearance of that small band of spruce and fir trees means, among other things, that even in these days of supposedly heightened environmental awareness, the struggle to save other lands and species will be long and difficult, perhaps even impossible in the end.

The tale of Mount Graham is an old, old story, repeated at many times and in many places. In the third-century *Aesopica,* the source of much moral wisdom in the West until television came along, we find a fable that may well have been set in southeastern Arizona at the dawn of the new millennium. It reads:

> An astronomer used to wander outside each night to look at the stars. One evening, as he walked through town staring at the sky, he fell into a deep well. He cried for help until a neighbor arrived and called down to him. Learning what had happened, the neighbor said, "Why pry into the heavens when you can't see what's right here on Earth?"

Until science is able to answer the villager's question, until the doctrine of multiple use of public lands is suspended, until our putative civilization holds the tops of mountains in the same regard as do the Apache, until political and economic corporatism is overthrown once and for all, we share *Tamiasciurus hudsonicus grahamensis*'s fate.

Jody Aliesan

This Is a Managed Forest

. . . formal speeches at Mescalero [Apache] community gatherings are organized into four parts. The speaker begins with a prologue that adheres to a standard formula, and in it he explains that he doesn't really know much about the topic at hand. This is followed by the speaker's thoughts on the subject. He then offers a brief summary of what he has said. Finally, he finishes with a standard closing in which he acknowledges his ignorance but says that his words have expressed how the situation looks to him.

—E.C. KRUPP, *Echoes of the Ancient Skies*

Fourteen years ago I got a ride from Puget Sound to Washington's wilderness coast with a man who operated his own bus line on the main road across the Olympic Peninsula. I sat in the back of his three-seat van looking out at the green tunnel we drove through: cedars, hemlocks, firs, growing right up to the highway shoulder. Behind him sat another man, who leaned forward to talk over the back of the seat. The second man laughed loudly and swore and told jokes about environmentalists, shouting over the travel noise that it was time to log the national forests. Now and then he glanced behind him at me and my backpack.

After he got off and we drove away, the first man said, "You were pretty quiet back there. You an environmentalist?" I said I wasn't calling myself anything, but I hoped there would be someplace left where the trees weren't all the same kind and the same age and planted in rows. He didn't speak for a while and then we talked quietly, the way people do when they don't know for certain and aren't trying to prove anything.

This spring my sweetheart and I drove to the same place on the same road. We thought we were prepared for what has happened to the forests. We'd read articles and seen aerial photographs of mountains shaved up to the national park boundaries, rivers clogged with debris and mudslides. But when we rounded the bend into familiar country, I couldn't help the tears. We turned off the car radio and passed through in silence. Everywhere we looked, great populations of trees had been mowed down, huge patches cut out of the blanket pelt of woods, steep slopes scraped and eroding, and where tree screens along the road thinned out, vast gray killing grounds stretched away and up the hills: everything dead, uprooted, tumbled, scraped, and burned.

This is not about aesthetics, although cultures the world over who have lived most harmoniously with the land have taught that doing something well or correctly usually means also doing it beautifully. My concern is manipulation: substituting something partial, superficial, and false for what is whole, genuine, and true.

They say the burning helps Douglas fir get started. They say they're planting this destroyed land. And here and there we did see tiny trees in the midst of the black and gray. But the plantings are not part of a natural succession from fireweed to bramble to alder to maple to conifers, with all the other life underfoot and beside and above. We will not get back what we lost. Later on we drove through stands of the results: spindly crowded trees all the same age, all the same kind. As we emerged into another blasted clearing, on a corner where a side road met the highway, in front of a small misshaped hemlock—all that was left of what had stood there—we saw the first sign. It said: This Is a Managed Forest.

Three months later, four of us sat around a table in a cabin in the woods of the San Juan Islands, talking by candlelight. I said:

> It looks to me like everything is getting steadily worse, and there is no hope. I can live without hope. I can even be happy without it. Who was it said, "I live every day with despair but I try not to let it depress me"? But it seems to me we've been born to live in a time of great loss, and the best we can do is slow it down. Help each other through it.

One of the others said:

> There are significant exceptions. People holding out, waking up, changing their minds and ways. Some of them in decision-making positions. There may be time enough, heart enough, intelligence enough, for turning things around.

I said:

> Maybe so. But where will things be turned to? Away from destruction and waste, yes. But toward management. There's nothing wrong with gardens. I keep one myself, and exert control and practice selection. But it's wrong for us to try to make the whole world our garden, with everything managed and in its place. We are a creature among creatures, one nation among nations, equals on the face of the earth.

He agreed that, in that case, things did look bleak.

> There are just too many of us, I said, looking at the candles. Or we're too greedy, desperate, ignorant, careless, insensitive, and downright evil for the good of the rest. It would be better for everything else if we all disappeared.

My sweetheart got up from the table, touched me on the shoulders as she passed behind my chair, crossed the small room and lay down on the futon, her back to the rest of us. When I joined her there after our friends climbed to the loft, she whispered:

> I don't understand you. You don't have faith in human beings.
> It's true, I said. Should I?

I do have faith in the balancing force of the universe, call it Providence, karma, natural law, or fate: whatever moves without either vengeance or compassion when we swing to excess or act in opposition to its unfolding. In the words of the biologist Kenneth Hsu, "The lesson learned from the history of life . . . is not the Darwinistic ideology, but the Taoistic teaching of symbiosis, coevolution, and an unfathomable combination of chance and inevitability."

We see this balancing most dramatically when events rush toward what physicists call turbulence: things get faster, more frequent, as they head toward chaos. Press hard enough, somet[illegible] will suddenly break open, then split again and again, bran[illegible] all directions, cracks in the mirrors of a fly's eye.

Life operates best, writes Freeman Dyson, in an atmosphere of loose structure and tolerance for error. Not in a managed garden. It may be that the earth as a whole, as part of the larger balancing, will take care of our problem, but not necessarily in our favor. Many prophesies—including Mayan, Christian, Hopi, geologic, and climatological—foretell a time soon of great catastrophe, and it seems to me we have it coming. When other living beings have increased their influence beyond bounds they have starved, succumbed to disease, or lost their responsiveness to change. Why should it be any different for us?

What is it about us that wants to manage? What does it fear? Why it is so destructive? Maybe the manager inside us wants control, and fears whatever it can't control. Fears what is wild, equating that with abandon rather than with self-sufficient independence. Prefers the tame, the predictable, the subdued. Thinks of abundance as threatening, goes into a killing frenzy to assert superiority over what outnumbers or weighs more or stands taller. Fears ambiguity, incompleteness, the unknown. Prefers what is black-and-white, thorough, *clear-cut*.

I understand that old-fashioned forestry doesn't argue in favor of clearcutting. I hear that sustained yield and selective logging are better practices, but they don't make as much money as quickly. That the older, more subtle and complicated ways could also provide more sustained employment, especially as clearcutting becomes automated and the trees are sent raw to other economies for processing. But it's too late now. It's easier to manipulate words, call old growth "decadent" and clearcuts "regeneration sales." It's easier to blame the loss of mills and timber jobs on environmentalists and the diminishing number of ancient trees still alive.

I understand that the quality of wood from the replanted monocrops is falling. The soil lacks trace elements, the trees are less healthy, less hardy, more vulnerable to insects and diseases. Bears strip them for cambium, since the usual fruit-bearing undergrowth has been suppressed with defoliants or the heavy metals in the urban sewage sludge that is sprayed as fertilizer. The stands have to be cut sooner, so the trees are smaller: less vertical grain, less clear wood. Carpenters say the best wood around anymore is being demolished by wreckers' balls and dumped into landfills because it takes effort and planning to salvage it.

What I don't understand is how someone can cut down a forest because it is in the budget and it's necessary to justify cutting the same number of acres next biennium. I don't understand cutting down a forest because a lot of money is being paid for big trees and it's important to make as much as possible as fast as possible. Or to ease the cash flow. Or to take advantage of tax breaks. I don't understand cutting down a forest to prevent it being set aside as wilderness, or out of hate for environmentalists and desire for revenge. I don't understand killing trees just because they are in the way.

My sweetheart called after a day over near the Dungeness Spit. "Do you want to know what we saw on the Peninsula? They're burning trees. They're just yanking them out of the ground with backhoes and tossing them into pickup trucks. And burning them. Both sides of the road. Conifers. I don't know why."

I write these words on paper. You are seeing them printed on paper. I live in a wood-frame cottage, and benefit from the death of trees in more ways than I'm aware of. But it looks to me like the deforestation of the Pacific Northwest is more than a matter of supply and demand and a free-market economy. Something more than the forests is being managed.

Trees are noble beings. They do a great deal of good and no purposeful harm. Maybe it's time for trees to manage us. By their absence, they will.

Waning moon
Duir, month of the oak
1991

Tim McNulty

Forests, Forestry, and the Land: An Ecosystem on Edge

Valley forests drew back into morning fog as our truck climbed a steep logging road in Washington's Olympic Mountains. The fresh clearcuts we had replanted earlier that season fell away into deep, glacier-hewn valleys, and patches of old-growth forest darkened the road with shade. After nearly an hour we followed a spur road to its end on a high broken ridge. As we stepped out to the edge of the landing to look over the day's work, our stomachs took a turn. Bare, eroded cliffs and rock faces dropped steeply to a rubble of boulders and slash. Large Douglas fir and hemlock stumps clung to cliff walls, and dry scraps of moss trailed from the rocks like battle-torn flags. From somewhere far below the sound of a creek lifted and fell with the mountain wind.

That was nearly twenty years ago, but the vision comes back to me clear and stark. I'd had a few seasons of tree planting behind me by that time, and I thought I'd seen something of logging on the Olympic Peninsula. I'd heard the term "timber mining" used to describe the heavily logged Shelton District of the Olympic National Forest, and I thought I knew what it meant. But the destruction I saw that day exceeded anything I had encountered. This went beyond the bounds of insensitive management; this was devastation.

As the timber industry turned up the pressure on Congress in the late 1970s and 1980s and the pace of clearcutting on national forests continued to accelerate, sights like this became altogether too common on the Olympic Peninsula. What I didn't know then was that in little more than a decade this type of volume-driven forestry would precipitate a crisis from which the timber industry and the land itself might not be able to recover.

On June 22, 1990, the U.S. Fish and Wildlife Service listed the northern spotted owl as a threatened species. The listing confirmed conservationists' contentions that the old-growth forest ecosystem of the Pacific Northwest was itself in jeopardy. The news hit particularly hard on the heavily forested Olympic Peninsula. In one sense, it was the closing argument in a long, ongoing debate about public land use here, a debate that has engulfed forests and rural communities throughout the Pacific Northwest.

The deep, rain-saturated forests of the mountainous Olympic Peninsula in the northwest corner of Washington state are among the richest, most diverse and biologically productive in the temperate world. Consequently, they're also among the most heavily cut. The port of Port Angeles alone ships as much as three hundred fifty million board feet of timber annually. Lumber and pulp mills dot the coast, and the small logging town of Forks on the peninsula's west end touts itself the "logging capitol of the world." With upwards of two billion board feet cut from peninsula forest lands each year, few question that claim.

But just inland from the broad, logged-over coastal lowlands that surround the community of Forks, there's an abrupt and dramatic change of scene. Ranks of even-aged second-growth plantations give way to the high mossy canopy of the Olympic rainforest. Nearly a million acres in the mountainous heart of the peninsula have been preserved intact as Olympic National Park. The park and adjacent national forest Wilderness areas make up the largest temperate old-growth forest preserve in the country. The world scientific community has twice affirmed the planetary significance of Olympic National Park, designating it both a Biosphere Reserve and a World Heritage Site. With over 95 percent of the park in the National Wilderness System, Olympic is North America's premier wilderness park outside of Alaska. It also holds the lesser distinction of having been, for its entire history, the park most embroiled in controversy in the entire national park system.

Caught between these poles and the seemingly irreconcilable world views and political agendas that accompany them, the Olympic Peninsula is a microcosm of the greater Pacific Northwest. Here the century-long debate between preservation and utilization, as championed by John Muir and Gifford Pinchot, has reached a climax. If a solution to this dichotomy is to work anywhere, it must be made to work here.

I've lived on the Olympic Peninsula for the past twenty years, and for most of that time I've drawn my livelihood from resource and forestry work. I've planted, thinned, and selectively logged in the forests. I've worked on watershed rehabilitation and timber stand management, salvaged cedar, fought fires, and cleared trails in the mountains. It's good work; it kept me in shape and gave me the sense that I was helping put something back into the land. There was time off in the winter to write, and the seasonal round suited me.

As is the case with many rural areas in the Pacific Northwest, forestry, fishing, and other resource-related work are the mainstay of the peninsula's economy. In the interest of pursuing a sustainable economy, and partly as a result of my experiences in the woods, I became involved in conservation politics early on. I served on committees and task forces; did grass-roots organizing on wilderness, wildlife, and forestry issues; attended meetings, testified at hearings and wrote articles. Two firmly held beliefs guided me in these efforts. One was the need to see the Olympic Peninsula as one place: a single living ecosystem functioning in splendid disregard for arbitrary jurisdictional boundaries. The other was the need to manage our resource use in a truly self-sustaining manner. As basic and elementary as these principles were to me, I encountered, among the agencies and political processes with which I was involved, an institutional unwillingness to consider or act on them.

As a rule the Forest Service, the Park Service, and the Washington Department of Natural Resources refused to look beyond their jurisdictional boundaries when making decisions, and were loath to take positions on issues that affected neighboring lands. Even the conservation community framed its agendas largely along boundary lines on public lands.

More problematic were the private and industry-owned forest lands. These are the lower elevation, deeply soiled, most productive timberlands on the peninsula. They provide critical year-round habitat for wildlife and fish, yet they were traditionally excluded from any public planning. Thus these lands, which virtually surround national park and national forest lands on the peninsula, were managed not to protect wildlife habitat, watersheds, fisheries, or recreational opportunities, or even to ensure a non-declining sustained yield of timber, but simply to serve the corporate bottom line.

Instability is a fact of life in the Northwest woods. Aside from breakdowns and seasonal slowdowns (summer fire season, winter snow), there's the market. When housing starts are up or export prices high, activity accelerates; when prices fall, the woods shut down. These ups and downs come with the country, and woods workers have always managed to suffer through them without much complaint. But other factors have come into the picture over the past several years, making the seasonal slumps and economic troughs of the past pale by comparison.

Today more timber is being cut on the Olympic Peninsula, by fewer workers, than ever before. Automation and mechanized harvest techniques have dramatically reduced the work force at the same time that timber companies have cut back on management of young stands. Many of the large timber companies with long histories on the peninsula have fallen prey to the corporate mergers, takeovers, and leveraged buyouts of the Reagan era. Mills were spun off to pay massive debts, and standing timber reserves were liquidated at a dizzying rate. The situation was compounded by a falling American dollar accompanied by an inflationary rise in prices that Asian buyers were paying for unprocessed logs. The result, an accelerating cycle of larger blocks of younger and younger stands being cut for export, spells disaster for the future of forestry on the peninsula and in the greater Northwest.

Not only are mature second-growth forests disappearing at a rate faster than they can be regrown, but younger stands, those that would come into maturity over the next two to three decades, are also being liquidated for the overseas market. The impact this frenzy of clearcutting has had on fish and wildlife can only be guessed, but its effect on the future of the peninsula's forest economy is clear.

This isn't the first time the coastal lowlands have been cut. Beginning in the middle part of the last century and reaching a peak in the 1920s and 1930s, logging companies reaped tremendous profits cutting the virgin forests of the Puget Sound basin and the coastal Northwest. Laying tracks and working with hand saws and steam yarders, logging crews ripped through tremendous expanses of lowland forest. They felled, cable-yarded, and hauled the choicest logs on flat cars to mills, then pulled up tracks, broke their camps, and moved on. It was as brutal a regime for the workers as for the land, and mortalities ran high. Reforestation was an unknown term in those days. In the years that followed, wildfires swept unchecked across the landscape like the wrath of an angry god.

Devastating as this early logging was, it was of a different nature than today's systematic, mechanical clearcut harvest methods. By comparison, in fact, it was almost benign. Limitations in technology and market forces helped ensure that everything in the forest ecosystem wasn't taken. Smaller and less desirable tree species were often left standing, as were trees on steep uplands, in gorges, and along narrow river canyons. Rail lines laid along larger valleys were incapable of reaching trees very far up the mountainsides, thus ensuring healthy, site-specific seed stock would remain. Large sections of felled trees were left, and crooked trees and dead snags were left standing. Even after the fires that followed logging, these elements of the original forest ecosystem—what ecologists refer to as a forest's biological legacy—remained. In short, the original logging of the Douglas fir forests mimicked, to a degree, natural catastrophic events such as wildfires and windstorms—precisely the conditions under which the forest ecosystems of the Douglas fir region evolved.

This is not to say that early twentieth century logging was done either sensitively or scientifically—far from it. But over the decades of benign neglect that followed, these elements of the original forest ecosystem helped the second-growth forest recover much of its biological richness, species diversity, and habitat value. Naturally the question arises, why couldn't some of these techniques be scientifically incorporated into industrial logging practices today?

In the late 1970s, prices for pulp wood on the Olympic Peninsula reached a level that encouraged this kind of selective management. I worked with a small cutting crew then, selecting and felling the smaller and more closely spaced trees in maturing second-growth stands to be skidder-yarded for pulp wood. We worked carefully, taking our time so as not to damage the remaining trees, and leaving a variety of age and species that would ensure the continued health and viability of the stand. I calculated that this kind of selective cutting could occur regularly on a twenty- to thirty-year basis, yielding saw logs as well as pulp wood, and not destroy the stand. The thought that stands like these would be leveled for the export market within a decade didn't enter my mind. As impressed as I was with the resilience of the forest community, I underestimated the ferocity of the market economy. Not only would those same market forces strip the lowland second-growth forests, but they would fuel a local political climate that apparently will stop at nothing short of the elimination of the last old-growth forests remaining on our public forest lands.

Timber industry propagandists and their operatives in the media and Congress have done an outstanding job of reducing a complicated, historical issue to bite-sized headlines. They've been equally adept at pitting constituencies most victimized by their actions against each other. But spotted owls vs. jobs has never been the issue in the Northwest, and rural communities and urban environmentalists have more in common than the industry's hired mouthpieces would ever admit. The overriding issue remains the survival of one of the earth's most complex temperate forest ecosystems, one that has been whittled down to remnants that may not be sufficient for its survival. Here, once again, the Olympic Peninsula is an acute example of the problem.

Separated from the mainland by tidewater on three sides and miles of heavily logged lowlands to the south, the old-growth forests of the Olympic Peninsula are cut off from the more extensive forests of the Cascade Range. Like the larger old-growth community itself, the peninsula is an isolated ecosystem. But this wasn't always the case.

The coniferous forests of the Pacific Northwest have a unique history. The north-south axis of our western mountain ranges allowed whole forest ecosystems to migrate with the advance and recession of the great Pleistocene glaciers. Unlike in Europe and Asia, where east-west ranges blocked the southern migration of temperate forests, Northwest forests were able to ride out this epoch of profound climatic change virtually intact. The wisdom of those millions of years of adaptation and change is written into the genetic material of the old-growth ecosystem as securely as if it were stored in the Library of Congress. It isn't just the trees that are old in the ancient forest: it's the whole, complex, interacting community.

Faced with the uncertainties of global warming and climatic change, our existing old-growth preserves can be crucial to the future restoration of altered and devastated landscapes. But as Aldo Leopold cautioned years ago, the first rule of intelligent tinkering is to save all the cogs and wheels. If the ecosystem is fragmented, if the habitat islands are too small to adapt, if the complex web of species is short-circuited, we may be facing an uncertain future with only half a world.

For many of us who were drawn to the peninsula by the deep forest wilderness at its heart, the ancient groves of the valleys and deeply-timbered slopes offered a sense of hope, a place to keep in our hearts while working among the cuts and scars of the commercial forest lands. But biologists investigating spotted owl populations here have interjected a sobering note. Viable owl habitat, the most biologically important part of the ancient forest, tapers off on the peninsula above 2,500 feet in elevation. Heavy snows and winter temperatures reduce the viability of those higher forests as habitat. We realized that most of the lands in Olympic National Park, and many parks and national forest wilderness areas throughout the Northwest, were no longer the ecological reserves we once thought them to be. Suddenly the narrow river corridors and the remaining stands of lowland old-growth forest assumed increasing importance.

It's now apparent that the health and long-term survival of our existing protected areas depended upon sound management of our low-lying commercial forests. The kind of selective management I was involved with in the 1970s now appears less a luxury afforded by high stumpage prices than a necessary prescription for sustainable management of the forest ecosystem.

It's no small irony that the old rip-'em-up logging practices of the last century could begin to appear progressive. But as modern, industrial forest management took hold in the decades that followed World War II, the rate and extent to which the Northwest landscape was transformed caused scientists and conservationists to take a closer look at both approaches.

In their fervor to manage forests like corn fields, industrial timber managers "sanitized" their forest lands over the last four decades, eradicating any trace of biological legacy. In the vast horizon-to-horizon clearcuts pioneered by such progressive land stewards as Weyerhaeuser and company, original forests were leveled, slash was burned, and a single species, Douglas fir, was planted in disciplined, even-aged ranks. To managers, these young, Christmas-tree-like plantations were pleasing to the eye; they were orderly, predictable, and performed well on paper. In fact, this approach was so successful in its liquidation of "decadent and diseased" old growth in favor of vigorous young plantations that it very nearly spelled the end of the lowland forest ecosystem.

What biologists studying spotted owl habitat on the Olympic Peninsula and elsewhere found was that remnants of natural forest processes—standing snags and down logs, a mix of ages and species in an uneven, partly open canopy—survived in the lowlands. Not in the managed forests of the timber industry, but in natural forest stands, those that grew up following natural disturbances like windstorms or wildfires. Not surprisingly, some of these characteristics were also found in the old railroad logging areas, although most of those sites had since succumbed to a third rotation of industrial forestry. Some of the species that depended upon old growth and mature forests were found using these stands, and productivity in these sites also seemed high. Researchers reasoned that if these elements could be factored into managed forests, then there might be hope for protecting ecological values in commercial forests that were managed for timber. With a modest reduction in volume and careful management, the "New Forestry" as it was called was the first alternative that offered something to both sides of the controversy.

In the field, the new forestry looks a lot like the old turn-of-the-century logging photos of Kinsey and Curtis: ragged and messy. Snags, whips, clusters of trees, slash everywhere. Yet as developed by old-growth ecologist Jerry Franklin and others, it may prove the best hope forests and forestry have got. The forest service and Washington Department of Natural Resources have begun experimenting with new forestry techniques on the Olympic Peninsula and elsewhere, but both forest ecologists and industry managers are quick to point out that it's no panacea. It may be fifteen or twenty years before any hard wildlife data is available, and even its proponents admit it's a gamble. But as Jerry Franklin has pointed out, so was clearcutting. What's more, we've been running an ecological deficit for so long now, we've *got* to try to envision forestry in a new way. Not only is the economic stability of the rural Northwest on the block, but so is the ecological integrity of some of our most outstanding natural areas, like Olympic National Park.

Trying to interject a sense of balance to the old-growth controversy, I joined Dr. Franklin and about thirty others on a government-appointed commission to try to resolve the deadlock over management of the Department of Natural Resources' remaining old-growth forest lands. We were a mixed group made up of representatives from environmental organizations, the timber industry, Indian tribes, educators, legislators, and specialists in economics, forestry, and law. We worked toward consensus for a year, and to everyone's surprise we agreed on a course of action. Our recommendations included deferring logging in some crucial owl nesting areas, as well as providing economic development assistance for local communities. The state forests of the Olympic Peninsula's west end were restored to non-declining sustained yield, which will slow the rate of cutting and supply some stability to forest-dependent communities.

Perhaps most important, an experimental forest was established for the western Olympic Peninsula, where new forestry techniques will be combined with integrated habitat management in an effort to make commercial forestry compatible with ecosystem protection. A research institute has been established to guide experiments and monitor results. The hope is for a working forest that will provide a richer habitat for old-growth– and mature-forest–dependent wildlife, that will protect wildlife migration corridors and fish habitat, and that will supply a steady flow of timber.

Can it be done? It's still too early to tell. But it's long been obvious that the ecological crisis in Northwest forests could never be resolved by merely preserving national parks and wilderness areas. The issue is too vast and far more complex than that. There's no question that additional ecologic reserves are needed, and needed badly, but somehow the issue of habitat protection on commercial forest lands must be addressed. I continue to hold onto the hope that a true sustainable forestry—sustainable for the ecosystem as well as for rural communities—will yet evolve here. Here, where healthy forests and small towns still survive, if anywhere.

A few weeks ago, taking a long "short cut" home through the mountains, I turned off on an old logging spur and took a walk into an old cut I'd reforested a good many years ago. The Douglas fir seedlings we'd planted had closed above me and were bolting skyward now at three to five feet per year. Among them were other trees we didn't plant: alders along the overgrown haul road, western hemlocks and red cedars blown in from an adjacent stand, an occasional white pine and Bigleaf maple, willows in the streamside draws. The land has a way of taking care of itself in spite of our designs. In time, third-growth forests will once more mantle the lowlands of the peninsula. There's no doubt that a forest industry will be here to draw from it a livelihood. I like to think that by then some lessons will be learned, that attitudes about the land and life here will evolve and change and that life in the woods won't be such a fast-moving, high-stakes game. I like to think that people will continue to be able to live and work in these forests, and that they will finally value this green, bountiful land for what it is.

John Daniel

Cuttings

1.

Sometimes the fallers would be working on a distant slope where we could see them, and when I wasn't wrestling a choker around a log I'd watch them drop the Douglas firs. As a tree toppled and then fell faster, its boughs would sweep back, the whole trunk would flex a little just before it hit the hillside, a flash of wood showing if it broke somewhere. Across the distance the sound came late, and small. The saws sounded like hornets.

The fallers worked in pairs, and they worked slowly. It's a dangerous job—the trees are big, the hills are steep. On any one day they never seemed to advance very far against the front of forest, but they worked slowly and steadily, and day by day they got the job done. They drove the back roads every morning, they laid the big trees down, they bucked them into standard lengths. All across Weyerhaeuser's Northwest empire, they turned the forest into pickup sticks.

2.

There are forests on the rainy side of the Cascade Range where the best way you can walk is on the trunks of fallen trees. Some of them are thicker through than you are tall. They make a random pathway through devil's club and thimbleberry, one to another and another, leading you nowhere except to more trunks with upthrust roots, more standing moss-coated stubs and skeletal snags, more bigleaf maples and western hemlocks and tall Douglas firs. The bark of the big trees is pocked and charred, and most of them lean, already beginning their eventual fall. The filtered light is clear and deep. The only sound you hear is the stepping of your feet among ferns and seedling trees that grow out of softening sapwood. And when you climb down from the pathway of trunks, your feet sink into a yielding matrix of moss and needles and rotting wood—trees becoming earth, earth becoming trees, the forest falling and gathering itself, rising from the abundance of its dying.

3. Up on the landing the steel tower stands a hundred feet tall, a diesel yarder at its base with a reel of heavy cable. When we've set the chokers and scrammed out of the way, the rigging slinger sounds his whistle. The yarder roars, the chokers cinch, and two or three logs start stubbornly up the hill like things alive, plunging and rolling, snagging on stumps and lurching free, dragging and gouging the ground, then dangling in air as they approach the landing, where they're deftly dropped in a neat deck for the waiting trucks. Everything goes to the landing—butt-cuts ten feet through, mature saw logs, buckskin snags, measly pecker-poles, even half-rotted slabs and splintered chunks. Nothing is wasted. The operation scours the hillside, as far as the cables can reach, and by the time we lower the tower and trundle along to a fresh show, only stumps and sticks and boughs are left, patches of sun-struck fern and sorrel, long raw furrows in the barren ground.

4. Like the sea, like the streams full of salmon, the ancient forest gave plenty—totem poles, tool shafts, bows, fishing floats, baskets, dishes, robes, roots, tubers, medicine. A good red cedar might be felled by storm, or they'd bring a tree down themselves by burning into its base. They hollowed the trunk with adzes, heated water in the cavity with hot stones, stretched out the softened sides with posts, lashed stern and bowsprit to the hull with cedar rope. For their houses they split cedar logs into wide boards, tapping horn or hardwood wedges with a hammerstone. And sometimes they split large planks from standing trees and let the trees live on. They still live on. Here and there in the silence of the rainy forest you can find them, you can stand inside those spaces that yielded good wood, where human hands selected a careful portion of what the trees could give.

5. We started out from Bagby Hot Springs in Mount Hood National Forest. As I remember the trail, it climbed along a stream bed and topped out on a sunny ridge, then turned north along the far ridge flank, easy ups and downs through fir and hemlock, gray cliffs on the right. We walked a day like that, then camped in thicker woods where patches of old snow remained and small sounds stirred around our sleeping bags. In the morning after breakfast we walked on, following the trail toward no certain destination. We climbed for a while, still in trees, and then saw light ahead—a meadow, we thought, or a small lake. We walked into a glare of stumps and piled boughs, sap-smell heavy in the air. We worked around the far edge of the cut, trying to pick up the trail. We found the logging road, of course—dry and dusty white, unearthed boulders by its side—but we never found the trail. We sat on stumps a while and walked back the way we had come.

I was new to the Northwest then. I'd been hearing about multiple-use on the public lands, and now I knew what multiple-use was. I decided that even a college drop-out could find better things to do than set chokers for a living.

6. The rain shadow east of the Cascades is the native home of the yellowbellies, ponderosa pines that can measure up to eight feet through and a hundred sixty feet tall. Where they've been left alone they tilt from the earth like great orange arrows, fletched with green, parceled out in a spacious array contrived by shallow soils and periodic sweeps of fire through the centuries. Logging here is usually called selective, like the fires, and sometimes that's exactly what it is. But clearcuts aren't too hard to find. The Forest Service has called them "group selections," and little blowdown patches sold for salvage have a way of expanding into sheared squares. The pine forest stands on gentle terrain. It's easy to get at. By the thirties many of the old yellowbelly groves were gone—*clean-cut,* in the usage of the day, the fat logs hauled out under ten-foot wheels. Now they're skidded out on chokers behind big Cats, and in most of ponderosa country, selective logging means that every thirty years or so the Cats drag out the biggest trees. It's called creaming, or high-grading, and it doesn't take everything. But the forest any kid sees is lesser than the one her father saw, diminishing toward little trees and big stumps, the ancient woods gradually brought down to human scale.

7. Junipers are stubby trees full of branches, and they often have several trunks. In most of them the grain is twisted, a natural tendency accentuated by the big Great Basin winds. He had to walk many dry hills and search many canyons to find a straight-grained tree, or a tree with one straight-grained trunk inside a thicket of outer trunks. He carefully stripped a length of bark to inspect the wood. With chiselstone and hammerstone he notched the top and bottom of the stave he wanted, about four feet long, two-and-a-half inches wide. He went away then, for a few years maybe, while the stave seasoned on the tree. When he came back, if it had seasoned well, without weather-checking, he split it from the tree with a tool of stone or antler. He carved and steamed and worked the stave until it curved in a deep belly and recurved at the ends. He boiled horn for glue, and glued on sinew fibers for strength and spring. He glued on rattlesnake skin to protect the backing, fashioned a grip of wrapped buckskin. He strung the bow with a length of sinew.

One juniper, a huge tree with several great trunks and limbs, shows scars of twelve staves removed. A scar heals as the tree lays in new wood, straight-grained wood laid down where straight-grained wood was taken. One scar shows clear evidence of having yielded four staves in sequence. The harvest interval was probably longer than a human life. In a crotch of one of the tree's big limbs, a hammerstone remains where it was placed.

8. Mount Adams, Mount Jefferson, Three Sisters, Diamond Peak—it doesn't matter which Cascade mountain you climb. From any of them you see a few singular volcanoes ranging away to north and south, studding an expanse of rolling green going blue in the distance. From most of the peaks you can see a lake, or several lakes. And always, more each year, on both flanks of the range and sometimes high up toward the crest, you can see the white squiggles of advancing roads and the bare geometric patches of sheared ground. From the highways you see mostly trees. From the summits you can see where all those trucks are coming from. And almost every acre in your view is public land, retained in the ownership of the American people, part of a national forest system established a hundred years ago to hold good woodlands in reserve against the aggressions of the timber barons.

Some of the cuts are greening up with a growth of genetically selected Douglas firs, which will yield a forest of identical clones, which will be cropped in sixty or eighty years and the clearcuts planted again, to raise another forest if they can. But many of the cuts are bare and brown, flecked with silver whiskers of culled wood. From this elevation they look neat and trim. Whenever I look down at them I search for a new metaphor. They aren't a quilt, not yet at least, but their clustered patchwork does suggest a farmer's fields. "Cascade crew cut" is a term you sometimes hear. *Mange* is the best that I've been able to do, a mange spreading through the mountains. But mange is scraggly and uneven. These clearcut barrens are too regular, too geometrical and clean-sided. Whatever is making them is working surgically, with fine precision. Mange doesn't know what it's doing to the animal. What's working at these mountains knows exactly what it's doing.

9. As my friend grows older he feels himself turning from a farmer to a forester. He walks his wooded hillside, which about the time that he was born was cleared and planted in crops. The topsoil ran away, the fields were left to scrub, and now he walks among the young trees that have reclaimed the hill. He names their kinds, delighting in their company. "Look at that oak there, isn't it pretty? That'll be an oak for a long time." He tells a story about a neighbor who swung his dog on one of the wild grape vines, a story that ends badly for the dog but brings laughter to the hillside decades later. Stories grow here like the trees. My friend comes to walk and talk sometimes, and other times to work. Low stumps are visible where he's thinned, the poles and logs hauled out behind his horses, seasoning now in neat piles below. In his mind he sees the cut wood forward to its good uses—fence posts, rafters, fuel for the winter—and the standing forest grows on in his mind too. "If I cut that sassafras," he says, "the little oak might grow." He opens such small spaces for the sun, opens and raises his hillside forest toward the beauty of the big hardwoods that once stood here, sunlight playing in their broad leaves, their roots grown deep in the rich soil of their making.

10. "No, it ain't pretty," a man said to me once, "but it's the only way to harvest these trees. It don't pay to go in there just for a few." We were standing in the rainy morning outside the Weyerhaeuser time shack. His tin hat battered by years in the woods, a lunch pail and steel thermos of coffee in his hands, he spoke those words with a certainty I remember clearly—just as I remember what a good man he was, how he cussed beautifully and told fine stories and was friendly to a green chokersetter, how he worked with an impossible appetite that left me panting and cussing unbeautifully behind him. I don't remember what I or someone said that drew his response, or whether he was answering some doubt he himself had raised. I only recall the authority of his voice, the rain dripping from his tin hat, and the idling crummies waiting to carry us out the muddy roads from camp, out through the stripped hills to another day of work.

The voice that spoke those words is my voice too. It's in all of us—the voice of practicality and common sense, the voice that understands that ugly things are necessary. It's a voice that values getting a hard job done and making an honest living. It has behind it certain assumptions, certain ideas about progress, economy, and standard of living, and it has behind it the evidence of certain numbers, of payrolls and balance sheets, of rotation cycles and board footage. It is not a heartless voice. It has love for wife and children in it, a concern for their future. It has love for the work itself and the way of life that surrounds the work. And it has at least a tinge of regret for the forest, a sense of beauty and a sorrow at the violation of beauty.

I must have nodded, those years ago, when a good man spoke those words. I didn't argue—against his experience and certainty, I had only a vague uneasiness. Now, I suppose, I would argue, but I know that arguing wouldn't change his mind, just as I know that he wouldn't change mine. As he defined the issue, he saw it truly. Many of us define the issue differently now, and we think we see it truly, and all of us on every side have studies and numbers and ideas to support what we believe. All of us have evidence.

The best evidence, though, is not a number or idea. The land itself is not a number or idea, and the land has an argument to make. Turn off the highway, some rainy day in the Northwest, and drive deep into a national forest on the broad gravel roads and the narrow muddy roads. Drive in the rain through one of the great forests of Earth. Drive past the stands that are left, drive past the gentle fields of little trees and big stumps. Pass the yellow machines at rest, the gravel heaps and sections of culvert pipe, the steel drums here and there, a rusting piece of choker in the ditch. Drive until you come to a steep mountainside stripped of its trees—you will come to it—where puke-outs have spewed stone rubble across the road, where perhaps the road itself, its work accomplished, has begun to sag and slide.

Stand in the rainfall, look at the stumps, and try to imagine the forest. You will have to imagine it, because on this steep slope no forest of that scale, very likely no forest at all, will stand again. The great trees, and the creatures that wove their countless strands of energy into a living, shifting tapestry, from deep in the rooted soil through all the reaches of shaded light to the crowning twig-tips with their new cones. . . The trees are gone, the creatures are gone, and the very genius of these hills, that gathered rain and changing light for centuries, that grew and deepened as it brought forth a green and towering stillness—it too is leaving. It's washing down in gullies to a muddy stream.

Peter Levitt

For the Trees

If a tree falls in the forest and there is no one there to hear it, does it make a sound?

—Question asked by the humans after they stopped living in forests

1.

If a tree falls in the forest and there is no one there to hear it, *it makes a sound.* (How could there be no one there to hear it?) That sound is heard simultaneously in all places around the earth and into the heavens, by all things. In that moment when the tree falls, it is the sound of our world.

2.

If a whole forest falls in the forest, the sound it makes is unbearable—so unbearable we pretend we can't even hear a single tree when it falls, and ask about it, lowering the two bats of our eyes.

3.

If a child falls in the forest, any child, your child, your sapling of a girl or boy, or one you are fond of, if this child falls, scraping a limb, perhaps, and cries out, and there is no one there to hear it, the sound never leaves you, but flies through the air of you like a wild parrot, repeating its cry. The forest is filled with the parents of these ones—the mothers and fathers who have come there for the comfort, the advice, of their elders, the trees, and to find their fallen young. After a while, these parents become birds themselves. You can hear them calling with a two or three note song:

> *Who's there? Who's there?*
> *Is it you? Is it you?*

4.

When we enter a forest, it is exactly like making love, for we are entering the body of a living being. A kind of sacredness is there. Who has not felt the silence move through them like a fragrant ghost, rising from their first steps on the forest floor? Who has walked through a forest and not felt the all-embracing air and limbs, the quality of the light, the sanctity rooted in this most ancient natural sanctuary our earth provides? Rare is the person who has truly been there and not, in some way, offered a bow.

Here is a story given to us from the ancient forests of India, although it could easily happen right here, say, up in Washington or among the last old-growth stands hugging our Pacific shore:

> *One day the Buddha was walking through the forest with some good friends. Suddenly he stopped and pointed to the ground. This would be a good spot for a sanctuary, he said. Indra, who was known as the Emperor of the gods, took a blade of grass and stuck it into the ground. The sanctuary is built, he said. And all of them smiled.*

The sanctuary is built. The sanctuary is already built. The sanctuary inherent in the smallest green shoot. The sanctuary of our elders' strong-hearted lives, rooted in the earth's deep bed. This sanctuary is built. Built from beginningless time. And isn't that why we go to the forest? To enter the sanctuary, to walk within it, to breathe its air, to hear its sudden, its subtle sounds, or the long weaving sigh wind makes high in its branches, needles, and leaves, to find that part of ourselves we did not even know we had lost, to ask about ourselves, *Who's there? Who's there? Is it you? Is it you?* To do all of this—isn't that why we go—and to remember?

How do we remember? How does the forest help us stitch and weave until the fabric of our memory is made whole again? We once lived in forests. Do you remember? It was a life before this human one. We were minerals. We were sunlight on the forest floor. We were spore, fungi, bacteria, plant-life, insect. We were the green leaf, the red vein. We were chlorophyll, photosynthesis. We were snowdrift. We were the sound of rain. It is in us. Do you remember? We once lived there. I know we can remember because just as we once *were* the life of the forest, the forest is still alive in us. Can it be that forests are lawyers, baseball players, poets, astronauts, loggers, school teachers, doctors, mathematicians, car mechanics? It can be. So how do we remember, we forest beings, currently called the human race? How does the forest help us see clearly enough for our memory to return?

We remember by going into the presence of the old ones, sitting beside them, or walking beneath their sheltering limbs. There is a quality that rises up from the fertility, the deep aroma of the soil we know we can trust. When we feel the texture of their roughened skins with our fingers, and see the ages gathered into those various bark patterns with our eyes, when we feel the air they create, that fullness, we know then that trees are our elders. We begin to recall. And when I say they are our elders, it is with gratitude, and with awe, for trees of the old-growth are the great-great-great-great-great-grandmother/grandfathers of our world. The kind of noble, reliable ancestors all people have looked to when they needed strength, or beauty, or protection, or grounding, or rest, shelter, warmth, security, and the kind of knowing where you do most of the listening because what's being told to you is like the beautiful silent voice it's being told to you with, rare. Rare as the air you breathe, *and from the same source.* Elders. The ones we go to so that we may learn from the long and broad lives they've lived, for our forests are tellers of part of our own history.

If a forest is whole (and this means that if, as part of the life of the forest, it is logged by women and men who see with the eyes of the forest itself), the history is one of nurturance, natural cycle, balance, rationality. Do forests think? Forests *are* thought. Thoughtfulness. A planning that ensures survival of great numbers and variety of beings and species. A mind that is a model of compassionate provision for the lives of squirrels, birds, snakes, bear, coyote, deer, elk, and humans. It is the natural way of forests to give us our lives, purifying and protecting the air of this breathing world. It is their natural way to nourish the soil, even as they are nourished by it, to provide food for millions of species, to become clothing, home to the marmot, woodpecker, wolf. It is their nature to offer their own lives for all the family of living things to thrive, each according to its various needs and way. It is their natural way to serve. Isn't that what true elders understand? But it is not part of their natural way for entire forests to be cut down. And it is not part of our natural way to cut them down. Not natural, not needed. It does not serve.

If each of us were to arrange to go to the forest, and live beneath a tree, as an apprentice, and observe the life and ways of that tree with great attention and care, for a cycle of just four seasons, we would know how to live with greater kindness, strength, grace, purpose, compassion. We would know how to live with proportion. We would learn—it would come back into our hands—how to serve. The tree would give us back to ourselves. In discovering our lineage, heart-line, history, in touching this one root of our ancient body, we would discover what it means to take root in this earth and emerge with new breath, new serenity and understanding, vigor and hope, new senses of meaning of our own lives. We would emerge like bright seedlings, carrying the essence of our ancestors. All of this with the fresh green moistness of new life. We would remember so well that we might even remember ourselves right into the present and begin to see our lives as the life of the forest itself. Are we not the air of the forest, her minerals, her rivers, the fruit of her soil? Isn't there still something of forest light, mountain slope, river-sound, in our visions and dreams? Isn't what we call spirit, which comes from the seed syllable for *breath* (*in*spiration, breathe in, *ex*piration, breathe out), isn't this too given to us by sunlight, earth, and rain ? And by the complex interacting life of the millions of creatures of the forest world? By natural diversity, fertility, by wild seed? Remember?

5. *Whatever befalls the Earth, befalls the sons and daughters of the Earth.* —CHIEF SEATTLE

Beside me, as I write this, there is a picture postcard. A miniature from our world. In the midst of the lush foliage of a forest, seven human figures have thrown their bodies in despair over the huge stump of a tree. By the size of the stump it is clear that this tree lived hundreds of years before it was felled. The circular cut of the stump they weep upon is so broad that their outstretched hands don't even approach the central birth-ring of the tree. And, there are no other ancient trees in view. On the back of the card it says this:

> *If trees could scream no one*
> *on earth would sleep peacefully again.*

The picture is from a painting by Jane Evershed, called *Mourning in the Rainforest.* The light in the painting is golden, early morning light. A new day's glow filters through the remaining leaves and needles onto the richly colored forest floor. It is beautiful. It is pained. What will this day bring?

The trees are screaming. The scream of the trees is everywhere about us. We can hear it in the way we turn from each other's eyes when we meet. What kind of light might we find arcing between us if we were to risk a look? We can hear it in the feeling of pressure that gathers in each of our bodies, like a tree contracting from the blow of the axe. We can hear it in the stiffening of our spines, the tightening of our lungs, and in that knot we carry like a stone just below the heart. That's the scream of the trees. They can be heard in our wasted cities, in the collapsed veins of our young, in the hopeless unwanted stare of our human elders, who have not been permitted the nobility of their ancestor-trees. That's the screaming too.

If you really believe there is no connection between these things, you haven't looked deeply enough. Because entire mountainsides are marked for the cut, it is easier for young gang members who have never been to a forest to cut each other down. The colors they wear, signifying their tribe, mark them for "the cut" as well. This, too, is the scream of the trees. It is easier to rape or kill people, once we *as a species,* rationalize (but not with the native rationality of the forest!) and accept the centuries-old wholesale destruction and looting of the mountains of China, India, Brazil, Mexico, U.S.A. with the false idea that *it serves our needs.* (It does not serve! These are not our needs!) The concept is the same. Doesn't the language of *slash and burn* feel almost identical with *search and destroy?* On and on. The violence of the clearcut and the violence which keeps us cowering behind the walls of our rooms, afraid to go out into the open air, are based on the same thoughtless, wasteful, delusion-centered mind. It is a stab into our own lungs, close to the heart. Every forest creature knows what happens when the machinery of the cut, carrying the full weight of its intention, dozes its way into the sacred body of the forest. It shakes the ground.

And our ground is shaking. I don't mean only the literal soil in which the forest community has taken root and grown, matured, propagated, and re-propagated again and again for millions of years, that miracle of interspecies development and interdependent cooperation, but the deeper, more extensive ground of being, *the root of the root,* until that shaking can be felt and is known everywhere, in each cell of the larger organism we call Earth, our home. That ground is shaking. And the ground on which we evolutionary newcomers have made our stand, the lands where human communities have taken root, grown, matured, propagated, and so on, shakes with a devastating fright. Because it is wanton, this destruction. It is wanton, to massacre the forests. Without true necessity. Without true cause, moral standard. Ignorant. Ignoring. Without the bounds of literal reality. Without.

Recently a rabbi friend told me that it is part of mystical Jewish thought that when we live in such a way that we do not acknowledge and honor our relationship to the Source, when we defile the sacred ground of our existence, we are not the only ones whose lives are diminished, but that *the ground* itself—the Source—diminishes as well. I was shocked. Could it be so? Is it possible that when we turn our backs and live out of relationship with the Source, *it* diminishes? Do we really have that kind of effect? To answer that question we only need to look carefully at our present world. Are we heading for a time when we will have cut down all the trees? A time, therefore, when we will no longer be there to hear the last tree as it falls, and will, ourselves, make no sound—our no-sound the final soundless scream of all the trees? Please look with me. The evidence is everywhere around.

6. Don't massacre the trees.

Art Goodtimes

Baptized Green

Born in the post-war boom, I was a child of the affluent Fifties. My parents moved my two brothers and me out of the city and into a tract-home bungalow south of San Francisco when I was five.

Youth for me and many of my generation was a blend of playground drama, the Baltimore catechism, and that newfangled programmed eye of television. I loved Lucy, tried to do what Sister Leo said, and wondered why Philbert led three lives instead of the comfortable one we all knew in the Santa Clara Valley—a Pacific Rim paradise of Mediterranean climate, endless orchards of apricots and almonds, and a million fewer people than today.

All that ever interrupted the routine of our "small lawns of hope," as George Oppen knew them, were the weekend trips into the Santa Cruz mountains to explore the preserved redwood groves of Big Basin State Park. It was there I learned the rhythms of another world, a pre-programmed profusion of natural wealth—the crackling of the fire logs, plush needle carpet underfoot on the trails, the pecking of the flickers, lively creeks where my brothers and I built rock dams, mud forts, and chased the quick crayfish.

And once a year we took a long vacation, two weeks at Big Basin at first, and then venturing further out, into the Sierras. When I was eleven we even made the grand West Coast tour up to Canada. It was then, tooling along in our big Buick station wagon through Oregon, that I first saw clearcuts, the distant bald hillsides swept clean of green and tucked far off from the highways. To be honest, they impressed me less at the time than the vast tracts "lost" to fire, like the huge Raymer Burn, with its roadside interpretive sign that explained the unmanaged tragedy of nature run amuck.

Indeed, while a sense of the wild had emerged from years of

camping, it had been strictly regulated by the state's campground mentality. Smokey the Bear was our hero. Fire was good only within prescribed rings. And the forest, as one placard I still keep extolled, was "an apartment house," with various levels of habitation, starting with the ground-floor insects and working its way up to the penthouse eagles. It was a neat, hierarchical, Industrial Growth framework into which the park rangers tried to stack trees, critters, and of course campers. Growing up with that mindset, I accepted my late technolithic culture at face value and took pleasure in feeding the tame Bambi fenced near the park headquarters.

Nature was a sanctuary of wild things kept safe and made accessible by wise management. That was the lesson. And I learned it.

But two weeks up in the Sierras, bivouacked far from campgrounds and other happy campers along a barely accessible National Forest road, playing Huck Finn on rafts, hunting under rocks for blue-belly lizards, and getting lost and found all on our own, taught my brothers and me a different kind of nature, a true wilderness that wasn't so neat, so safe—an unpredictable forest where mountain lion roamed and black bear scratched deep petroglyphs in the bark of giant ponderosa.

But driving a car is much different than walking in the forest.

On our Canadian vacation, the vast wilderness of Northern California, Oregon, Washington, and British Columbia impressed me through the mediating glass of a speeding windshield that summer of 1956 with their seemingly unending dimensions. The family stayed in hotels, ate at restaurants. We were tourists, bought trinkets, took photographs of each other posed beside wooden Indians.

It wasn't until many years later that I came to really understand what a clearcut was. Old enough to be on my own, I chose to return to the city of my birth, where my mother's family had lived for several generations, the San Francisco of childhood stories and Gold Rush legend. It was the Sixties, and I soon joined the hordes of flower children flocking into "Baghdad-by-the-Bay," as *San Francisco Chronicle* columnist Herb Caen had tagged this ex-beatnik haven.

Married after the riots at San Francisco State (where we met), my wife and I cut a crazy Dead figure in those days, zooming around the Haight on my Honda, bird's nest basket I'd woven cradled over the 250's headlight, my brocaded Don Giovanni jacket cutting the fog and Karen's rainbow scarf snapping zigzag behind us Isadora Duncan style all the way down Mission to the financial center where she worked.

But the city wasn't our main focus.

Almost every free weekend we drove a couple hundred miles south to a small river pool near Camp Hunter-Liggett's San Antonio Mission, our valley retreat, to lounge in the adobe sun with off-duty soldiers and Mill Creek hippies, naked, telling tales and seeing visions.

Even after I'd finished school and my marriage dissolved, I kept up the bifurcated pattern. Moving to a relic earthquake cottage in the Richmond District just a couple of blocks from Golden Gate Park, I did my conscientious objector work as a busdriver for a handicapped center during the week, and on the weekends I would hitchhike north or south along the coast highway, bushwhacking into roadless areas, camping out alone. On Sunday afternoons I'd hitchhike back. Those two or three days often seemed to stretch time and usually I'd swear I'd been gone for weeks. On those larks I'd go as far as the rides would take me if they were congenial, or stop at a favorite haunt en route if they were not.

Fort Ross was one such layover.

This relic, square-log, southernmost outpost of Russian-American expansionism held a special fascination beyond its Orthodox crosses. My great-grandfather's family had logged the giant *Sempervirens* along the Russian River and my great-grandmother's ancestor had been *jefe de policia* in Monterey, 1794. My roots ran deep in California history. Like the many romantic ruins of Franciscan missions along El Camino Real (concentration camps for the captured *indigenas,* as I later learned), Fort Ross was a seemingly charming reminder of bygone eras. Old Highway One ran through the middle of the reconstructed fort, and I'd visited it several times as a youth on road trips with my family.

Just below the fort was a delightful angler's trail along Fort Ross Creek that gradually disappeared into a sinuous labyrinth of winter windblow, beaver dams, polished agate falls, and black oak acorn groves. Many times I'd hopped out of the car with my pack where the highway crossed the creek, thanked the driver, and walked off into the coastal rainforest of Northern California's marine terraces. Years later, my daughter, Iris Willow, would be conceived on a sandbar far up this obscure swordfern gulch.

Another favorite haunt was a nearby sheep-meadow wagon road up the shortgrass ridge, fanning deep into the old Pomo forests—fragrant bay laurel, Douglas fir, cypress, and ocean mist redwood. There I camped and dreamt, wrote and huddled over small pit fires. One weekend I dared the spring stars without a bag, curled up in a coat, sweater stretched over me. On and off all night I shivered, teeth dancing like time-lapse shellfish, until curling ever closer round the embers I once again got up and ignited them, calling back the heat.

As I studied the natural history of the Bay Area of my birth—roaming Mt. Tam and Mt. San Bruno, making a trek to the top of Diablo, and all of Inverness—I fell in love with mushrooms.

A waxy red *Hygrophorus* in a Santa Cruz canyon was the siren that won me, and I was soon joining Land's End forays with the San Francisco Mycological Society. My companion Francesca and I would find oyster mushrooms along Steep Ravine in Marin and bundle them home for sizzling meatless stroganoff, wild rice, and hot sake by candlelight. Alone at Point Reyes, I knelt at the stipe of the *Destroying Angel,* coifed in a veil of perfect white, or chummed with the patrician *boletes,* staining blue when bruised (while the *B. eastwoodiae* stained red—poisonous, deadly).

Some of the region's best fields of the delicate and delicious *shaggy manes* were to be found above Fort Ross, along that ancient Russian wagon road into two hundred-year-old groves of second-growth climax. All day I'd amble in the pierced shadows, basking in heat on the roots of an uprooted giant, or trace the limpid amperage of water splashing over moss-edged igneous. Monarchs and swallowtails would leapfrog through the carpeting sorrel with its trillium blooms and alight on a huckleberry bush, whose berries quickly stained my palm and tongue.

I slept in that forest many nights. Heard *los tecalotes,* the owls, calling in the moonlight. Watched voles tunnel around my tent. Saw tracks of mountain lion just above camp. Indeed, certain Fort Ross redwoods became my friends. I'd camp under this one, find banana slugs at another, and mark where a third twisted in spiral dance with a cottonwood trunk. I spent hours discovering new wonders each time I visited.

Then, of course, since it's a Christian mythos we live under and Fort Ross was as close to Eden as I could recall, came the Fall.

I hiked up the wagon road one weekend, intent on hunting up a pack load of *Coprinus* and sleeping under a heaven of shooting stars, and disaster! Heavy tire tracks led like cruel footsteps into my sanctuary along a newly carved logging road. I felt myself drawn irrevocably along the soil scars to a clearing I could see up ahead in the canopy—a clearcut!

This wasn't obliteration, like a Pacific atoll stripped bare by a hurricane. This was slaughter, mayhem and the tortured bodies of the dead and dying. Busted trees tilted everywhichway. Peeled limbs hung from downed giants. The once placid duff churned with scarred furrows, spent chainsaw oil cans leaking a rainbow film of crud in puddled water. I began to weep unashamedly. I could hear from deep within the ravaged grove the cry of the dinosaur sequoias. I walked around in a daze, unable to fathom the cultivated separation from sense of place that let an "owner" wipe out this magic web of leaf and antennae, wings and roots, pollen and song.

Suddenly every clearcut I'd ever seen at a distance grabbed at my throat, like fingers round the neck of a drowning man. I could smell death in the running sap. It was my flesh ripped up on this killing floor. It was my pain, my earth. And, as in a forced christening in the mean-spirited blood of empire, pitiless bottomline trickledown profitshare battlefield, this have-you-no-shame greed of Industrial Growth Society, I was baptized green.

"No," I said. "Yes." I declare my interdependence. In the name of the land, and the sky and the holy sea, I pledge allegiance to the stars stripped of myth, this planet full of wonders, the Mother whose children we all are—sun that wakes us, air that breathes us, green that feeds us, water that connects us all in the hoop. Goodbye empire. Goodbye pin-striped suits. I embrace this everywhere around us always nurturing Earth First!

Not long after that I left the city, and I've lived in the mountains ever since.

Dian Million

K'enq'a: The Depth of Stillness

In this rock we
see the beginning the weight
and depth of stillness
as old as any beginning
older than
those of us who choose the motion
spinning higher out, our fragile
writhings familiar
with destruction.

Who will imagine the world in a hundred years; who will imagine even now what all this may have been. I grew up in Alaska, Oregon, and Washington, and I live among the remnants of these places as I write this. It was to have knowledge of immensity—to know that the non-human world was a beautiful place to live in. No one thought it consciously of course. It was just where we lived, following my father as he went from job to job in the 1950 Northwestern world of one-store towns and among people who had a sense of themselves as free of "the system." They weren't kind to people who lived "stuck in some city." Actually most of them were logging towns, and it was the beginning of the end. My father drove log trucks, and we often lived in places where logging is what people did for money. In the winters he would hunt those same forests. He wanted to be free, and to this day he recounts that theme over and over, an "old-timer" in his seventies, living alone in Valdez, Alaska, and he still believes it is about living without being "told what to do."

I do not believe he knows about environmentalism or thinks of his role in the opening of Alaska to development. He thinks of the job, that it was a job where a man could be free, so to speak. He thought of the woods as a place to live out some internal vision that he had of freedom from "civilization." I loved living under the 200-foot fir groves that were everywhere up the sweep of the north coasts. I love those places now, and in the bare and torn places where the trees were ripped out, I imagine them in the mists like ghosts, so thickly that the smell and sound of them are everywhere and are indelible.

It is hard to explain to someone who never knew the world then. That you could walk out your back yard and never be seen again; that in the forests there was a life that had nothing to do with humans, that the fish are born there, and that life in these places is old and tenacious.

We are Alaskan Native through my mother who was born in Nenana, Alaska, and from my relations of blood on that side I learned that nothing is forever in this time, because change and want and need are in voracious control. That under the control of these forces all is expendable; the Native peoples, countless lives that do not communicate in a human value system, the water that makes all this life possible, the trees that live to some of the greatest ages on earth. Life is about change, and to a great degree about want and need, but something is speeded up here. We live beyond cycles now; we live consciously making the choices to change it all at faster and faster rates.

In the 1950s we lived in the shacks and the lean-to's of the towns that made it their business to take the trees. I suppose that my father and the men who thought like him did not know they were mortal, because they often acted as if nothing was sacred. They acted on the land and on the Native people in a very similar manner. Everything this country prizes was embodied in my father and others of his mien, the hard-drinking, hard-working, conqueror of Native women; the I can-do-anything-I-want iconoclastic frontier Man. I suggest that it is this man who was the pioneer. You could "tame" the wilderness, and you could escape your own society's mores by not having any. Thus, the guiding light ahead of progress was always lawlessness.

In the scheme of things for the world, logging is the industry that made it possible to put the non-Indian human life in those places on the map. I suppose many people grew rich from the offering of the trees—ironically not the people who raped their own places to earn money to feed their families. They are as expendable as the trees; many just do not know this yet. It is particularly hard for people, because no one who ever lived and earned a living amongst the spiritual splendor of the mountainsides and free-running rivers ever hated living there. You can live within what is "wild" only if you live lightly. When you live within a nonhuman construct and take for the taking, something else occurs.

People who may have never *experienced* a forest thought of millions of uses for paper and other wood products; industrialists made fortunes; loggers got settled into needing their jobs. Not many people wanted to know what was going on behind the polite fringe of trees left next to the highways (so as not to ruin the scenery). The people who cut the trees and scraped the land, and who know and love the forests well, will be the last to admit to this ruin. Too bad for them.

There is nowhere to go now. We cannot imagine this place, or even this continent, as it was when it lay pristine and sweet within its own heart.

> We go out among the still places
> the fear
> that it is havoc we render
> too eager to destroy
> every vestige of what we did not make ourselves
> and not ever know this
> so fast the vision of our own worth,
> frightened by our powerlessness . . .

The great hunting and gathering cultures who had from four to fourteen thousand years of experience here knew the forest's endless bounty and its power; they knew it as a cyclical process that was always renewed and renewing.

That we do not imagine the coastal forests as they were in the early part of this century means that we do not mourn, for we do not mourn what we do not remember. It was a necessity to kill the wilderness, those places that brought terror and fear of chaos to settler minds. It was on purpose that the land was cleared, and that wild things, including the cultures that didn't share the settlers' view of what wild and tame meant, were destroyed. Necessary evil or necessary harvest. What competed with settlers, or what settlers coveted, could be killed or taken.

So the old photographs capture the smiles and proud stances of men on carcasses of the gargantuan old trees; photographs which figure prominently in all the museums and roadside diners of the North country. These are the pictures of the victors and the victory of men who knew they were first and last, because no forest would ever again attain the great ages of the ones they had cut. They were pioneer in the meaning of first—in a world that was fast running out of firsts. The trees lay quietly on the specially built wagons and trucks made for the occasion, sometimes so big that thirteen men would stand across one stump. The western coastal forests were continuous from Alaska to California across a land changing with each wagon.

The 1930s was the last time in the Pacific Northwest great forests lay thick upon the land. Technology hadn't quite caught up with the dream yet, but it began to. In the 1930s and 1940s three great fires caused by logging in tinder-hot, dry summer weather became known as the Tillamook Burn. Fire raged so hot that smoke could be seen all over the Western United States from the air. It burned for months. It darkened the sky over much of the West. Those who saw the smoke likened it to what was later known as nuclear holocaust. School children from Portland and the vicinity worked for years to replant the area, which is now mostly managed tree farm. In Washington and Oregon, the speed of the cutting grew dizzying.

What had been ancient forest is only described in a few places now, and the generation that actually saw those forests is not here anymore to tell what they saw.

The mourning for the great forests has begun. It has only been the last generation that has taken notice that little old growth even exists in the Northwest any longer; that many species dependent on the life of a forest also sink toward extinction. Few salmon come to spawn naturally, to dance with the rivers for life and regeneration.

What are we interdependent with? We, who are a part of this. We, who have made the most impact upon it. Creation and destruction lie within us, and yet we strangely are not moved to great passion by its passing; in great numbers we don't know yet what it is we lose. We can barely envision what we never knew. I don't think that the heads of timber companies as they sat in the great urban centers of the east ever knew. "Heads" is a good word, because they were disconnected from their souls, which can't be reached by calculation.

Trees, as other substantial life on earth. We, who are so lonely that we reach out poignantly to the stars for communication while we so studiously destroy the other life forms here.

The trees are not the forest. Planting trees will not a forest make. The forest is a living force in retreat now. In some places the earth is scorched from the destruction of trees and other plant cover, vulnerable now and in time and place probably irreplaceable. It would take a thousand years for it all to come back in some healthy form. Because we do not think in those frames of time, it will not be done.

> We sit among the rock people
> for the length that light retreats;
> I feel the first gentle touch of rain
> and you are crying without sound
> the warm rivulets among the cool.
> I cannot breathe
> the wind has caught it up in my throat
> and we walk into the arbor
> and lay upon the land.

We lived in the forest, hearing it breathe at night; the wind put us to sleep that way. We could burn wood to stay warm when it got thirty degrees below, and in the summer could seek the cool moistness within those boreal glens, still places always. I live in the forest's shelter now, because I, like many Northern people, don't like the sun all the time. I like the sun in the winter when the trees have made the world brilliant green against the equally luminous white of the snow and fathomless teal of the water. It is life I think of always in the shaded corridors of filtered sunlight, the life which is so extravagant here where water is abundant.

I believe that the living force of the trees and the water are being sucked out of the land because the land is a commodity, bought and sold. Whatever exists on it is usable or expendable, and I wonder at it. Life is sacred to whom? Only human life. Only what we deem. Life in all forms beyond our imaginations, life in forms we have no senses to comprehend. I mourn the great proclamations of living force that manifested themselves as forests, while I am human and also must use them. It is for consciousness, for longer memory span that I argue.

As we expand humanity and expend the earth, we must *remember.* We will never miss what we do not remember. Scarcity will be our future, as bounty is what we seem to know here in the North still. If oil moves people to the same greedy lust as gold, what lust will we know someday for the places that have water when the aquifers to the south of us are gone. Would the water seem like the forest: without end?

Life is tough. I have learned from the grass in the cracks of the sidewalks. If grass needs to grow, it will break the concrete. I will never really suffer what concrete stands for to live in my heart: I will break it.

to learn old stillness
I walk toward you on the land
Out towards the mouth of the gate
a halfmoon place where we find the bones
of a young deer
and wonder at the faces of the rock people   knowing
they lead out
and we follow
bonded.

Let the land speak for itself.

Reginald Gibbons

The Destruction of Forests, of Peoples, of Persons

Trees are clearcut from slopes that were never so devastated by men in the history of the planet, even when they were burnt off by all-consuming fire, which can restore as well as destroy. The offense of clearcutting is not only to the plant and animal life that is destroyed; it is not only to the men and women who find spiritual depth and physical pleasure in wilderness. Clearcutting adds another notch to a long and evil list of triumphant human destruction, much of it vocally defended by persons of small vision and even less understanding.

I cannot agree with the argument that clearcutting is fundamentally a matter of employment for the thousands of men who work in the trade. It is true that without trees to cut, these men will be out of work, discarded as workers, perhaps impoverished, along with their families. However, clearcutting is fundamentally a matter of ownership and rights to property. These owners and managers are often only too happy for the loggers themselves to argue their case for them, and thus shift the focus away from those who truly have the power of decision to those who, even if they were ordered to cut down every plant on the entire earth, would never become wealthy or powerful as a result. That the suffering of loggers who lose work is real does not justify the offense of clearcutting. The onus of this offense lies on the owners and managers who choose to harvest trees in a short-term fashion rather than preserve and protect what can never be replaced, while establishing methods that allow a sustainable renewable forest.

We must regard the natural world in a respectful—not necessarily worshipful, but at least stewardly—way if it is to replenish our spirits as well as our economy and the economy of future generations. The natural heritage of the planet, forever in flux, forever evolving with and without the added factor of human agency, must be managed, to the necessary extent, with the greatest care if it is to continue to sustain life in variety and health. But today, corporate power and governmental complicity continue despite their rhetoric of concern. They continue to prepare for more destruction, insulated from societal control. To paraphrase poet Karl Shapiro, the purpose of public relations is to convince the victims that they are happy. However, such destructive power must always be challenged whenever possible. Why should corporations and the governing officials in corporate pockets control the fate of forests and all the life and ecological resources within them?

Some power to shape our lives and environment will be necessary if we hope to end human illness and hunger and servitude and violence, but the power to raid and exploit either people or the natural world must be fought steadily and with hope. There is a deep connection between the way men in power, whether their power is corporate or governmental, view the natural world as primarily a mass of renewable resources to be sold and the way they view the lives of human beings—a viewpoint that says both human beings and the natural world can be destroyed for any justifiable economic purpose.

How can one entirely separate the destruction of the natural world from a government's actions, even war? What was the war in the Persian Gulf if not a way to create the opportunity to control a natural resource—oil—and to create profits in reconstruction of industry? The human industry required to restore life and health to the Persian Gulf is, as usual, left to find its own slow and agonized way forward, offering as it does no great markup. What can we expect of the same power's attitudes toward forests when the head of the Environmental Protection Agency of our government says that the environmental destruction of the Gulf War is not *so* bad? How can one entirely distinguish the scars on the earth left by clearcutting from those left by wars? Clearcutting does not *look like* husbandry or natural-resource management; it *looks like,* and it is, a war against nature. As war is a kind of clearcutting of human beings.

Such destruction was not possible before the invention and manufacture of the machines of mass destruction. In earlier times, it took centuries in such places as Greece and Spain for men to destroy forests covering entire regions with the strength of just their hands. Nor could whole nations of people be easily destroyed by the sword, even when it was wielded by the most tireless and cold-blooded human hands. But neither human justice nor responsible husbandry appear to be present in the great machinery of destruction at work today.

So, how can the desire for profit and the rationalizations of power, whether in the U.S. or the Soviet Union or South Africa or Brazil (where destruction of forests means the destruction of peoples) or anywhere else, be supplanted by a joy in the air and prospect of wilderness? How can pleasure in destruction and damage be changed to pleasure in conservation and service?

Over generations, one must speak out against the manufacture of more machinery of death and against the impunity of the agents of destructive political power and of wealth. One must regard all peoples and all places, both man-formed and natural, with equal care not to cause devastation and suffering. This will, in turn, bring safety and dignity to human beings while preserving the natural environment. One must refuse to regard any people or tribe or nation or race as essentially different from one's self. The natural world is the home from which human beings arose. Places felt as sacred—shores, deep woods, mountains, deserts—are the sources from which our species' capacity for inner life arose. One must protect the destruction of people; and the clearcutting of forests.

W.S. Merwin

Who Cares for Forests?

Many Americans who have become aware recently of the accelerating destruction of the world's forests, particularly rain forests, seem to be better informed about the devastation in Latin America and even in Asia than about anything of the kind in the U.S. It is sometimes forgotten that major sections of North America were once magnificent climax forests which have been destroyed as a matter of course, for most of four centuries, until less than 5% of them are left in the lower 48 states, and even that remnant is threatened. And the menace to them, when it is mentioned at all, is often spoken of as though it were in no way related to the human ruin of the earth's forests elsewhere. There is a suggestion—and its origins are easy to guess—that it is all right to be concerned about the forests of the Amazon or Malaysia (where Americans have no vote and cannot do much to obstruct the course of business) but that persistent defense of forests within the U.S. is politically unacceptable. Yet such a concern continues to exist, and has seemed important enough to merit responses from the companies in the form of full-page ads in expensive publications, showing great vistas of mountain ranges covered with trees, the ads financed by consortiums with sylvan names, composed of corporations in the tree-felling business. If one believed the accompanying copy one would get the notion that because of the generous foresight of these companies the forests of North America have never done so well. The message informs the reader that there are more trees now than even a society that runs on pulp can need.

And the trees they are talking about? A monoculture of genetically manipulated species bred to grow fast on soil laced from the air with a spectrum of additives ranging from pesticides to defoliants, their lives inseparable from spraying schedules and the ground that holds them up chemically emptied of any other growing thing that might impede their rate of increase. To suggest that these toxic plantations are forests, or as good as forests, or even better than forests requires a highly evolved disregard for biological fact and for the intelligence of the subscribers to such publications.

But real forests—remnants of them—do survive within the political limits of the U.S., and they include tropical forests, in Hawaii, that are threatened and are being destroyed as they are in other parts of the world. On the island of Hawaii U.S. Army engineers are currently bulldozing a native dry-land forest—which some biologists regard as one of the rarest and most easily lost of forestry biotypes—off the planet to make way for a firing range, and they are doing so with the full backing of the Federal government. On December 6, 1989, visiting U.S. judge Samuel Conti refused to issue a restraining order for the operation, saying that the work was already well under way and a delay would cost the Army a lot of money.

The project, in fact, had moved quite far before word of it spread sufficiently to permit effective organized opposition—a familiar situation in Hawaii. But a few miles away on the same island there is another area of native forest—lowland rain forest, this one—that is beginning to be better known. Its Hawaiian name is the Wao Kele O Puna—the Forest Upland of Puna—and it is situated on the eastern slope of the island, a few miles above the old one-street town of Pahoa. The present threat to the Wao Kele O Puna is a plan involving several development companies, and financial backing from the U.S. mainland, Israel and Japan. The idea is to use the area for drilling geothermal wells—there are different stories about what the resultant energy would be used for and how it would be transported. The plan is eagerly endorsed by the State of Hawaii, whose representatives have remained impervious to growing opposition on that island and throughout the state.

Of course the geothermal plan is not the first threat to Hawaiian rain forests. The forests of the island of Hawaii, and the lowland forests in particular, have been cut, burned, grazed, plowed, "developed" in one way or another, until by the time the necessary permits had been acquired for the bulldozers to enter the Wao Kele O Puna in early autumn 1989 there were only some 27,000 acres of lowland rain forest left in one place, and the Wao Kele O Puna was the last major area of its kind anywhere in the islands, and anywhere in the world. Much of its flora had yet to be studied by botanists, and it included many species that had evolved only within the Hawaiian islands, far from any other land—a situation which makes the remnant native ecosystems of the islands, in the opinion of many biologists, among the most valuable sources of evolutionary information on earth.

The Wao Kele O Puna, besides, is one of the very few places in the islands where native birds, wiped out throughout the lowlands by habitat destruction and the European introduction of the mosquito and avian malaria, have been able to evolve an immunity to the disease, and establish populations again. They are important, and in some cases essential, pollinators of some species of Hawaiian flora, and they are sensitive to the toxins and other disturbances generated by geothermal development.

Furthermore, the forest is part of the "ceded lands" that were legally set aside for the benefit of the Hawaiian people. In 1985 the state made a deal "swapping" it for an adjoining piece of disturbed and replanted land, the original drilling site. That land, the drilling of which was also fiercely disputed, is now covered with 300 feet of fresh lava. Now the state has given the geothermal developers a chance at the Wao Kele O Puna. Native Hawaiians in the area, some of whom had used the forest, as their parents and forebears had done for generations, for gathering medicinal plants and materials important to the survival of a variety of cultural practices, were never consulted about the exchange. They have challenged it in the courts, but for the time being they are denied entry to the forest at an iron gate put there by the developers and kept guarded.

Beyond the gate the bulldozed road that was gouged into the forest in autumn 1989 runs straight ahead for three miles (the developers, True Geothermal Ventures, of Wyoming, had secured a permit for a few acres) to an area the size of a parking lot at a shopping mall, part of which has been scooped out, draped with waterproof material and left to fill with rain, as a reservoir: the drilling requires large amounts of water.

Arrangements between the land-owner, developers, and officials had been pushed through with the undisguised intent of avoiding the need for a new, undisputed Environmental Impact Statement. A hired expert had provided the opinion that the forest was not of indispensable quality—a tactic polished with successful use. In early October 1989, with a large group of Hawaiians, I trespassed the full length of the three-mile road to the plastic reservoir and the prospective drill site. I walked with an independent biologist who pointed out to me, species by species, the indigenous flora that was there, the damage that had already been done to it, the weeds from outside the forest and outside Hawaii that were already growing in the churned ruts and turnouts, and described the further damage, the chain reaction that would inevitably follow. The native Hawaiians, walking barefoot on the crushed lava, left offerings to the fire goddess Pele at the foot of one regal *o'hia* tree (sacred to her) that had somehow been left standing near the earth-moving machinery. Some days later that tree was bulldozed, the drills came up the road, the drilling began. In December the State Board of Land and Natural Resources, one of the agencies pushing the project, approved a further 50-foot wide easement for two geothermal transmission lines to cross the state's nearby Nalowale (appropriately enough, the Hawaiian word means "lost, gone, forgotten, vanished") Reserve. Though Pahoa residents were not allowed into the forest, the developers' trucks came out of it and backed up to the public water mains in Pahoa where they tanked up to fill the reservoir faster, keeping locals who also depend on that water and pay taxes for it, waiting in line.

But the people of Pahoa already had an idea of what to expect of geothermal development as a neighbor. In the early 80's a relatively modest experimental well was sunk not far from the town in an area that normally teems with tropical growth. The noise was deafening; the ground for some distance around the site was soon so poisoned that it looked like an industrial dump, and the fumes from the plant were so toxic that even the nearby residents who had tried to stay had to be evacuated, and the plant was closed. Proponents say their technology has improved, but they have preferred to have their next try in dispensable forest, three miles from a guarded gate.

One of the claims made by proponents of geothermal development in Hawaii is that it is "clean," in contrast to the exhaust from fossil fuels. They have suddenly evinced a laudable concern about global warming, which geothermal development, they insist, would reduce dramatically. Some of their statements to the press make it sound as though they were offering a choice between their own clean plans and the greenhouse effect.

Their regard for environmental consequences would be more convincing if the interested parties had directed much attention to such matters before pre-empting them in support of their own venture. The real nature of the state's zeal for conservation can be assessed from the fact that the Wao Kele O Puna was in fact an area theoretically protected as conservation land, and the state simply removed the protective category to allow the developers to exploit it. It can be summed up by the fact that the State of Hawaii presently spends a mere two million dollars on conservation (just 0.3% of its electric utility revenues)—one of the lowest figures of any state in the nation.

Geothermal wells may not produce much carbon dioxide, but they do produce unpredictable amounts of lethal hydrogen sulfide, as neighbors of the first Hawaiian experimental well know. Engineers' reports of geothermal development elsewhere indicate that although there have been improvements, the gas is a continuing problem. And protestations from the state's Department of Health about how carefully they intend to monitor emissions are not wholly reassuring to those who recall the same department's implication, only a few years ago, in a cover-up of heptachlor in the islands' milk, and its maneuvers to permit massive air pollution (and contributions to the greenhouse effect) caused by the use of coal and by the burning of sugar cane before harvest in Hawaii.

Besides the emission of hydrogen sulfide, such wells produce large quantities of brine containing toxic heavy metals including mercury, boron, cadmium, manganese and possibly lead and arsenic; and for this waste no really satisfactory method of disposal has been found. In some parts of the world the effluvium has simply been allowed to run off into streams or the ocean, killing wherever it goes. In October, at the site in the forest, I listened to a conversation between a lawyer, a biologist and a drilling engineer from the company. When the latter was asked what provision would be made for the brine from the well he said he had not heard anything about that; he did not know whether there were any plans for it at all. He was just in the oil drilling business normally, he said.

But the geothermal advocates talk confidently of "reinjecting" these great quantities of liquid into the ground, a process which engineers with no stake in the project say is risky and uncertain at best. Even where the process had been possible the "reinjected" material has been known to back up and return, and there is no guarantee that it will not find its way into ground water sooner or later. The practice, besides, has been known to cause seismic activity, including earthquakes of some seriousness. A recent geologist's report prepared for Hawaiian Electric has stated that such injection "may prove difficult to integrate with production objectives," and has suggested as an alternative putting the stuff into "deep seawater zones immediately south of the expected geothermal reservoirs"—possibly polluting offshore fresh water aquifers.

Evidently geothermal is not so "clean" after all. Nor is it, as its proponents claim, "renewable" unless one is prepared to envisage well after well being dug to replace those that never produce, those that produce disappointingly or cease to produce either at their maximum life of twenty years or at some point before that, which cannot be predicted. At The Geysers near Clear Lake, California, the world's largest geothermal-power producing field, steam pressure has dropped 20 percent since 1987 and could be down by half by the year 2000, rendering more than two billion dollars' worth of power plants obsolete. A well, therefore, comes with no promises, and so back-ups are assumed, and successors, which means more area—in this case more rain forest—turned into industrial wasteland. It is not surprising that the present developers in the Wao Kele O Puna, before the first drilling has been completed, have applied for a permit to expand their original bite of forest land.

One of the geothermal advocates' chief arguments is that their plan would relieve Hawaii of dependence on oil, but it is hard to imagine that they believe their own words. The same representatives of state agencies who addressed Secretary of Energy James Watkins at the regional hearing in Honolulu, in January 1990, requesting Federal funding for the project, in the same speeches asked the Secretary of Energy for a greatly increased stockpile of oil in Hawaii. No one who has spent much time in Hawaii since the post-war spate of development began can doubt that any prospective increase in energy will be echoed immediately by an increase in development and the demands of development. Roughly 60 percent of the oil used in Hawaii, in any case, is consumed for transportation, and no amount of geothermal would change that. The oil used for electricity is residual oil left over from the two Hawaiian refineries. It is hard to see how geothermal energy would be likely to make much difference there. Evidently the geothermal proponents want *both* oil and geothermal—and whatever capital they can drum up with them.

A serious conservation program, of the kind outlined by energy consultant Robert Mowris, on the other hand, could cut Hawaii's energy consumption by more than half—five times the maximum claimed by the geothermal advocates, and at a fraction of the cost. And of course without the loss of the rain forest, whose importance the geothermal proponents are now minimizing. After all, they insist, there are bits of rain forest elsewhere. Why fuss about their taking just a little of this one?

The Sierra Club and other environmental groups in Hawaii are urging an energy conservation plan as the solution, one that would include more efficient appliances, use of solar water heaters—devices that are operating successfully, and at a great savings, elsewhere. But not geothermal. Besides the destruction, the risks, the economic burden of geothermal development, they argue that a project of that size, and a serious conservation program, are simply not compatible. Their goals are opposed. One would draw resources away from the other.

After hearing the arguments that are presented for the vast geothermal venture—the largest economic gamble ever proposed for Hawaii—one person after another has come to the conclusion that something is missing that would help explain why the proponents are so determined to push through a plan that is clearly so costly, dangerous, and destructive. Some essential piece seems to have been withheld from the public. It may have to do with the backers or prospective backers, promises of capital, subsequent plans such as the one for strip-mining the Pacific for manganese and smelting the ore in Hawaii (it is an odd coincidence that one of the most influential geothermal advocates, State Senator Matsuura, has several large lumps on his desk clearly labeled "manganese") but evidently the proponents are not eager for the public to know the whole truth.

If the state officials really believed in the goals they pretend are theirs they would be working for an effective conservation program and considering making Hawaii the world capital for the research and development of solar energy. The islands are ideally placed for such development, and only economics—and the economics of oil at that—have prevented solar energy from becoming a major alternative long before this. Instead, such foresight is being left to the Japanese.

In the immediate present it is imperative to save the Wao Kele O Puna forest instead of allowing it to be fragmented, polluted and lost. If enough people care about that, and act in time, it can be saved—what is left of it. If they do not, it will go the way of the forests whose fate we lament in South America and Asia.

Christopher Harris

Getting Used to Clearcuts

When I was young, a wooded hill behind my grandparents' house defined how I thought of forests. A spring on the hill fed water to the house. This was a mystery to me. What did a spring look like? How could the water my grandmother used to wash dishes, the water I drank and bathed in, originate in the forest? I begged my grandfather to take me there. One day, much to my surprise and delight, my grandfather relented. He led me to the sitting room, pulled a pair of boots from the closet, and held them to my feet. They were my grandmother's, small, high-topped, and made of supple leather. They fit well.

It was a dry, mid-summer morning. Small clouds of dust rose as we walked down the town's only road. We soon came to a bridge. Seeing the road end in woods on the other side, I hesitated. I wanted to ask why a bridge went nowhere. My grandfather turned to look at me, his eyes hidden in the shadow cast by the brim of his hat. "Come on. It'll be okay," he coaxed. I took his offered hand and crossed the bridge beside him.

I cannot recall how we made our way to the spring, even though I returned to it many times after my grandfather first took me there. I remember the small concrete box built over the spring. Cold water trickled from its base. My grandfather and I sat for a time, listening to squirrels chatter and looking at sunlight filter through the canopy of the forest, which was largely hardwoods. My grandfather sauntered from tree to tree, identifying different species for me. When he thought I had been at the spring long enough, we returned to the bridge and the road home.

Revealing the spring, my grandfather introduced me to the magic of the forest, replacing one mystery with another. Because I was a child, I did not concern myself with understanding why the spring had a quality unlike any other place I knew. Years later my inchoate feeling became clearer when I read John Muir. Trees, he wrote, are "temples" and the forest is infused with "one smooth, pure wild glow of Heaven's love." I thought of the forest as a source of inspiration, a place where one could rest and be in Nature.

Lately I find myself thinking of trees as a crop instead of a source of inspiration. This change may be inevitable after spending a lot of time where trees have been cut down. Now I look with perhaps too much irony at stands of old-growth forest with names like Cathedral Grove, Fisher-Scott Memorial Pines, Roosevelt Grove of Ancient Cedars, Grove of the Patriarchs, and Carlisle Pines.

I have walked through the Carlisle Pines, marveling at the beauty of the trees, trying to ignore the vast metropolis that surrounds the preserve. Some of the largest white pines in New England grow on these 22 acres in suburban Boston. The trees are 100 to 136 feet tall, the tallest having a diameter of 3.5 feet. When Europeans began settling New England in the seventeenth century, white pines as tall as the Carlisle pines were plentiful in much of the region. The pines were ideal for masts of the Royal Navy, and the British government decreed that trees with diameters larger than 24 inches be used for that purpose. Colonists cut smaller trees to supply lumber for houses, staves, hoops, beds, tables, chairs, fences, shingles, and firewood. As the population grew, doubling every 25 to 27 years, the demand for lumber and arable land increased. By the late eighteenth century so much of the New England forest had fallen to the lumber man and farmer that reseeding began. I have tried to envision New England three centuries ago, when white pines as tall and magnificent as the Carlisle pines were common.

On Canada's Vancouver Island, I am unsettled when I glimpse clearcut hills from Cathedral Grove, a small patch of virgin timber set aside by the island's major logging company. Cathedral Grove. The name suggests a place where one's vision is directed upward, away from worldly concerns. However, as my eyes follow the boles of these old-growth trees toward the sky, I have difficulty being grateful that the owner forfeited as much as $750 per 1,000 board feet by sparing them. In Cathedral Grove, I cannot forget that the demand for this old-growth timber is great, especially in Japan, where construction practices necessitate using strong vertical-grained beams made from spruce, ponderosa, and Douglas fir, and where the veneration of quality, knot-free wood puts a premium on cedar and western hemlocks. Seventy-thousand acres of virgin forest have been cut every year since 1980.

I will not saunter through the Grove of the Patriarchs, a stand of Douglas fir, western red cedar, and hemlock on the eastern border of Washington's Mount Rainier National Park. The memory of clearcuts I traveled by to get to the park would disturb my enjoyment of the trees; views of deforested land I had passed would linger like the afterimage of an intense light.

On the other hand, I know it is easy to become used to clearcuts. Like the quirks of an old acquaintance, they are made invisible by familiarity. To see them anew, go to Washington's Olympic Peninsula. Start at Gray's Harbor. Traveling route 101 north, you'll pass through more than fifty cuts before reaching the Olympic National Park at Kalaloch. When you finally arrive at Kalaloch, you'll need this oasis of uncut forest. Or, begin your journey from the north at Lake Crescent. There the park lulls you into believing that uninterrupted forest covers the Olympic Mountains. Quickly enough, however, you come upon clearcuts at Sappho, and you realize that it's one and the same for the National Park Service to care for trees in Olympic National Park and artifacts at a national historic site. Logging has destroyed so much of the virgin forest that a majestic spruce, fir, or cedar is as quaint as Benjamin Franklin's desk at Independence Hall.

Better yet, wander from the comfortable highway of the tourist. There are plenty of roads into the mountains; each square mile of logged forest requires five miles of road. Any narrow, unassuming dirt road off the highway may take you to a cut. If you happen upon a large site, the road branches into many. Take your pick. They all end at bluffs where lumber men have skidded logs up mountain slopes. Along the way you'll pass rusting cables, shredded tires, empty oil cans, pieces of abandoned equipment, and pile after pile of dead wood. If the cut is old, the mountain may have begun eroding, causing an uphill bank to collapse onto the road. Don't be disappointed if a landslide thwarts your journey. Step from your car, breathe the mountain air, and try not to think of what the forest once was.

List of Photographs

Gary Snyder

Ancient Forests of the Far West

But ye shall destroy their altars, break their images, and cut down their groves.

—*Exodus* 34:13

After the Clearcut

We had a tiny dairy farm between Puget Sound and the north end of Lake Washington, out in the cutover countryside. The bioregionalists call that part of northwestern Washington state "Ish" after the suffix that means "river" in Salish. Rivers flowing into Puget Sound are the Snohomish, Skykomish, Samamish, Duwamish, Stillaguamish.

I remember my father dynamiting stumps and pulling the shards out with a team. He cleared two acres and fenced it for three Guernseys. He built a two-story barn with stalls and storage for the cows below and chickens above. He and my mother planted fruit trees, kept geese, sold milk. Behind the back fence were the woods: a second-growth jungle of alder and cascara trees with native blackberry vines sprawling over the stumps. Some of the stumps were ten feet high and eight or ten feet in diameter at the ground. High up the sides were the notches the fallers had chopped in to support the steel-tipped planks, the springboards, they stood on while felling. This got them above the huge swell of girth at the bottom. Two or three of the old trees had survived—small ones by comparison—and I climbed those, especially one Western Red Cedar (*xelpai'its* in Snohomish) that I fancied became my advisor. Over the years I roamed the second-growth Douglas Fir, Western Hemlock, and cedar forest beyond the cow pasture, across the swamp, up a long slope, and into a droughty stand of pines. The woods were more of a home than home. I had a permanent campsite where I would sometimes cook and spend the night.

When I was older I hiked into the old-growth stands of the

foothill valleys of the Cascades and the Olympics where the shade-tolerant skunk cabbage and devil's club underbrush is higher than your head and the moss carpets are a foot thick. Here there is always a deep aroma of crumbled wet organisms—fungus—and red rotten logs and a few bushes of tart red thimbleberries. At the forest edges are the thickets of salal with their bland seedy berries, the yellow salmonberries, and the tangles of vine-maples. Standing in the shade you look out into the burns and the logged-off land and see the fireweed in bloom.

A bit older, I made it into the high mountains. The snowpeaks were visible from near our place: in particular Mt. Baker and Glacier Peak to the north and Mt. Rainier to the south. To the west, across Puget Sound, the Olympics. Those unearthly glowing floating snowy summits are a promise to the spirit. I first experienced one of those distant peaks up close at fifteen, when I climbed Mt. Saint Helens. Rising at 3 A.M. at timberline and breaking camp so as to be on glacier ice by six; standing in the rosy sunrise at nine thousand feet on a frozen slope to the crisp tinkle of crampon points on ice—these are some of the esoteric delights of mountaineering. To be immersed in ice and rock and cold and upper space is to undergo an eery, rigorous initiation and transformation. Being above all the clouds with only a few other high mountains also in the sunshine, the human world still asleep under its gray dawn cloud blanket, is one of the first small steps toward Aldo Leopold's "think like a mountain." I made my way to most of the summits of the Northwest—Mt. Hood, Mt. Baker, Mt. Rainier, Mt. Adams, Mt. Stuart, and more—in subsequent years.

At the same time, I became more aware of the lowlands. Trucks ceaselessly rolled down the river valleys out of the Cascades loaded with great logs. Walking the low hills around our place near Lake City I realized that I had grown up in the aftermath of a clearcut, and that it had been only thirty-five or forty years since all those hills had been logged. I know now that the area had been home to some of the largest and finest trees the world has ever seen, an ancient forest of hemlock and Douglas Fir, a temperate-zone rainforest since before the glaciers. And I suspect that I was to some extent instructed by the ghosts of those ancient trees as they hovered near their stumps. I joined the Wilderness

Society at seventeen, subscribed to *Living Wilderness,* and wrote letters to Congress about forestry issues in the Olympics.

But I was also instructed by the kind of work done by my uncles, our neighbors, the workers of the whole Pacific Northwest. My father put me on one end of a two-man crosscut saw when I was ten and gave me the classic instruction of "don't ride the saw"—don't push, only pull—and I loved the clean swish and ring of the blade, the rhythm, the comradeship, the white curl of the wood that came out with the rakers, the ritual of setting the handles, and the sprinkle of kerosene (to dissolve pitch) on the blade and into the kerf. We cut rounds out of down logs to split for firewood. (Unemployed men during the Depression felled the tall cedar stumps left from the first round of logging to buck them into blanks and split them with froes for the hand-split cedar shake trade.) We felled trees to clear pasture. We burned huge brushpiles.

People love to do hard work together and to feel that the work is real; that is to say primary, productive, needed. Knowing and enjoying the skills of our hands and our well-made tools is fundamental. It is a tragic dilemma that much of the best work men do together is no longer quite right. The fine information on the techniques of hand-whaling and all the steps of the flensing and rendering described in *Moby Dick* must now, we know, be measured against the terrible specter of the extinction of whales. Even the farmer or the carpenter is uneasy: pesticides, herbicides, creepy subsidies, welfare water, cheap materials, ugly subdivisions, walls that won't last. Who can be proud? And our conservationist-environmentalist-moral outrage is often (in its frustration) aimed at the logger or the rancher, when the real power is in the hands of people who make unimaginably larger sums of money, people impeccably groomed, excellently educated at the best universities—male and female alike—eating fine foods and reading classy literature, while orchestrating the investment and legislation that ruin the world. As I grew into young manhood in the Pacific Northwest, advised by a cedar tree, learning the history of my region, practicing mountaineering, studying the native cultures, and inventing the little rituals that kept my spirit sane, I was often supporting myself by the woodcutting skills I learned on the Depression stump-farm.

At Work in the Woods In 1952 and '53 I worked for the Forest Service as a lookout in the northern Cascades. The following summer, wanting to see new mountains, I applied to a national forest in the Mt. Rainier area. I had already made my way to the Packwood Ranger Station and purchased my summer's supply of lookout groceries when the word came to the district (from Washington, D.C.) that I should be fired. That was the McCarthy era and the Velde Committee hearings were taking place in Portland. Many of my acquaintances were being named on TV. It was the end of my career as a seasonal forestry worker for the government.

I was totally broke, so I decided to go back to the logging industry. I hitched east of the Oregon Cascades to the Warm Springs Indian Reservation and checked in with the Warm Springs Lumber Company. I had scaled timber here the summer of '51, and now they hired me on as a chokersetter. This is the lava plateau country south of the Columbia River and in the drainage of the Deschutes, up to the headwaters of the Warm Springs River. We were cutting old-growth Ponderosa Pine on the middle slopes of the east side, a fragrant open forest of massive straight-trunked trees growing on volcanic soils. The upper edge verged into the alpine life-zone, and the lower edge—farther and farther out into the desert—became sagebrush by degrees. The logging was under contract with the tribal council. The proceeds were to benefit the people as a whole.

> *11 August '54*
> *Chokersetting today. Madras in the evening for beer. Under the shadow of Mt. Jefferson. Long cinnamon-colored logs. This is "pine" and it belongs to "Indians"—what a curious knotting-up. That these Indians & these trees, that coexisted for centuries, should suddenly be possessor and possessed.* Our *concepts to be sure.*

I had no great problem with that job. Unlike the thick-growing Douglas Fir rainforests west of the Cascades, where there are arguments for clearcutting, the drier pine forests are perfect for selective cutting. Here the slopes were gentle and they were taking no more than 40 percent of the canopy. A number of healthy mid-sized seed trees were left standing. The D8 Cats could weave their way through without barking the standing trees.

Chokersetting is part of the skidding operation. First into the woods are the timber cruisers who estimate the standing board feet and mark the trees. Then come the road-building Cats and graders. Right on their heels are the gypo fallers—gypos get paid for quantity produced rather than a set wage—and then comes the skidding crew. West-of-the-mountains skidding is typically a high-lead or skyline cable operation where the logs are yarded in via a cable system strung out of a tall spar tree. In the east-side pine forest the skidding is done with top-size Caterpillar tractors. The Cat pulls a crawler-tread "arch" trailer behind it with a cable running from the Cat's aft winch up and over the pulley-wheel at the top of the arch, and then down where the cable divides into three massive chains that end in heavy steel hooks, the butt-hooks. I was on a team of two that worked behind one Cat. It was a two-Cat show.

Each Cat drags the felled and bucked logs to the landing—where they are loaded on trucks—from its own set of skid trails. While it is dragging a load of logs in, the chokersetters (who stay behind up the skid trails) are studying the next haul. You pick out the logs you'll give the Cat next trip, and determine the sequence in which you'll hook them so they will not cross each other, flip, twist over, snap live trees down, hang up on stumps, or make other dangerous and complicating moves. Chokersetters should be light and wiry. I wore White's caulked logger boots with steel points like tiny weasel-fangs set in the sole. I was thus enabled to run out and along a huge log or up its slope with perfect footing, while looking at the lay and guessing the physics of its mass in motion. The Cat would be coming back up the skid trail dragging the empty choker cables and would swing in where I signaled. I'd pluck two or three chokers off the butt-hooks and drag the sixteen-foot cables behind me into the logs and brush. The Cat would go on out to the other chokersetter who would take off his cables and do the same.

As the Cat swung out and was making its turnaround, the chokersetters would be down in dirt and duff, ramming the knobbed end of the choker under the log, bringing it up and around, and hooking it into the sliding steel catch called a "bell" that would noose up on the log when the choker pulled taut. The Cat would back its arch into where I stood, holding up chokers. I'd hook the first "D"—the ring on the free end of the choker—over the butt-hook and send the Cat to the next log. It could swing ahead and pull alongside while I leaped atop another load and hung the next choker onto the butt-hook. Then the winch on the rear of the Cat would wind in, and the butts of the logs would be lifted clear of the ground, hanging them up in the arch between the two crawler-tread wheels.

Stood straight
                holding the choker high
As the Cat swung back the arch
                piss-firs falling,
Limbs snapping on the tin hat
                bright D caught on
Swinging butt-hooks
                ringing against cold steel.

(from *Myths and Texts*)

The next question was, how would they fan out? My Cat-skinner was Little Joe, nineteen and just recently married, chewing plug and always joking. I'd give him the highball sign and at the same time run back out the logs, even as he started pulling, to leap off the back end. Never stand between a fan of lying logs, they say. When the tractor hauls out they might swing in and snap together—"Chokersetters lose their legs that way." And don't stand anywhere near a snag when the load goes out. If the load even lightly brushes it, the top of the snag, or the whole thing, might come down. I saw a dead schoolmarm (a tree with a crotch in its top third) snap off and fall like that, grazing the tin hat of a chokersetter called Stubby. He was lucky.

The D8 tears through piss-fir
Scrapes the seed-pine
                chipmunks flee,
A black ant carries an egg
Aimlessly from the battered ground.
Yellowjackets swarm and circle
Above the crushed dead log, their home.
Pitch oozes from barked
                trees still standing,

Mashed bushes make strange smells.
Lodgepole pines are brittle.
Camprobbers flutter to watch.

I learned tricks, placements, pulls from the experienced chokersetters—ways to make a choker cable swing a log over, even to make it jump out from under. Ways and sequences of hooking on chokers that when first in place looked like a messy spiderweb, but when the Cat pulled out, the tangle of logs would right itself and the cables mysteriously fan out into a perfect pull with nothing crossed. We were getting an occasional eight-foot-diameter tree and many five and six footers: these were some of the most perfect Ponderosa Pine I have ever seen. We also had White Fir, Douglas Fir, and some larch.

I was soon used to the grinding squeaking roar and rattle of the Cat, the dust, and the rich smells that rose from the bruised and stirred-up soil and plant life. At lunchtime, when the machinery was silent, we'd see deer picking their way through the torn-up woods. A Black Bear kept breaking into the crummy truck to get at the lunches until someone shot him and the whole camp ate him for dinner. There was no rancor about the bear, and no sense of conquest about the logging work. The men were stoic, skillful, a bit overworked, and full of terrible (but funny!) jokes and expressions. Many of them were living on the Rez, which was shared by Wasco, Wishram, and Shoshone people. The lumber company gave priority to the Native American locals in hiring.

Ray Wells, a big Nisqually, and I
                    each set a choker
On the butt-logs of two big Larch
In a thornapple thicket and a swamp.
                    waiting for the Cat to come back,
"Yesterday we gelded some ponies
"My father-in-law cut the skin on the balls
"He's a Wasco and don't speak English
"He grabs a handful of tubes and somehow
                    cuts the right ones.
"The ball jumps out, the horse screams
"But he's all tied up.

The Caterpillar clanked back down.
In the shadow of that racket
                    diesel and iron tread
I thought of Ray Wells' tipi out on the sage flat
The gelded ponies
Healing and grazing in the dead white heat.

There were also old white guys who had worked in the lumber industry all their lives: one had been active in the Industrial Workers of the World, the "Wobblies," and had no use for the later unions. I told him about my grandfather, who had soapboxed for the Wobblies in Seattle's Yesler Square, and my Uncle Roy, whose wife Anna was also the chief cook at a huge logging camp at Gray's Harbor around World War I. I told him of the revived interest in anarchosyndicalism among some circles in Portland. He said he hadn't had anyone talk Wobbly talk with him in twenty years, and he relished it. His job, knotbumper, kept him at the landing where the skidding Cats dropped the logs off. Although the buckers cut the limbs off, sometimes they left stubs which would make the logs hard to load and stack. He chopped off stubs with a double-bitted axe. Ed had a circular wear-mark impressed in the rear pocket of his stagged jeans: it was from his round axe-sharpening stone. Between loads he constantly sharpened his axe, and he could shave a paper-thin slice off a Day's Work plug, his chew, with the blade.

Ed McCullough, a logger for thirty-five years
Reduced by the advent of chainsaws
To chopping off knots at the landing:
"I don't have to take this kind of shit,
Another twenty years
                    and I'll tell 'em to shove it"
                    (he was sixty-five then)
In 1934 they lived in shanties
At Hooverville, Sullivan's Gulch.
When the Portland-bound train came through
The trainmen tossed off coal.
"Thousands of boys shot and beat up

For wanting a good bed, good pay,
decent food, in the woods—"
No one knew what it meant:
"Soldiers of Discontent."

On one occasion a Cat went to the landing pulling only one log, and not the usual 32-foot length but a 16. Even though it was only half-length the Cat could barely drag it. We had to rig two chokers to get around it, and there was not much pigtail left. I know now that the tree had been close to being of record size. The largest Ponderosa Pine in the world, near Mt. Adams, which I went out some miles of dust dirt roads to see, isn't much larger around than was that tree.

How could one not regret seeing such a massive tree go out for lumber? It was an elder, a being of great presence, a witness to the centuries. I saved a few of the tan free-form scales from the bark of that log and placed them on the tiny altar I kept on a box by my bunk at the logging camp. It and the other offerings (a flicker feather, a bit of broken bird's-egg, some obsidian, and a postcard picture of the Bodhisattva of Transcendent Intelligence, Manjusri) were not "my" offerings to the forest, but the forest's offerings to all of us. I guess I was just keeping some small note of it.

All of the trees in the Warm Springs forest were old growth. They were perfect for timber, too, most of them rot-free. I don't doubt that the many seed-trees and smaller trees left standing have flourished, and that the forest came back in good shape. A forester working for the Bureau of Indian Affairs and the tribal council had planned that cut.

Or did it come back in good shape? I don't know if the Warm Springs timber stands have already been logged again. They should not have been, but—

There was a comforting conservationist rhetoric in the world of forestry and lumber from the mid-thirties to the late fifties. The heavy clearcutting that has now devastated the whole Pacific slope from the Kern River to Sitka, Alaska, had not yet begun. In those days forestry professionals still believed in selective logging and actually practiced sustained yield. Those were, in hindsight, the last years of righteous forest management in the United States.

Evergreen The raw dry country of the American West had an odd effect on American politics. It transformed and even radicalized some people. Once the West was closed to homesteading and the unclaimed lands became public domain, a few individuals realized that the future of these lands was open to public discussion. Some went from exploration and appreciation of wilderness to political activism.

Daoist philosophers tell us that surprise and subtle instruction might come forth from the Useless. So it was with the wastelands of the American West—inaccessible, inhospitable, arid, and forbidding to the eyes of most early Euro-Americans. The Useless Lands became the dreaming place of a few nineteenth- and early-twentieth-century men and women (John Wesley Powell on matters of water and public lands, Mary Austin on Native Americans, deserts, women) who went out into the space and loneliness and returned from their quests not only to criticize the policies and assumptions of the expanding United States but, in the name of wilderness and the commons, to hoist the sails that are filling with wind today. Some of the newly established public lands did have potential uses for lumber, grazing, and mining. But in the case of timber and grass, the best lands were already in private hands. What went into the public domain (or occasionally into Indian reservation status) was—by the standards of those days—marginal land. The off-limits bombing ranges and nuclear test sites of the Great Basin are public domain lands, too, borrowed by the military from the BLM.

So the forests that were set aside for the initial Forest Reserves were not at that time considered prime timber land. Early-day lumber interests in the Pacific Northwest went for the dense, low-elevation conifer forests like those around the house I grew up in or those forests right on saltwater or near rivers. This accessible land, once clearcut, became real estate, but the farther reaches were kept by the big companies as commercial forest. Much of the Olympic Peninsula forest land is privately held. Only by luck and chance did an occasional low-elevation stand such as the Hoh River forest in Olympic National Park, or Jedediah Smith redwoods in California, end up in public domain. It is by virtue of these islands of forest survivors that we can still see what the primeval forest of the West Coast—in its densest and most concentrated incarnation—was like. "Virgin forest" it was once called, a telling term. Then it was called "old growth" or in certain cases "climax." Now we begin to call it "ancient forest."

On the rainy Pacific slope there were million-acre stands that had been coevolving for millennia, possibly for over a million years. Such forests are the fullest examples of ecological process, containing as they do huge quantities of dead and decaying matter as well as the new green and preserving the energy pathways of both detritus and growth. An ancient forest will have many truly large old trees—some having craggy, broken-topped, mossy "dirty" crowns with much organic accumulation, most with holes and rot in them. There will be standing snags and tons of dead down logs. These characteristics, although not delightful to lumbermen ("overripe"), are what make an ancient forest more than a stand of timber: it is a palace of organisms, a heaven for many beings, a temple where life deeply investigates the puzzle of itself. Living activity goes right down to and under the "ground"—the litter, the duff. There are termites, larvae, millipedes, mites, earthworms, springtails, pillbugs, and the fine threads of fungus woven through. "There are as many as 5,500 individuals (not counting the earthworms and nematodes) per square foot of soil to a depth of 13 inches. As many as 70 different species have been collected from less than a square foot of rich forest soil. The total animal population of the soil and litter together probably approaches 10,000 animals per square foot" (Robinson, 1988, 87).

The dominant conifers in this forest, Douglas Fir, Western Red Cedar, Western Hemlock, Noble Fir, Sitka Spruce, and Coastal Redwood, are all long-lived and grow to great size. They are often the longest-lived of their genera. The old forests of the western slopes support some of the highest per-acre biomass—total living matter—the world has seen, approached only by some of the Australian eucalyptus forests. An old-growth temperate hardwood forest, and also the tropical forests, average around 153 tons per acre. The west slope forests of the Oregon Cascades averaged 433 tons per acre. At the very top of the scale, the coastal redwood forests have been as high as 1,831 tons per acre (Waring and Franklin, 1979).

Forest ecologists and paleoecologists speculate on how such a massive forest came into existence. It seems the western forest of twenty or so million years ago was largely deciduous hardwoods—ash, maple, beech, oak, chestnut, elm, gingko—with conifers only at the highest elevations. Twelve to eighteen million years ago, the conifers began to occupy larger areas and then made continuous connection with each other along the uplands. By a million and a half years ago, in the early Pleistocene, the conifers had completely taken over and the forest was essentially as it is now. Forests of the type that had prevailed earlier, the hardwoods, survive today in the eastern United States and were also the original vegetation (before agriculture and early logging) of China and Japan. Visiting Great Smoky Mountains National Park today might give you an idea of what the mountain forests outside the old Chinese capital of Xian, known earlier as Ch'ang-an, looked like in the ninth century.

In the other temperate-zone forests of the world, conifers are a secondary and occasional presence. The success of the West Coast conifers can be attributed, it seems, to a combination of conditions: relatively cool and quite dry summers (which do not serve deciduous trees so well) combined with mild wet winters (during which the conifers continue to photosynthesize) and an almost total absence of typhoons. The enormous size of the trunks helps to store moisture and nutrients against drought years. The forests are steady-growing and productive (from a timber standpoint) while young, and these particular species keep growing and accumulating biomass long after most other temperate-zone trees have reached equilibrium.

Here we find the northern Flying Squirrel (which lives on truffles) and its sacred enemy the Spotted Owl. The Douglas Squirrel (or Chickaree) lives here, as does its sacred enemy the treetop-dashing Pine Marten that can run a squirrel down. Black Bear seeks the grubs in long-dead logs in her steady ambling search. These and hosts of others occupy the deep shady stable halls—less wind, less swing of temperature, steady moisture—of the huge tree groves. There are treetop-dwelling Red-backed Voles who have been two hundred feet high in the canopy for hundreds of generations, some of whom have never descended to the ground (Maser, 1989). In a way the web that holds it all together is the mycelia, the fungus-threads that mediate between root-tips of plants and chemistry of soils, bringing nutrients in. This association is as old as plants with roots. The whole of the forest is supported by this buried network.

The forests of the maritime Pacific Northwest are the last remaining forests of any size left in the temperate zone. Plato's *Critias* passage (¶III) says: "In the primitive state of the country [Attica] its mountains were high hills covered with soil . . . and there was abundance of wood in the mountains. Of this last the traces still remain, for although some of the mountains now only afford sustenance to bees, not so very long ago there were still to be seen roofs of timber cut from trees growing there . . . and there were many other high trees. . . . Moreover the land reaped the benefit of the annual rainfall, not as now losing the water which flows off the bare earth into the sea." The cautionary history of the Mediterranean forests is well known. Much of this destruction has taken place in recent centuries, but it was already well under way, especially in the lowlands, during the classical period. In neolithic times the whole basin had perhaps 500 million acres of forest. The higher-elevation forests are all that survive, and even they occupy only 30 percent of the mountain zone—about 45 million acres. Some 100 million acres of land once densely covered with pine, oak, ash, laurel, and myrtle now have only traces of vegetation. There is a more sophisticated vocabulary in the Mediterranean for postforest or nonforest plant communities than we have in California (where everything scrubby is called chaparral). *Maquis* is the term for oak, olive, myrtle, and juniper scrub. An assembly of low waxy drought-resistant shrubs is called *garrigue. Batha* is open bare rock and eroding ground with scattered low shrubs and annuals.

People who live there today do not even know that their gray rocky hills were once rich in groves and wildlife. The intensified destruction was a function of the *type* of agriculture. The small self-sufficient peasant farms and their commons began to be replaced by the huge slave-run *latifundia* estates owned in absentia and planned according to central markets. What wildlife was left in the commons might then be hunted out by the new owners, the forest sold for cash, and field crops extended for what they were worth. "The cities of the Mediterranean littoral became deeply involved in an intensive region-wide trade, with cheap manufactured products, intensified markets and factory-like industrial production.... These developments in planned colonization, economic planning, world currencies and media for exchange had drastic consequences for the natural vegetation from Spain through to India" (Thirgood, 1981, 29).

China's lowland hardwood forests gradually disappeared as agriculture spread and were mostly gone by about thirty-five hundred years ago. (The Chinese philosopher Meng-zi commented on the risks of clearcutting in the fourth century B.C.) The composition of the Japanese forest has been altered by centuries of continuous logging. The Japanese sawmills are now geared down to about eight-inch logs. The original deciduous hardwoods are found only in the most remote mountains. The prized aromatic Hinoki (the Japanese chamaecypress), which is essential to shrine and temple buildings, is now so rare that logs large enough for renovating traditional structures must be imported from the West Coast. Here it is known as Port Orford Cedar, found only in southern Oregon and in the Siskiyou Mountains of northern California. It was used for years to make arrow-shafts. Now Americans cannot afford it. No other softwood on earth commands such prices as the Japanese buyers are willing to pay for this species.

Commercial West Coast logging started around the 1870s. For decades it was all below the four-thousand-foot level. That was the era of the two-man saw, the double-bitted axe-cut undercuts, springboards, the kerosene bottle with a hook wired onto it stuck in the bark. Gypo handloggers felled into the saltwater bays of Puget Sound and rafted their logs to the mills. Then came steam donkey-engine yarders and ox teams, dragging the huge logs down corduroy skidroads or using immense wooden logging wheels that held the butt end aloft as the tail of the log dragged. The ox teams were replaced by narrow-gauge trains, and the steam donkeys by diesel. The lower elevations of the West Coast were effectively totally clearcut.

Chris Maser (1989, xviii) says: "Every increase in the technology of logging and the utilization of wood fiber has expedited the exploitation of forests; thus from 1935 through 1980 the annual volume of timber cut has increased geometrically by 4.7% per year.... By the 1970s, 65% of the timber cut occurred above 4,000 feet in elevation, and because the average tree harvested has become progressively younger and smaller, the increase in annual acreage cut has been five times greater than the increase in volume cut during the last 40 years."

During these years the trains were replaced by trucks, and the high-lead yarders in many cases were replaced by the more mobile crawler-tread tractors we call Cats. From the late forties on, the graceful, musical Royal Chinook two-man falling saws were hung up on the walls of the barns, and the gasoline chainsaw became the faller's tool of choice. By the end of World War II the big logging companies had (with a few notable exceptions) managed to overexploit and mismanage their own timberlands and so they now turned to the federal lands, the people's forests, hoping for a bailout. So much for the virtues of private forest landowners—their history is abysmal—but there are still ill-informed privatization romantics who argue that the public lands should be sold to the highest bidders.

> San Francisco 2 × 4s
>   were the woods around Seattle:
> Someone killed and someone built, a house,
>   a forest, wrecked or raised
> All America hung on a hook
>   & burned by men in their own praise.

Before World War II the U.S. Forest Service played the role of a true conservation agency and spoke against the earlier era of clearcutting. It usually required its contractors to do selective logging to high standards. The allowable cut was much smaller. It went from 3.5 billion board feet in 1950 to 13.5 billion feet in 1970. After 1961 the new Forest Service leadership cosied up to the industry, and the older conservation-oriented personnel were washed out in waves through the sixties and seventies. The USFS now hires mostly road-building engineers. Their silviculturists think of themselves as fiber-growing engineers, and some profess to see no difference between a monoculture plantation of even-age seedlings and a wild forest (or so said Tahoe National Forest silviculturist Phil Aune at a public hearing on the management plan in

1986). The public relations people still cycle the conservation rhetoric of the thirties, as though the Forest Service had never permitted a questionable clearcut or sold old-growth timber at a financial loss.

The legislative mandate of the Forest Service leaves no doubt about its responsibility to manage the forest lands *as forests,* which means that lumber is only one of the values to be considered. It is clear that the forests must be managed in a way that makes them permanently sustainable. But Congress, the Department of Agriculture, and business combine to find ways around these restraints. *Renewable* is confused with *sustainable* (just because certain organisms keep renewing themselves does not mean they will do so—especially if abused—forever), and *forever*—the length of time a forest should continue to flourish—is changed to mean "about a hundred and fifty years." Despite the overwhelming evidence of mismanagement that environmental groups have brought against the Forest Service bureaucracy, it arrogantly and stubbornly resists what has become a clear public call for change. So much for the icon of "management" with its uncritical acceptance of the economic speed-trip of modern times (generating faster and faster logging rotations in the woods) as against: slow cycles.

We ask for slower rotations, genuine streamside protection, fewer roads, no cuts on steep slopes, only occasional shelterwood cuts, and only the most prudent application of the appropriate smaller clearcut. We call for a return to selective logging, and to all-age trees, and to serious heart and mind for the protection of endangered species. (The Spotted Owl, the Fisher, and the Pine Marten are only part of the picture.) There should be *absolutely no more logging* in the remaining ancient forests. In addition, we need the establishment of habitat corridors to keep the old-growth stands from becoming impoverished biological islands.

Many of the people in the U.S. Forest Service would agree that such practices are essential to genuine sustainability. They are constrained by the tight net of exploitative policies forced on them by Congress and industry. With good practices North America could maintain a lumber industry and protect a halfway decent amount of wild forest for ten thousand years. That is about the same number of years as the age of the continuously settled village culture of the Wei River valley in China, a span of time which is not excessive for humans to consider and plan by. As it is, the United States is suffering a net loss of 900,000 acres of forest per year (*Newsweek*, 2 October 1989). Of that loss, an estimated 60,000 acres is ancient forest (Wilson, 1989, II2).

The deep woods turn, turn, and turn again. The ancient forests of the West are still around us. All the houses of San Francisco, Eureka, Corvallis, Portland, Seattle, Longview, are built with those old bodies: the 2×4s and siding are from the logging of the 1910s and 1920s. Strip the paint in an old San Francisco apartment and you find prime-quality coastal redwood panels. We live out our daily lives in the shelter of ancient trees. Our great-grandchildren will more likely have to live in the shelter of riverbed-aggregate. Then the forests of the past will be truly entirely gone.

Out in the forest it takes the same number of years as the tree lived for a fallen tree to totally return to the soil. If societies could learn to live by such a pace there would be no shortages, no extinctions. There would be clear streams, and the salmon would always return to spawn.

A virgin
Forest
Is ancient; many-
Breasted,
Stable; at
Climax.

Excursus: Sailor Meadow, Sierra Nevada We were walking in mid-October down to Sailor Meadow (about 5,800 feet), to see an old stand on a broad bench above the north fork of the American River in the northern Sierra Nevada. At first we descended a ridge-crest through chinquapin and manzanita, looking north to the wide dome of Snow Mountain and the cliffs above Royal Gorge. The faint trail leveled out and we left it to go to the stony hills at the north edge of the hanging basin. Sitting beneath a cedar growing at the top of the rocks we ate lunch.

Then we headed southwest over rolls of forested stony formations and eventually more gentle slopes into a world of greater and greater trees. For hours we were in the company of elders.

Sugar Pines predominate. There are properly mature symmetrical trees a hundred and fifty feet high that hold themselves upright and keep their branches neatly arranged. But then *beyond* them, *above* them, loom the *ancient trees:* huge, loopy, trashy, and irregular. Their bark is redder and the plates more spread, they have fewer branches, and those surviving branches are great in girth and curve wildly. Each one is unique and goofy. Mature Incense Cedar. Some large Red Fir. An odd Douglas Fir. A few great Jeffrey Pine. (Some of the cedars have catface burn marks from some far-back fire at their bases—all on the northwest side. None of the other trees show these burn marks.)

And many snags, in all conditions: some just recently expired with red or brown dead needles still clinging, some deader yet with plates of bark hanging from the trunk (where bats nest), some pure white smooth dead ones with hardly any limbs left, but with an occasional neat woodpecker hole; and finally the ancient dead: all soft and rotten while yet standing.

Many have fallen. There are freshly fallen snags (which often take a few trees with them) and the older fallen snags. Firm down logs you must climb over, or sometimes you can walk their length, and logs that crumble as you climb them. Logs of still another age have gotten soft and begun to fade, leaving just the pitchy heartwood core and some pitchy rot-proof limbs as signs. And then there are some long subtle hummocks that are the last trace of an old gone log. The straight line of mushrooms sprouting along a smooth ground surface is the final sign, the last ghost, of a tree that "died" centuries ago.

A carpet of young trees coming in—from six inches tall to twenty feet, all sizes—waiting down here on the forest floor for the big snags standing up there dead to keel over and make more canopy space. Sunny, breezy, warm, open, light—but the great trees are all around us. Their trunks fill the sky and reflect a warm golden light. The whole canopy has that sinewy look of ancient trees. Their needles are distinctive tiny patterns against the sky—the Red Fir most strict and fine.

The forests of the Sierra Nevada, like those farther up the West Coast, date from that time when the earlier deciduous hardwood forests were beginning to fade away before the spreading success of the conifers. It is a million years of "family" here, too, the particular composition of local forest falling and rising in elevation with the ice age temperature fluctuations, advancing or retreating from north and south slope positions, but keeping the several plant communities together even as the boundaries of their zones flowed uphill or down through the centuries. Absorbing fire, adapting to the summer drought, flowing through the beetle-kill years; always a web reweaving. Acorns feeding deer, manzanita feeding robins and raccoons, Madrone feeding Band-tailed Pigeon, porcupine gnawing young cedar bark, bucks thrashing their antlers in the willows.

The middle-elevation Sierra forest is composed of Sugar Pine, Ponderosa Pine, Incense Cedar, Douglas Fir, and at slightly higher elevations Jeffrey Pine, White Fir, and Red Fir. All of these trees are long-lived. The Sugar Pine and Ponderosa are the largest of all pines. Black Oak, Live Oak, Tanbark Oak, and Madrone are the common hardwoods.

The Sierra forest is sunny-shady and dry for fully half the year. The loose litter, the crackliness, the dustiness of the duff, the curl of crisp Madrone leaves on the ground, the little coins of fallen manzanita leaves. The pine-needle floor is crunchy, the air is slightly resinous and aromatic, there is a delicate brushing of spiderwebs everywhere. Summer forest: intense play of sun and the vegetation in still steady presence—not giving up water, not wilting, not stressing, just quietly holding. Shrubs with small, aromatic, waxy, tough leaves. The shrub color is often blue-gray.

The forest was fire-adapted over the millennia and is extremely resistant to wildfire once the larger underbrush has burnt or died away. The early emigrants described driving their wagons through park-like forests of great trees as they descended the west slope of the range. The early logging was followed by devastating fires. Then came the suppression of fires by the forest agencies, and that led to the brushy understory that is so common to the Sierra now. The Sailor Meadow forest is a spacious, open, fireproof forest from the past.

At the south end of the small meadow the area is named for, beyond a thicket of aspen, standing within a grove of flourishing fir, is a remarkably advanced snag. It once was a pine over two hundred feet tall. Now around the base all the sapwood has peeled away, and what's holding the bulky trunk up is a thin column of heartwood which is itself all punky, shedding, and frazzled. The great rotten thing has a lean as well! Any moment it might go.

How curious it would be to die and then remain standing for another century or two. To enjoy "dead verticality." If humans could do it we would hear news like, "Henry David Thoreau finally toppled over." The human community, when healthy, is like an ancient forest. The little ones are in the shade and shelter of the big ones, even rooted in their lost old bodies. All ages, and all together growing and dying. What some silviculturists call for—"even-age management," plantations of trees the same size growing up together—seems like rationalistic utopian totalitarianism. We wouldn't think of letting our children live in regimented institutions with no parental visits and all their thinking shaped by a corps of professionals who just follow official manuals (written by people who never raised kids). Why should we do it to our forests?

"All-age unmanaged"—that's a natural community, human or other. The industry prizes the younger and middle-aged trees that keep their symmetry, keep their branches even of length and angle. But let there also be really old trees who can give up all sense of propriety and begin throwing their limbs out in extravagant gestures, dancelike poses, displaying their insouciance in the face of mortality, holding themselves available to whatever the world and the weather might propose. I look up to them: they are like the Chinese Immortals, they are Han-shan and Shi-de sorts of characters—to have lived that long is to have permission to be eccentric, to be the poets and painters among trees, laughing, ragged, and fearless. They make me almost look forward to old age.

In the fir grove we can smell mushrooms, and then we spot them along the base of rotten logs. A cluster of Elegant Polypores, a Cortinarius, and in the open, pushing up dry needles from below, lots of russula and boletus. Some scooped-out hollows where the deer have dug them out. Deer love mushrooms.

We tried to go straight across the southern end of the meadow but it was squishy wet beneath the dry-looking collapsed dead plants and grasses, so we went all the way around the south end through more aspen and found (and saved) more mushrooms. Clouds started blowing in from the south and the breeze filled the sky with dry pine needles raining down. It was late afternoon, so we angled up steep slopes cross-country following deer-paths for an hour and found the overgrown trail to an abandoned mine, and it led us back to the truck.

Us Yokels This little account of the great forests of the West Coast can be taken as a model of what has been happening elsewhere on the planet. All the natural communities of the world have been, in their own way, "ancient" and every natural community, like a family, includes the infants, the adolescents, the mature adults, the elders. From the corner of the forest that has had a recent burn, with its fireweed and blackberries, to the elder moist dark groves—this is the range of the integrity of the whole. The old stands of hoary trees (or half-rotten saguaro in the Sonoran Desert or thick-boled well-established old manzanita in the Sierra foothills) are the grandparents and information-holders of their communities. A community needs its elders to continue. Just as you could not grow culture out of a population of kindergarten children, a forest cannot realize its own natural potential without the seed-reservoirs, root-fungus threads, birdcalls, and magical deposits of tiny feces that are the gift from the old to the young. Chris Maser says, "We need ancient forests for the survival of ancient forests."

When the moldboard plows of the early midwestern farmers "cut the grass roots—a sound that reminded one of a zipper being opened or closed—a new way of life opened, which simultaneously closed, probably forever, a long line of ecosystems stretching back thirty million years" (Jackson, 1987, 78). But the oldest continuous ecosystems on earth are the moist tropical forests, which in Southeast Asia are estimated to date back one hundred million years.

> Thin arching buttressing boles of the white-barked tall
> straight trees, Staghorn ferns leaning out from the limbs
> and the crotches up high. Trees they call brushbox,
> coachwood, crabapple, Australian red cedar (names
> brought from Europe)—and Red carrabeen, Yellow
> carrabeen, Stinging-trees, Deep blue openings leaning
> onward.

Light of green arch of leaves far above
Drinking the water that flows through the roots
Of the forest, Terania creek, flowing out of Pangaia,
Down from Gondwanaland,
Stony soil, sky bottom shade

Long ago stone deep
Roots from the sky
Clear water down through the roots
Of the trees that reach high in the shade
Birdcalls bring us awake
Whiplash birdcalls laugh us awake—

Booyong, Carabeen, Brushbox, Black butt, Wait-a-while
(Eucalypts dry land thin soil succeeders
Searching scrabbly ground for seventy million years—)

But these older tribes of trees
Travel always as a group.
Looking out from the cliffs
On the ridge above treetops,
Sitting up in the dust ledge shelter
Where we lived all those lives.

Queensland, 1981

A multitude of corporations are involved in the deforestation of the tropics. Some got their start logging in Michigan or the Pacific Northwest—Georgia Pacific and Scott Paper are now in the Philippines, Southeast Asia, or Latin America with the same bright-colored crawler tractors and the buzzing yellow chainsaws. In the summer of 1987 in Brazil's western territory of Rondonia—as part of the chaotic "conversion" of Amazonia to other uses—an area of forest the size of Oregon was in flames. One sometimes hears the innocent opinion that everyone is a city-dweller now. That time may be coming, but at the moment the largest single population in the world is people of several shades of color farming in the warmer zones. Up until recently a large part of that realm was in trees, and the deep-forest-dwelling cultures had diverse and successful ways to live there. In those times of smaller population, the long-rotation slash-and-burn style of farming mixed with foraging posed no ecological threat. Today a combination of large-scale logging, agri-business development, and massive dam projects threatens every corner of the backcountry.

In Brazil there is a complex set of adversaries. On one side the national government with its plans for development is allied with multinationals, wealthy cattle interests, and impoverished mainstream peasants. On the other side, resisting deforestation, are the public and private foresters and scientists making cause with the small local lumber firms, the established jungle-edge peasants, environmental organizations, and the forest-dwelling tribes. The Third World governments usually deny "native title" and the validity of communal forest ownership histories, such as the *adat* system of the Penan of Sarawak, a sophisticated multidimensional type of commons. The Penan people must put their bodies in the road to protest logging trucks *in their own homeland* and then go to jail as criminals.

Third World policies in regard to wilderness all too often run a direction set by India in 1938 when it opened the tribal forest lands of Assam to outside settlement saying "indigenous people alone would be unable, without the aid of immigrant settlers, to develop the province's enormous wasteland resources within a reasonable period" (Richards and Tucker, 1988, 107). All too many people in power in the governments and universities of the world seem to carry a prejudice against the natural world—and also against the past, against history. It seems Americans would live by a Chamber-of-Commerce Creationism that declares itself satisfied with a divinely presented Shopping Mall. The integrity and character of our own ancestors is dismissed with "I couldn't live like that" by people who barely know how to live *at all.* An ancient forest is seen as a kind of overripe garbage, not unlike the embarrassing elderly.

Forestry. "How
Many people
Were harvested
In Viet-nam?"

Clear-cut. "Some
Were children,
Some were over-ripe."

The societies that live by the old ways (Snyder, 1977) had some remarkable skills. For those who live by foraging—the original forest botanists and zoologists—the jungle is a rich supply of fibers, poisons, medicines, intoxicants, detoxicants, containers, water-proofing, food, dyes, glues, incense, amusement, companionship, inspiration, and also stings, blows, and bites. These primary societies are like the ancient forests of our human history, with similar depths and diversities (and simultaneously "ancient" and "virgin"). The *lore* of wild nature is being lost along with the inhabitory human cultures. Each has its own humus of custom, myth, and lore that is now being swiftly lost—a tragedy for us all.

Brazil provides incentives for this kind of destructive development. Even as some mitigations are promised, there are policies in place that actively favor large corporations, displace natives, and at the same time do nothing for the mainstream poor. America disempowers Third World farmers by subsidizing overproduction at home. Capitalism plus big government often looks like welfare for the rich, providing breaks to companies that clearcut timber at a financial loss to the public. The largest single importer of tropical hardwoods is Japan (Mazda, Mitsubishi) and the second largest is the USA.

We must hammer on the capitalist economies to be at least capitalist enough to see to it that the corporations which buy timber off our public lands pay a fair market price for it. We must make the hard-boiled point that the world's trees are virtually worth more standing than they would be as lumber, because of such diverse results of deforestation as life-destroying flooding in Bangladesh and Thailand, the extinction of millions of species of animals and plants, and global warming. And, finally, we are not speaking only of forest-dwelling cultures or endangered species like voles or lemurs when we talk of ecological integrity and sustainability. We are looking at the future of our contemporary urban-industrial society as well. Not so long ago the forests were our depth, a sun-dappled underworld, an inexhaustible timeless source. Now they are vanishing. We are all endangered yokels.

(*Yokel:* some English dialect, originally meaning "a green woodpecker or yellowhammer.")

Notes

Jackson, Wes. *Altars of Unhewn Stone: Science and the Earth.* San Francisco: North Point, 1987.

Maser, Chris. *Primeval Forest.* San Francisco: Sierra Club, 1989.

Richards, John F., and Richard P. Tucker. *World Deforestation in the Twentieth Century.* Durham, N.C.: Duke University Press, 1988.

Robinson, Gordon. *The Forest and the Trees: A Guide to Excellent Forestry.* Covelo, Calif.: Island Press, 1988.

Snyder, Gary. *Myths and Texts.* New York: New Directions, 1960.

———. *The Old Ways.* San Francisco: City Lights, 1977.

Thirgood, J.V. *Man and the Mediterranean Forest: A History of Resource Depletion.* New York: Academic Press, 1981.

Waring, R.H., and Jerry Franklin. "Evergreen Coniferous Forests of the Pacific Northwest." *Science,* 29 June 1979.

Wilson, E.O. "Threats to Biodiversity." *Scientific American,* September 1989.

Catherine Caufield

The Ancient Forest

Ours was once a forested planet. The rocky hillsides of Greece were covered with trees. Syria was known for its forests, not its deserts. Lebanon had vast cedar forests, from which the navies of Phoenicia, Persia, and Macedonia took their ship timber, and which provided the wood that Solomon used to build the temple at Jerusalem. Oak and beech forests dominated the landscapes of England and Ireland. In Germany and Sweden, bears and wolves roamed through wild forests where manicured tree farms now stand. Columbus saw the moonscape that we call Haiti "filled with trees of a thousand kinds." Exploring the east coast of North America in 1524, Verrazano wrote of "a land full of the largest forests . . . with as much beauty and delectable appearance as it would be possible to express." The first European settlers gazed upon these forests with a mixture of awe, fear, and greed. To them the forests were both a terrible wilderness and a source of riches. Cutting them down was the way to security and prosperity. "The very notion of advancement, or civilization, or prosperity, seems inseparably connected with the total extirpation of the forest," one settler observed. At first, forests were cleared mainly for subsistence purposes—to get land for farming or wood for homebuilding—but large-scale commercial logging was under way by the early eighteen-hundreds. In 1850, according to the book "This Well-Wooded Land," lumber production was the No. 1 manufacturing industry in the United States.

The loggers started in the great hardwood and white-pine forests of the Northeast. By the time of the Civil War, those forests had largely been exhausted. Logging then moved to the pineries, the cypress swamps, and the live-oak stands of the South and to the pine forests of the Great Lakes region. It took only fifty years to deplete the latter. One writer of the time described logging as "the great nomad among American industries, driving from one virgin forest to another, like a threshing machine from one ripe wheat field to the next." In Canada, the progression followed a similar line—from new Brunswick to Quebec and on to the Pacific Coast.

In the West, the loggers came up against their last frontier—the most magnificent forest on the continent and the greatest conifer forest on earth. The Pacific forest curves along the coast for nearly two thousand miles, from the Alaska Panhandle to just north of the Golden Gate; it stretches inland as far as the Cascade Range and the Coast Ranges. The trees—spruces, cedars, redwoods, hemlocks, and Douglas firs—are immense, many three hundred feet or higher and fifty feet around. Five-hundred-year-old trees are not uncommon here, and some of the trees are more than two thousand years old. These are the largest and oldest trees in the world, and their age and size imbue this forest with a solemnity so deep it seems to many visitors spiritual. This forest is home to a greater mass of life than even the tropical rain forests. It is crucial to the stability of the region's and the world's climate: it causes up to a third of the local precipitation, and it stores more carbon than any other terrestrial ecosystem. It is the breeding ground for the most productive salmon fisheries in the world—fisheries that support an industry worth billions of dollars annually. It is home to little-known species, such as the marbled murrelet, one of the last birds in North America to have its nesting place discovered, and the Pacific yew, a tree that contains an important anti-tumor agent. Above all, this forest is a remnant of the world as it was before man appeared, as it was when water was fit to drink and air was fit to breathe.

Originally, the Pacific forest covered seventy thousand square miles of Canada and the United States. About sixty per cent of Canada's Pacific forest has by now been destroyed, mostly in the past forty years. In the United States, less than ten per cent survives. Almost all that remains in both countries is on public lands, and it is scheduled to be cut for lumber, plywood, and pulp, much of it for export to Japan. Conservationists estimate that these forests will be gone in less than twenty years. Government and timber-industry officials disagree; they say it will be fifty to eighty years before the forests are exterminated.

From the air or from a mountaintop, the forest may seem at first like a single entity—a homogeneous swath of green that blankets hills and valleys. A closer look contradicts this picture. The forest is really many forests—a patchwork of different colors, shapes, and textures. The ribbon of deep green snaking through the forest is made by spruce trees lining a stream bank. Circular patches of green and rust colors are bare boggy areas too wet to support trees. A set of pick-up-sticks on a hillside is a five-acre patch of wind throw—huge trees tossed to the ground by fierce winds several years ago and now bleached a deathly, leafless white. A blackened patch with many trees still standing is where fire, perhaps set by lightning, ran through a grove. Bare treetops rising from the green forest like enormous white candelabras are the sign of an ancient cedar forest. Some areas are well stocked, densely packed with big trees. Others, perhaps on rocky hillsides or acid soils, have fewer and smaller trees.

The Pacific forest is essentially a coastal forest. The close connection between land, river, and ocean is especially noticeable in Alaska and Canada, where glaciers and shifting tectonic plates have created a landscape of hills and valleys and a jagged coastline with innumerable islands and inlets. The result is thousands of small watersheds, each draining into the ocean through its own little estuary, and each with its own character.

Tenakee Inlet almost bisects Chichagof Island, one of the main islands of the Alexander Archipelago, in southeastern Alaska. With Jason Carter, who lives in one of the island's three small towns, I cruised the inlet on a sunny April day and found it alive with wildlife that depend on it and on the forest that borders it. In just a few hours, we saw countless bald eagles, a colony of harbor seals, several groups of deer standing on the beach or swimming across the inlet, a mink scuttling across some rocks, a school of Dall's porpoises that played with us, diving and jumping in front of our boat, a brown bear loping across some tidal flats, a colony of sea lions, Canada geese and sandhill cranes flying in formation, two humpback whales blowing and diving, great blue herons, and numerous ducks, including some beautiful green-wing teal. For dinner that night, we ate enormous shrimp and Dungeness crabs that Jason had caught that morning. A day or two earlier, someone had said to me, "How many places in the world can you sit and watch humpback whales and brown bears at the same time? Here you can."

One of the things that make the Pacific Northwest forest so unusual is that it is a forest of conifers, and not broad-leaved trees. In "Ancient Forests of the Pacific Northwest" Elliott Norse, a senior ecologist at the Wilderness Society, explains that eighty million years ago conifers were the dominant vegetation on earth. Even then, however, a new, more diverse and adaptable type of plant was evolving—one that reproduces by means of flowers. The flowering plants, including broad-leaved trees, have evolved and adapted so well to different habitats that in most parts of the world they have pushed the less versatile conifers into a mere supporting role. True conifer forests are now restricted mostly to the Arctic regions—the far-northern reaches of Canada and the Soviet Union. But in the Pacific Northwest conifers have retained their prehistoric majesty. The reason for this anomaly is the region's strange climate: the winters are wet with regular freezes, and the summers are hot and dry. In most parts of the world, there is a season of moisture and warmth, when plants have the water and the sunlight they need for photosynthesis. In the Pacific Northwest during the summer, there is enough light for photosynthesis but not enough water. In the winter, when there is enough light and water for photosynthesis, temperatures often dip below freezing, and cause most broad-leaved plants to lose their leaves. Conifers, however, are well adapted to exploiting the opportunities for growth in these forests. Most conifers keep their leaves all year, so they are able to photosynthesize and grow during the winter months. And conifers, because they use water more efficiently than broad-leaved trees do, can also grow during the dry summer months.

Though the climate in the southern reaches of the Pacific forest is relatively dry, Alaska, British Columbia, and part of Washington State receive as much as a hundred and eighty inches of rain a year and have true temperate rain forests. As one walks through these forests, one is struck by the sheer volume of green stuff and by the exuberance with which it strives to live. Things grow in the oddest places. Every tree is hung with epiphytes and ferns. More than a hundred species of mosses and lichens grow high in the canopy. Fifty or a hundred feet above the ground, large trees sprout from the trunks of even larger trees. This sense of abundance is not deceptive. The Pacific rain forest cannot compete with tropical rain forests in the variety of plants and animals that it supports, but it supports a greater mass of living things by far. "Secrets of the Old Growth Forest," by David Kelly, tells us that the most productive tropical rain forests that have been measured contain a hundred and eighty-five tons of plants an acre. The average Pacific Northwest forest contains just under four hundred tons an acre. Some redwood forests contain eighteen hundred tons an acre. If human beings were as efficient in supporting themselves as these forests are, one square mile would be enough land to sustain nearly three million people.

Disasters—floods, volcanic eruptions, avalanches, lightning strikes, fires, and windstorms—have shaped the Pacific forest, and they continue to do so. Douglas fir, for example, owes its dominance of the Cascade region to the area's frequent fires. Douglas firs cannot grow in shade, and they do not germinate well on the layer of decaying vegetation that covers the soil in a Pacific Northwest forest. But after a fire reduces tree cover and burns off the litter, Douglas-fir seedlings germinate, and then they grow faster than their competitors. In the wet forests of Alaska and Canada, where fires are rare, hemlock and spruce are the dominant species.

The Pacific forest is a triumph of life over adversity. It thrives on thin, nutrient-poor, unstable soils, on steep hillsides, and under extremely difficult climatic conditions. Unfortunately for the forest, man took its magnificence at face value and inquired no further. How do its trees achieve their great size? How do they flourish in a difficult climate and terrain? How can it support such a large population of wild creatures? Those questions went unasked. In 1952, a Forest Service silviculturist called the great forests "biological deserts." The world's tropical rain forests, which scientists complain are ignored and misunderstood, have been far more intensively studied, and for a far longer time, than has their forgotten sister in the Pacific Northwest. The first comprehensive ecological study of the Pacific forest—a forty-eight-page report—was published in 1981. By contrast, a classic text on tropical-rain-forest ecology, by Paul Richards, was published in 1952, and in writing it Richards was able to draw on a body of published work about rain forests extending back at least to 1891.

The principal author of that 1981 report, "Ecological Characteristics of Old-Growth Douglas-Fir Forests," was a Forest Service scientist named Jerry Franklin, the son of a pulp-and-paper-mill employee in Washington State. Like many forestry students, Franklin helped put himself through school by working for the Forest Service. He did research on subalpine forests while he was studying for a Ph.D. in botany and soil science from Washington State University. His true love, though, was the Douglas-fir forest in which he had played and camped as a boy. In 1969, the National Science Foundation, in association with the Forest Service, financed a new program to study the ecology of the Pacific forest. Franklin became one of the project's leaders. "I was thinking, My God, here are these incredible forests, and nobody really knows a damn thing about them," Franklin told me as we walked through the Mt. Baker–Snoqualmie National Forest, in Washington State, last May. "They sort of got lost in the cracks, because the academic biologists and ecologists wanted to go down to the tropics, and the foresters thought they knew all they needed to know about the forests here, which was how to cut them down."

Forests, like human beings, have a natural life span. Once they reach maturity, at about two hundred years, growth slows down considerably, and most of their energy goes into sustaining themselves. Eventually, though it may take several centuries more, decay sets in, and the trees die and fall down. To a logger, leaving trees in the ground beyond their point of maximum annual wood production makes no sense. Since the Pacific forest consists of trees that tend to live for centuries beyond that point, it has been regarded by loggers and foresters alike as decadent. The professional forester's view is that such forests should be cleared and replanted with healthy young trees as quickly as possible. Franklin and his colleagues, however, found that this post-mature phase, now generally called old-growth, is the richest, most complex stage of the forest's life. For the first few decades after a patch of forest is cleared—by fire, wind, or logging—it is an open, grassy area, a good feeding ground for wildlife such as deer, bears, and elk. During severe winters, though, when these open areas are blanketed with several feet of snow, the animals take refuge in old-growth stands, where the ground is protected from snow, and food is still available. At about thirty years, the young stand enters an almost sterile period that lasts for up to a hundred years. This occurs because the trees, all the same age, have formed a dense, unbroken canopy, which blocks the sun and shades out understory growth. As the stand ages, trees die and fall, allowing sunlight to penetrate to the forest floor and stimulate another layer of growth. When the stand achieves a certain complexity of structure—shrubs, herbs, and trees of varying heights creating a multistoried canopy—it has become old-growth.

It is impossible to come up with a description of old-growth forest that fits the whole Pacific region, since, as Franklin points out, "nature is just too complex and variable to fit into neat conceptual boxes." Still, there is general agreement that true old-growth forests are characterized by large, old living trees; a multilayered canopy; large standing dead trees, called snags; and large dead trees on the ground and in streams. The dead trees are essential to the health of the forest, and are the basis of its astonishing productivity. The nutrients that the forest needs are not mainly in the soil but in the living and dead plant material itself. As leaves and branches fall to the forest floor, as trees and plants die and decay, this material is recycled to the living forest. With this highly efficient and almost closed system, the forest feeds itself, wasting nothing.

Though the great old giants of the forest may be beyond their wood-producing prime, they are at their prime for many other functions. Scientists have lately discovered that there are lichens that grow only on the canopies of the old-growth trees and can capture nitrogen from the atmosphere. A steady, barely noticeable rain of these lichens constantly enriches the layer of nutrients on the forest floor. A single old-growth tree may have sixty to seventy million needles, and a total of forty-three thousand square feet of leaf surface. The needles are astonishingly successful at collecting moisture and chemical nutrients from the atmosphere. When forests were cut around the Bull Run watershed, from which Portland, Oregon, gets some of its water supply, Forest Service scientists expected more water to enter the reservoir, because of reduced evaporation and transpiration. Instead, water levels in the reservoir dropped. Surprised researchers found that almost a third of the water in the Bull Run reservoir has never come from rain. Rather, the tall trees in old-growth forests collect it from passing clouds and fog banks. When the trees are cut down, the moisture banks waft by without depositing the water they hold.

Old-growth trees also protect the soil and the wildlife from the extreme effects of the region's wet, cold winters and dry summers: first, the dense canopy breaks the impact of the intense rain and snow, helping to prevent disastrous floods, landslides, and soil erosion, and providing a sheltered environment for wildlife in winter; second, the huge trunks can store thousands of gallons of water for the trees' own use and that of other species in the dry season.

One of the most important features of the old-growth forest is the variety of habitats it provides for wildlife. More than a hundred and fifty species of mammals live in such forests, and as many as fifteen hundred invertebrate species may live in a single stand. So far, according to Kelly's book, scientists have found a hundred and eighteen vertebrate species (mammals, birds, reptiles, amphibians, and fishes) whose primary habitat is old-growth. The large old trees, merely by virtue of their great height, create a continuum of climatic conditions, from the cool, dark, moist forest floor to the harsher environment of the canopy, exposed to the sun, rain, snow, fog, and wind. Every part of the tree—living or dead, including the roots—is home to a whole community of plants, insects, birds, and mammals. The plants and the animals that dwell in the canopy are different from those which nest in a snag, live halfway down a tree trunk, or stay on the forest floor. One species, the tiny red tree vole, which is found only in these forests, spends its entire life high up in a Douglas fir. It makes its nest there, eats almost nothing but Douglas-fir needles, and gets its water by licking rain from the needles.

A tree that is killed by fire, lightning, insects, or disease may remain standing for two hundred years or more. These huge snags are colonized by many types of insects, birds, and mammals. Several species of bats and birds breed under patches of loose bark. Ospreys and bald eagles use the snags as lookout posts. But the most valuable feature of the snags is the cavities that develop in their trunks and branches. At least forty-five vertebrate species, from the northern flying squirrel to the rare and beautiful northern spotted owl, will nest or feed only in the cavities of old-growth trees. These animals eat the mosses, lichens, and insects that invade dead or dying trees, and they in turn are eaten by animals higher up the food chain—animals like black bears, pine martens, and bobcats, all of which take shelter in snags.

In the very act of falling, a tree contributes to forest diversity in several ways. Its fall creates a light gap—a hole in the canopy through which sunlight can penetrate to the forest floor and stimulate the growth of plants, such as Western hemlock, that have survived for years in the deep shade but needed this burst of light to grow to full size. A tree that is uprooted creates two new wildlife habitats: the pit where its roots used to be, and the exposed roots themselves. A walk through any old-growth forest will take one past several fallen trees, their huge but shallow roots sticking ten or fifteen feet into the air and overgrown with mosses, lichens, ferns, and shrubs. The wresting of the roots from the ground allows organic matter to mix in with the mineral soil—an essential ecological service in the Sitka-spruce forests of Alaska, where the soil has a tendency to harden and form an impervious pan.

A thousand-year-old tree that falls to the forest floor may take four hundred years more to decay completely. During those centuries, it contributes in many ways to the life and the balance of the forest. Downed logs reduce soil erosion by creating a natural terracing effect on hillsides. They contain enormous amounts of water—enough to see many forest creatures through the dry season. A fallen tree supports an amazing, though still not entirely charted, variety of wildlife—at least a hundred and sixty-three species of birds, mammals, reptiles, and amphibians, and more invertebrates than have yet been counted. Most old-growth forests contain more than fifty tons of downed wood per acre. As much as a third of the forest's soil organic matter comes from these decaying logs; hemlock seedlings and other shade-tolerant plants take root in them as if in a rich plot of soil. In some areas, these "nurse logs" are the primary sites for tree reproduction.

Perhaps the most important and interesting aspect of the decay cycle is the interplay between certain fungi, which grow on decaying trees, and the roots of living trees. These fungi, called mycorrhizae, infect the root tips of many tree species, including all the conifers in the Pacific Northwest forest. In doing so, they promote the growth of tiny root hairs that spread across the forest floor searching for nutrients, and so help trees absorb nutrients that are unavailable to uninfected roots. Without mycorrhizae, trees cannot obtain the phosphorus, the nitrogen, and the water they need to survive and grow. An experiment that was conducted in Oregon's Siskiyou National Forest by Oregon State University in coöperation with the Forest Service found that Douglas-fir seedlings died within two years of planting when they were deprived of mycorrhizae. In turn, mycorrhizae, which cannot photosynthesize, obtain their food from trees.

Some mycorrhizal fungi, such as chanterelle mushrooms, reproduce aboveground. Others, like truffles, do so underground, and only in the wild. (In Europe, the black truffle, a mycorrhizal fungus, fetches four hundred to six hundred dollars a pound. A market in domestic truffles is just beginning, but the Oregon white truffle is already a valuable commercial crop.) Truffle spores are dispersed in the droppings of the mice, squirrels, chipmunks, and voles that eat the fungus. Since fungi can infect only those roots with which they come into direct contact, these small animals are essential to the survival of the forest. They are also essential to the spotted owl, which relies in large part on truffle-eating mammals for food. A decline of a forest's spotted-owl population might mean that there are not enough truffles to support a healthy population of these mammals, and therefore that the young trees in that forest are not being inoculated with the mycorrhizae upon which their survival depends. Thus the Forest Service has designated the spotted owl an "indicator species"—a species by which one can to some extent gauge the health of the forest.

In the midst of the nineteenth century's orgy of logging, there dawned the realization that the North American forest was finite. By 1879, according to a study by Michael Williams in "World Deforestation in the Twentieth Century," more than two hundred million acres—a quarter of the country's forestland—was gone, and the rate of deforestation was increasing. There was talk of a timber famine, and the talk was frightening, because at that time and for many decades to come the United States was at base a timber economy.

Many people, perhaps most, simply denied or were unaware that careless land-clearing caused serious problems. Others saw such problems as the unavoidable cost of the need to turn forests into farmland and timber. A few raised their voices in warning. One such as George Perkins Marsh, a Vermont lawyer, businessman, congressman, and diplomat. Marsh had extensive experience of deforestation. He was briefly a lumber dealer in Burlington, a town that in the space of twenty years went from selling timber from the nearby Green Mountains to having to buy it, because those woods were exhausted. Marsh also spent some time as Ambassador to Turkey, and was struck by the effects of deforestation in that country and in the Mediterranean region as a whole. In 1864, he published "Man and Nature," a book that Lewis Mumford later called "the fountainhead of the conservation movement." In it Marsh explained how "indiscriminate clearing of the woods" in other countries had damaged water supplies, agriculture, and commerce and had led to the downfall of cities and nations. "Man has too long forgotten that the earth was given to him for usufruct alone, not for consumption, still less for profligate waste," he wrote. He called for a new treatment of the natural world, based not on a romantic view of nature as an inspiration or a challenge to mankind, and not on a political philosophy that says the land belongs to the people, but on a scientific understanding of how natural systems work.

In 1891, Congress gave the President authority to create forest "reservations." No one was clear about the purpose of the forests until 1897, when Congress decided that they should be managed to protect watersheds and "to furnish a continuous supply of timber for the use and necessities of citizens of the United States." In 1905, President Theodore Roosevelt, an ardent conservationist, gave authority for managing these reservations, or national forests, to the Department of Agriculture's forestry division, renamed the Forest Service. By 1913, there were a hundred and eighty-seven million acres of national forests, and four million acres have been added since. While most of the national forests are in the West, the system also includes over twenty-four million acres of lands in the Eastern and Southern states, most of which have already been logged.

The first head of the Forest Service was an aristocratic Easterner, Gifford Pinchot. Though Pinchot had been trained in forestry in France, he was more of a politician and a crusader than a technician. He deplored the way private landowners were treating the nation's forests, and he argued, unsuccessfully, that the government should take control of all the country's forestlands. Pinchot was an inspirational figure and—especially with the backing of his ally Teddy Roosevelt—a powerful one. As David Clary points out in "Timber and the Forest Service," Pinchot believed deeply in scientific forestry as a tool of social progress. It was up to the Forest Service, he said, to replace the rootless, boom-and-bust logging economy with stable communities able to count on a continuing supply of timber from the national forests.

The Forest Service also played a part in advancing another rationale for forest protection—the preservation of wilderness. Private landowners, who were cutting their trees as fast as they could, pressured the Forest Service to keep national-forest timber off the already glutted market. The agency therefore kept its forests intact, waiting in gloomy anticipation of the day when the private forests would be exhausted and it could step in to avert the long-dreaded timber famine. In the meantime, "the national forests were de-facto wilderness, largely unaltered from their primeval conditions, seldom visited by man, and the 'hard-rock' forest rangers came to hold a deep affection for this wild uninhabited country," according to the forestry scholar Richard Behan, quoted in Dennis Roth's "The Wilderness Movement and the National Forests." Many of the leading advocates of wilderness in the first decades of this century were Forest Service employees—men who lived close to nature the year-round and wanted to see its beauty protected.

The greatest of the Forest Service's wilderness advocates was Aldo Leopold, a forester and game manager for the agency and a founder of the Wilderness Society, which is now one of the agency's strongest critics. Leopold believed that encounters with wilderness had formed the American spirit, and that taming the American landscape would cut the country off from the roots of its vitality. "Is it not a bit beside the point for us to be so solicitous about preserving institutions without giving so much as a thought to preserving the environment which produced them and which may now be one of our effective means of keeping them alive?" he asked. Inspired by the infant science of ecology, Leopold also argued that mankind needed to preserve natural areas for study. It was at Leopold's urging that, in 1924, the Forest Service set aside its first wilderness area—five hundred thousand acres around New Mexico's Gila River.

The idea that national forests could harbor wilderness areas and produce timber was consistent with the Forest Service's philosophy that forests offer many benefits, not only timber, wilderness, and the protection of water quality but also fishing, hunting, and recreation. For many years, the agency had no difficulty in reconciling these often conflicting interests, because there was no pressure to cut the national forests. The Second World War changed that. The Forest Service responded to the military's urgent need for wood by more than doubling its timber production in three years. As the country settled back into civilian life, the demand for wood continued to soar, but private forestlands were almost exhausted, and could not meet the demand. This was the timber famine that the Forest Service had long anticipated—the moment when it would step in to keep the American people in timber and the American timber industry in business.

The Forest Service had been set up to demonstrate to a sloppy and reckless timber industry how forests should be managed, but, early on, it came under pressure to violate its own guidelines. In the immediate postwar period, the harvest from the national forests was just a fraction of its potential. But, because the national forests were then still largely inaccessible, pressure on the few areas that logging trucks *could* reach was intense. By 1948, according to Clary's book, B.H. Payne, a Forest Service timber manager, was ruing the fact that "the Forest Service was forced to accept in part the highly undesirable practice of over-cutting on some of the developed areas in order to increase the over-all supply of timber." The demand for timber from the national forests climbed all through the fifties and sixties. "Land and Resource Planning in the National Forests," by Charles Wilkinson and H. Michael Anderson, shows that from 1944 to 1966 the amount of timber cut annually from the national forests almost quadrupled. Because of the quality and the volume of their timber, the ancient Pacific forests have been the most heavily cut. Since the mid-sixties, the hundred and fifty-six national forests have produced around twelve billion board feet of timber a year, and about a quarter of it comes from the thirteen old-growth national forests of the Pacific Northwest. (Board feet are the measure of the amount of usable wood in a tree. One board foot is one foot square and one inch thick. It takes about ten thousand board feet of timber to build the average single-family house. A large, old Douglas fir may contain that much timber; some giants are on record as containing thirty thousand board feet.)

Throughout the nineteen-sixties, evidence mounted that the Forest Service was mismanaging and overcutting the national forests. A 1969 Forest Service study concluded that its Douglas-fir forests were being overcut, and predicted that harvests would drop by forty-five per cent once the old-growth trees were gone. In 1970, a group of highly respected foresters issued a report criticizing the Forest Service for ignoring its legal obligation to protect all the resources of the forest. "Multiple-use management, in fact, does not exist as the governing principle," the report said. And in 1975 the Fourth Circuit Court of Appeals, in Virginia, banned clear-cutting in the Monongahela National Forest, in West Virginia. To cope with this emergency, Congress in 1976 adopted the National Forest Management Act, which ordered the agency to limit the timber cut to an amount that each forest could sustain in perpetuity. Under the N.F.M.A., the agency was also ordered to prepare, as part of its ten-year management plans, harvesting schedules, based on realistic analyses of each forest's timber potential. In these plans roads, meadows, lakes, and rocky areas may not be counted as forestland. The plans must also eliminate from the timber base land on which trees will not grow back within five years of logging, and must make more accurate estimates of the amount of forest to be set aside to protect other values, including water quality, wildlife, and recreation. On the other hand, the plans allow the agency to assume that it will be able to increase productivity by using fertilizers, pesticides, and specially selected seedlings in growing the next generation of trees. Taking all this information together, the Forest Service has determined that the sustainable harvest level for forests in Washington and Oregon is substantially lower than had been thought. The sustainability of even these lower levels has been called into question by some prominent foresters. James Torrence, the regional forester in charge of all the national forests in Washington and Oregon, told the Portland *Oregonian* shortly before his retirement, last summer, "We can do it"—harvest at the new levels. "We can physically do it. But we can't do it for the 10-year life of the plans."

In any case, none of the new forest plans for the Pacific Northwest are yet in effect. Draft plans for those forests indicated that the sustainable harvest level was about twenty per cent lower than had been assumed. In 1983, John Crowell, the Assistant Secretary of Agriculture who was responsible for the Forest Service, and had previously been general counsel to Louisiana-Pacific, one of the country's largest purchasers of federal timber, ordered the plans withdrawn and revised, and that process took six years to complete. In the course of this delay, additional scientific evidence of the ecological damage caused by high timber harvests was amassed. The new draft plans indicate that sustainable yield for the forests is about twenty-five per cent lower than current cutting levels. In addition, planners in several national forests have indicated privately that the final plans should have even lower harvest levels than the draft plans specify.

While the forest plans are slowly being completed, Congress has been directing the Forest Service to increase its planned cut above the sustainable yields reflected in the draft forest plans, and even above the historically high levels still being proposed by the Forest Service. In 1987—the last year for which analyzed figures are available—Congress ordered the Forest Service to cut eighteen per cent more timber from the nine old-growth national forests in western Washington and Oregon than the agency had proposed, or almost eleven per cent more than the draft plans for the forests say is sustainable. The Siskiyou National Forest, for example, has been ordered to harvest 46.7 per cent more than the Forest Service itself proposed, the Rogue River National Forest 35.8 per cent more, and the Mt. Baker–Snoqualmie National Forest 28.8 per cent more.

Overcutting is also a serious problem in British Columbia's forests, and provincial government ministers as well as industry officials expect timber yields to drop by at least twenty-five per cent as the old-growth runs out. More than ninety per cent of British Columbia's forests are publicly owned, and under the Canadian system publicly owned forests are the responsibility of the provincial governments. The system of allocating timber harvests in British Columbia is very different from that in the United States, where the Forest Service manages the forests on a day-to-day basis and awards onetime logging rights through competitive bidding. In British Columbia, the provincial Ministry of Forests licenses private companies to log and *manage* large areas of the public forests in perpetuity, with minimal oversight from its forest service and with virtually no public oversight. A study by Bill Wagner, at the University of Victoria, shows that more than ninety per cent of the province's public forests are under the control of just four groups of linked companies—the Bentley-Prentice group, the Mead-Scott group, the Bronfman, Reichmann & Desmarais group, and the Sauder, Champion, Ketcham & Fletcher group.

Most data on public forests in Canada, including the amount of timber cut in each licensed area and the price the government charges licensees for logs, are kept private, on the ground that licensees have a right to commercial confidentiality. Therefore, it is virtually impossible for citizens or academics to check either government's or industry's claims about the condition of the public forests. Licensees are required to adhere to vaguely worded management plans, among whose many shortcomings are that they do not require the use of the most up-to-date scientific data available and that they make little pretense of giving equal weight to the protection of such non-timber resources as fisheries, wildlife habitat, archeological sites, and endangered species. Management plans are public documents, but they can be amended in private, with no public notice. Citizens have no right to take either licensees or the government to court for alleged violations of management plans.

In the ancient coastal forests of British Columbia, the most extensive tenures are so-called tree-farm licenses, under which a company is given rights, renewable in perpetuity, over a large area of forest. The company does not pay for the license, even though tree-farm licenses, which can be used as collateral or sold, are valuable assets, and can be worth billions of dollars. If for any reason—including the creation of a national park, the settlement of native-land claims, or the protection of wildlife and fisheries—the government causes the cut on a licensed area to be reduced by more than five per cent over twenty-five years, it must compensate the licensee for lost future profits. The Ministry of Forests sets the allowable cut for each licensed area on the basis of forest inventories, which the licensees carry out periodically. In general, the inventories do not exclude all areas that are inaccessible, environmentally sensitive, or valuable for wildlife, scenery, or archeology, or that have uneconomic timber.

Neither the province nor the timber industry claims that l ging at present levels is sustainable. In 1979, the province ab doned sustained yield as a goal of its forestry program. A 1984 report by the Ministry of Forests noted, "British Columbia's forests are commonly thought to be managed under a policy of constant production over time. This is not true. Many future second-growth stands will yield smaller harvests at maturity than the existing old-growth forests." Worries about this so-called falldown problem are being pushed into the future, though its effects are already being felt in parts of the province where the old-growth has run out. Peter Pearse, British Columbia's leading forest economist, argues that "this complication ought not to worry us much if the impact is not felt until the mid-twenty-first century." And Norm Godfrey, who until recently was the forestry manager for Vancouver Island's Alberni tree-farm-license area—one of the largest such areas in British Columbia, and licensed to the conglomerate MacMillan Bloedel—says, "You have to look at it a different way. It's not that we'll get less later but that we're getting more now."

Today, the effects of almost fifty years of intensive logging in the publicly owned forests of the Pacific Northwest are clear. The logging industry has been unable to take large amounts of timber out of the forest without damaging water quality, wildlife, and even the forest's capacity for regeneration. Clear-cuts, once regarded as appropriate only in special circumstances, cover—or uncover—the landscape. The United States Forest Service makes an effort to protect the public from the mournful sight of clear-cuts by leaving "visual-protection corridors" of tall trees along the roadsides, but as the cutting has progressed from the valley floors up the steep hillsides clear-cuts have become harder and harder to hide; some spread across thousands of acres. It is not merely the sight of large areas of deforested land that upsets and confuses visitors; the jagged stumps, broken branches, and shredded bark that clutter the logging sites, and are bleached by the sun or blackened by fires set to destroy them, accentuate the sense of devastation, and so do the landslides that commonly scar steep denuded slopes. Senator Gale McGee, of Wyoming, called clear-cutting "a shocking desecration that has to be seen to be believed," and described one clear-cut as looking "as if a squadron of B-52s had ravaged the pristine beauty of the Wind River Mountains." In British Columbia, there is no limit on the size of clear-cuts. The limit on clear-cuts in the United States is forty acres in most national forests, sixty acres in Douglas-fir forests, and a hundred acres in Alaska, but exceptions can be granted. Observers estimate that up to half the clear-cuts in Alaska's Tongass National Forest are larger than a hundred acres.

Flying over the forests of Oregon, Washington, British Columbia, and Alaska, I have seen mile after mile of contiguous or nearly contiguous clearcuts, and they are among the ugliest scars on the planet. One near the Bowron Lakes, in British Columbia, covers more than a hundred and eighty square miles: it is one of the few manifestations of man visible from space. But looks are not everything. If this temporarily barren ground is only one stage in a cycle of growth and renewal, it may be a price worth paying for our use of wood. Assuming that we need trees and are going to cut them, perhaps the question should be not "Is it ugly?" but "Does it work?" What method of tree cutting has the least impact on the surrounding area and on the ability of the land to grow more trees? Clear-cutting, despite its ugliness, has several advantages over selection logging, in which only a few trees are taken out at a time. That clear-cutting is more economical is obvious. Also, some species, such as Douglas fir, do not regenerate well after selection logging, because they cannot grow in deep shade. Initially, clear-cutting has a greater impact on a site than selection logging has, but selection logging subjects a site to repeated invasions with heavy equipment and new roads. And there is some concern that in selection logging the best specimens—the biggest, straightest trees—are cut first, with only comparatively stunted, scrawny trees left behind to form a degraded genetic reservoir for succeeding generations. In some circumstances, then, clear-cutting is an appropriate method of logging. But clear-cutting—especially as it is practiced today—is a drastic operation, which carries the risk of serious damage and is not suitable for fragile soils or steep slopes.

National forests are generally less suitable for clear-cutting than private lands are, because private owners claimed the accessible, lowland forests first, leaving the national forests to be carved out of the steepest, most remote, and most easily damaged lands.

As a result, erosion and landslides after clear-cuts are particular problems on public forestland. The high rainfall that is common along the Pacific Coast increases the instability of the soil. When the protective tree cover and the thick layer of organic matter are removed, there is nothing to absorb and store the available moisture. Consequently, a heavily logged area will have more intense runoff in the wet season and less water available in the dry season. In winter and spring, the creeks will run dark with silt; in summer and fall, they will be dry and choked with logging debris.

Neither the United States Forest Service nor the British Columbia forest service bans cutting on steep hillsides; each situation is evaluated individually. The result is that throughout the region slopes as steep as forty-five degrees have been clear-cut. One of the most common sights on clear-cut slopes is a logging road running straight across a mountainside, with the earth crumbling away every few hundred yards. The washed-down soil chokes creeks and rivers.

To survive, forest streams must flow through corridors of living trees, and must contain a certain amount of wood—often more than sixty pounds for every square yard of stream—from large trees that have fallen into them. These accumulations of wood create the plunge pools, side channels, and gravel beds that are important fish habitats. Without them, sediment and logging debris flow downstream unimpeded, smothering the bottom-dwelling insects, scouring the streambed, and eroding the stream bank. Yet one frequently sees lakes and streams with no buffer at all, or with a hopelessly inadequate fringe, one or two trees deep. "We did that in the sixties and seventies, and now we're dragging the wood back into the streams," David Gibbons, until recently the regional fisheries-program manager for the Forest Service in Alaska, told me, adding that the state is introducing new guidelines for logging near forest streams.

When a forest has been clear-cut and the timber removed, there are literally tons of woody debris left behind—broken trees, branches, huge stumps, twigs, piles of bark. This unsightly mess, called slash, is sometimes allowed to decay and return nutrients to the soil, but more often it is burned, in order to destroy debris that might fuel wildfires, and to make replanting easier. Slash burning is a significant contributor to air pollution in Oregon and

Washington.

Proponents of logging often argue—erroneously—that cutting old-growth forests counteracts global warming, which is caused by the buildup in the atmosphere of carbon dioxide and other gases. Their argument is based on the fact that young trees absorb carbon dioxide at a faster rate than do old trees. This is true, but as Mark Harmon, a forest scientist at Oregon State University, explains, "even though the young forest is taking up carbon real fast, it can never—or not for hundreds of years—make up for the huge amount of carbon that was released when that old-growth forest was cut."

Simply cutting a tree does not cause the carbon stored within it to escape into the atmosphere. Only as the tree decomposes is the carbon released. When a forest is cut, the logging debris, leaf litter, and other organic matter left behind are exposed to sunlight, which speeds up decomposition. Often, a logging site is deliberately burned after clear-cutting, sending carbon into the air immediately. The soil is another storehouse of carbon, and as it is torn up and exposed to the air and sun during logging operations it also decomposes, sending its carbon load up to the atmosphere. Of the timber that is taken away, less than half is made into long-lived items, such as lumber or plywood. Fifty-two per cent is burned as fuel or made into paper or fibre products, which are soon thrown away, to decompose or be burned. Thus, Harmon says, "a great big chunk of this huge storehouse of carbon that is the old-growth forest is converted back into carbon dioxide within a few years."

If an area is to be clear-cut, there must, of course, be a road into it, and the United States Forest Service has become the biggest road-building agency in the world. Into the fragile landscape of the national forests it has carved hundreds of thousands of miles of roads. Many have been abandoned, but today the national forests contain more than three hundred and forty thousand miles of operable roads. That is eight times the mileage of the entire interstate-highway system. Over the next fifty years, the Forest Service plans to build about a hundred thousand miles of new roads, and to rebuild over three hundred thousand miles. Despite the fact that most logging roads are not paved, they are expensive to build and maintain, because of the rough terrain they must penetrate and the disturbances to which they are always subject. Major logging roads cost forty-five thousand dollars a mile on the average, and secondary ones average fifteen thousand dollars a mile. The Forest Service pays for roads by the sale of timber and by direct grants from the federal government; in 1988, the grants amounted to a hundred and seventy-five million dollars.

Cutting across mountainsides, crossing streams, dislodging rocks, creating piles of excess earth, roads are inherently destabilizing. When a road is bulldozed or blasted across a slope, tons of earth and rocks are moved. Often the excess soil is simply pushed over the side of the road, and there it forms a nucleus for future landslides. Every year, newly built logging roads make about a hundred and eighty thousand stream crossings. Each crossing involves a risk of damage to the stream. Ideally, roads should be engineered to allow streams to flow freely under them. In many cases, however, logging roads are simply cut across streambeds. Streams are often forced into drainage culverts that are inadequate to cope with the high-water flow or with the deluges of large branches, boulders, and logging waste, called debris torrents, that may be swept into the stream channel. Such debris torrents choke streambeds, causing floods, washouts, and landslides, which erode slopes, destroy the road, and silt up larger streams below.

Whatever the failures of the Forest Service in maintaining high standards of logging-road design and construction, those of British Columbia's Ministry of Forests are far worse. "We seem to be ten years behind in Canada in terms of forest legislation," Norm Godfrey told me. "There are laws telling our U.S. operation what to do in a way that doesn't exist in British Columbia at this time." As I toured MacMillan Bloedel's Vancouver Island concessions by plane with Godfrey and a group of other company officials, in the spring of 1989, and later, on my own, I saw plenty of evidence to support his statement.

Since the discovery, in 1988, that the Carmanah Valley, which is part of a MacMillan Bloedel concession on Vancouver Island, contains some spectacularly large ancient trees, including the world's tallest spruce, this remote valley has become a tourist attraction and a cause célèbre among Canadian environmentalists. They have enlisted much support from hikers shocked by what they have seen of a logging operation that was not meant to be on public display. Staring down at the clear-cuts, Godfrey shook his head and said, "If we had thought ahead, we'd have planned the road to minimize the visual impact."

"You'd love to turn the clock back," Dennis Bendickson, the company's divisional engineer, murmured in assent.

Later, as we passed over the Cypre region, a mountainous coastal area where huge clear-cuts are crisscrossed by poorly designed logging roads, Godfrey said, "We wouldn't do it that way now. The cuts would be smaller. Not because we know something now that we didn't then but because of the changing expectations of the public." MacMillan Bloedel is still logging at Cypre. In the winter of 1988, erosion from the denuded slopes was so bad that the company had to spread a slurry containing legumes and grasses over the hills in a bid to save both the hills and Cypress Bay, which they were falling into. Environmentalists are particularly upset by the devastation of Cypre and nearby watersheds, because they are part of Clayoquot Sound, a beautiful area of coastal mountains, fjords, forested islands, and white sand beaches that together make up one of two of Vancouver Island's last large expanses of coastal rain forest. The Ucluelet forest, some miles farther south, adjoins the Pacific Rim National Park, a long, narrow expanse of pristine beaches. "We logged every square foot of Ucluelet," Godfrey commented. "But we wouldn't do it that way now."

Half a century of clear-cutting and road building has left North America with a severely fragmented forest. The northeastern area of Alaska's Chichagof Island is a poignant illustration. Almost every watershed of this once-perfect landscape of forests, rivers, white sand beaches, and snowcapped mountain ridges has been violated, largely as a result of the Forest Service's allowing loggers to search out and take the biggest trees, which are scattered in small stands—a process known as high-grading. Though these old-growth stands are a small part of the forest, they are the most profitable to cut. But they are also the heart of the forest ecosystem, supporting both a mass of timber and a mass of life. Many of the clear-cuts are separated from each other by narrow strips of standing trees. These strips are supposed to serve as wildlife refuges, but they are utterly inadequate to support the animals displaced by logging, according to John Schoen, a wildlife biologist with Alaska's Department of Fish and Game. Moreover, some of these narrow strips have been largely or completely destroyed by wind. Many rivers and lakes are logged right down to their edges. Pointing to Kook Lake, a sockeye-salmon fishery severely damaged by overlogging, Schoen exploded, "Has that been high-graded? Man, I tell you it has!"

According to the Forest Service, only twelve per cent of the forest of northeastern Chichagof Island has been logged. But the logging has been concentrated in the high-volume old-growth forest, and clear-cuts are spread over almost every one of the region's watersheds. Near the coastal town of Tenakee Springs, the watersheds of Basket Bay, Kook Lake, Crab Bay, Corner Bay, Indian River, Pavlof Harbor, and Kennel Creek have all been high-graded, and severely damaged from an ecological point of view. Gone are dense, low-elevation forests where deer sheltered and fed in winter, and riparian forests where brown bears lived and in whose waters millions of salmon spawned each spring. The four hundred square miles of northeastern Chichagof Island is now laced by two hundred miles of logging roads, and the Forest Service plans to build another two hundred miles of roads over the next twenty-two years. These roads will take loggers into the few remaining pristine watersheds and drastically change the lives of Tenakee Springs' hundred residents.

Tenakee Springs is isolated, and the residents like it that way. Outsiders can get there only by boat or floatplane. There are no roads, and so there are no automobiles. The town has a small electric generator, limited indoor plumbing, and, at the time I visited, last spring, two communal telephones. The townspeople bathe together, too—women in the morning and evening, men in the afternoon and at night—in hot springs that bubble up in the center of town. There are few jobs in Tenakee, and many of the residents go off for a few months each year to earn some cash; in 1988, several worked on the Exxon Valdez oil-spill cleanup. But the ocean, the rivers, and the forest provide much of what people need—food, firewood, and building materials.

In the early nineteen-seventies, the Forest Service decided that Tenakee Springs should be linked by a road to the larger town of Hoonah, twenty-four miles to the northwest, "for administrative reasons." (The road would connect two Forest Service districts.) Almost everyone in Tenakee is vehemently opposed to that plan.

Even the Forest Service concedes that the road is unpopular. Helen Clough, then the district ranger who had jurisdiction over the road, told me, "A great majority of the Tenakee residents don't want a road to their town. They value that isolation, that remoteness—that's why they live there. It's one of the few remaining communities in Alaska—or America—where you can live that way."

The opponents of the road believe that an influx of cars and hunters will destroy the environment they love, and depend on for a living. Hoonah is already plagued by an excess of hunters. Because it is one of the hunting areas closest to Juneau, scores of hunters in camper vans make the short ferry trip to Hoonah each weekend during the hunting season. The pressure of hunting and the destruction of the animals' habitat by logging have reduced the island's bear population so much that the state Department of Fish and Game has had to drastically restrict hunting in the northeastern Chichagof. Commercial guides, who must pay the Forest Service a small percentage of their gross income for the right to operate in the national forest, have been forced to cut back or abandon their businesses in the area.

Despite the opposition, the Forest Service went ahead and built a road from Tenakee to within six miles of the Hoonah road system. Because the road had to traverse town land for a short distance to reach the coast, the City of Tenakee Springs threatened to deny access unless the Forest Service and the Alaska Pulp Company, which has logging rights in the area, agreed not to connect the road with other road systems. In response, the Forest Service in 1988 used its power as a federal agency to condemn the right-of-way, offering to pay Tenakee Springs a hundred dollars in compensation. Meanwhile, both Tenakee Springs and three clans of Tlingit Indians have gone to court to force the Forest Service to consider what effect the road link and increased logging might have on wildlife and water quality. Tenakee Springs has also appealed to Congress to include a clause banning a road link across the island in forthcoming legislation. That is probably Tenakee's last hope in its nearly twenty-year-long struggle to preserve its isolation and its way of life.

No one knows exactly how much of the ancient Pacific forest is left. There are no comprehensive maps or surveys of old-growth, and the little information that has been gathered is fragmentary and inconsistent. The United States Forest Service is only now developing a definition of old-growth—a step that British Columbia's forest service has not yet taken. One thing that is known is that the greatest extent of old-growth forest left is in coastal British Columbia, which also has the highest old-growth logging rates. And sixty per cent of British Columbia's coastal old-growth forest is estimated to have already been destroyed. Of perhaps seven million acres left, fewer than four hundred and fifty thousand have been set aside in parks and preserves. At the present cutting rate—about a hundred and twenty-five thousand acres a year—it is estimated that virtually all unprotected coastal old-growth will be gone by the year 2020. According to Douglas Williams and Robert Gasson, University of British Columbia forest analysts, the high-volume forests that both ecologists and economists value most will be gone even sooner—in fifteen years.

The Tongass National Forest takes in almost seventeen million acres and stretches across thousands of watersheds, over scores of islands, from valley bottoms to mountaintops, covering virtually the whole of southeastern Alaska. The general impression, even among foresters and environmentalists, is that the Tongass is the continent's great reservoir of old-growth. But although much of the Tongass is covered by very old trees only a small part of the region has the ecological and topographical conditions needed to support true old-growth forest. This classic high-volume old-growth, which originally covered almost a million acres, is being logged much faster than the rest of the forest, according to a study by Matthew Kirchhoff, a research biologist with the Alaska Department of Fish and Game. Twenty-five per cent of the classic old-growth is already gone, twenty per cent is legally protected, and thirty per cent is scheduled to be cut; the remaining twenty-five per cent is not scheduled for cutting at this time, because of technical and economic constraints.

Old-growth forests in the lower forty-eight states originally covered twenty-five million acres. The Forest Service estimates that the twelve old-growth national forests in Washington, Oregon, and Northern California have four million one hundred thousand acres of old-growth left. Adding in all other old-growth forests—those owned by the states or by the federal Bureau of

Land Management, and those in national parks—brings the total for the region up to five million four hundred thousand acres, of which a million acres are under permanent protection. According to the Wilderness Society, however, the Forest Service has greatly exaggerated the extent of the remaining ancient forests. In the most comprehensive independent study of old-growth so far conducted, Peter Morrison, a forest ecologist, analyzed old-growth in six Pacific Northwest national forests for the Wilderness Society in 1988. Using Forest Service data and aerial photographs, Morrison and his colleagues found that the six national forests contained a total of one million one hundred thousand acres of old-growth, and not two and a half million acres, as the Forest Service had estimated.

The Forest Service, which is now conducting its own old-growth inventory, has reacted mildly to the society's study. "I have no problem with it," Karl Bergsvik, the agency's assistant director for timber management, told me a year ago in his office, in Washington, D.C. "The only problem I have—and it applies to our data as well—is that they used information from inventories that weren't designed to provide the kind of information we're developing." Old-growth estimates for several of the six forests studied by the Wilderness Society have since been revised. The estimate for the Gifford Pinchot National Forest, for example, has been lowered from two hundred and thirty-one thousand acres to a hundred and ninety-three thousand; the society's figure, however, was a hundred and nineteen thousand acres.

The Wilderness Society figures indicate that the ancient forests are much closer to extinction than was realized. Forest Service officials say, for example, that the Siskiyou National Forest has four hundred and forty-three thousand acres of old-growth now, and after fifty more years of logging it will have a hundred and eighty-one thousand acres left. But the Wilderness Society says that the Siskiyou has less than this already—only a hundred and forty-one thousand acres. Extrapolating from its study and taking into account state, private, and other federal lands, the Wilderness Society estimates that the unprotected old-growth in all of western Washington and Oregon comes to under a million five hundred thousand acres—less than half the official estimate. If this estimate is correct, at the present rates of logging every bit of unprotected old-growth in western Washington and Oregon will be gone in less than twenty years.

Efforts to protect the ancient forests have so far been inadequate. Less than five per cent of the original forest has some sort of legal protection. The situation in British Columbia is particularly worrying, for neither of the two biggest reserves there is completely secure. One, the South Moresby National Park Reserve, is the subject of unsettled native-land claims, and the government of British Columbia has already seriously eroded the other, its Strathcona Provincial Park, by opening it to hydroelectric development, mining, and logging. Insuring the survival of the ancient forests is not merely a matter of protecting a certain percentage of the original forest. A system of parks and reserves is adequate only if it reflects the diversity of the original forest—including, for example, the Sitka-spruce and Western-hemlock forests along the coast from Northern California to Alaska, the Douglas-fir forests of Oregon and Washington, the Western-red-cedar forests of coastal British Columbia and Washington, and the mixed evergreen-hardwood forest of Oregon's Siskiyou Mountains. The reserves should also contain a significant proportion of the forests that have the greatest degree of biological diversity—the low-elevation forests on good growing sites. "There's damn little of the lower-elevation forest set aside," Jerry Franklin, now of the University of Washington, says. "In our wilderness areas, it's mostly higher-elevation forest with poor biological diversity. So the wilderness areas don't do a good job of protecting biological diversity. And the parks, with the exception of the Olympic National Park, don't really do a good job, either." In both the United States and Canada, parks have been chosen for their dramatic scenery rather than for their biological significance. Most of the parks in the Pacific area are centered on mountain ranges. They consist largely of rocks and snow and ice, with perhaps a fringe of old-growth forest on the lower slopes.

Reserves must also be big enough to accommodate the needs of their native species. Charles Meslow, a spotted-owl specialist with the Fish and Wildlife Service, has said that each mating pair of spotted owls, for example, requires from fifteen hundred to four thousand acres of old-growth forest, depending on where the forest is. In general, according to Franklin, "it is preferable to have reserves of several hundred acres, but smaller patches may also be worth saving, depending on a number of circumstances, including the type of forest, how isolated it is, and how rare it is." In 1986, the Forest Service's Old Growth Definition Task Group, a committee of government and university scientists, concluded that stands of less than eighty acres are ordinarily too small to be viable in the Pacific Northwest. As the climate heats up, it is going to be important to have not only reserves of a viable size but also corridors of forest linking those reserves, so that plants and animals can migrate among different latitudes. The corridors would also allow several small reserves to function as one larger unit. Unfortunately, no such corridors exist, and much of what remains of the ancient forest consists of small, isolated patches surrounded by clear-cuts or bisected by logging roads. The majority of the old-growth patches in the Siuslaw National Forest, in Oregon, for example, consist of less than forty acres.

"It's interesting that we're telling Third World countries, 'Don't cut your forests,' and yet look at the things we're doing here. We're wiping out our fish runs, we're wiping out our biotic diversity; we're sending species to extinction," Andy Kerr, of the Oregon Natural Resources Council, says. "You know, we're not a Third World country. We're not so poor that we have to destroy our ancient forests. And we're not so rich that we can afford to."

Our destruction of the greatest forests remaining on this continent has many consequences, certain to be long-lasting and in some cases irreversible. Fishing, tourism, and recreation are already suffering. It is harder for people who wish to do so to make a subsistence living. An ecological system that we do not yet understand is disappearing. Plant and animal species are being driven to the edge of extinction. Rivers and streams are dying. Drastic changes in our planet's climate are being hastened. In exchange, we are getting wood. But for how long? Instead of waiting the two hundred years it would take for the next generation of trees to produce as much wood as the ancient forest has produced, foresters are trying to speed up growth through the development of better seedlings, through the use of chemical fertilizers and pesticides, and through more intensive care of young trees. By these methods, the foresters figure, an eighty-year-old plantation could produce the same volume of timber as a forest two hundred and fifty, or even five hundred, years old—from thirty to fifty thousand board feet of timber an acre. The plantation trees will not be as big as those of the ancient forest, but there will be more of them per acre. "We know what nature can do, and we're relatively certain that we can do better than nature," George Leonard, the associate chief of the Forest Service, says.

Though the Forest Service insists that its reforestation program is a success, it is difficult to know for certain. The agency's records on reforestation and growth rates are incomplete and, in some cases, unreliable. The Forest Service defines reforestation so narrowly that it can claim very high rates of restocking, but these claims may be misleading. In 1988, for example, officials of the Siskiyou National Forest said that more than ninety-nine per cent of the forest's logged-over areas had been replanted to Forest Service standards. But the agency sets standards only for the number of trees planted, not for the number that survive. Thus one area in the Siskiyou National Forest has been reforested to agency standards six times since 1961—and there is every indication that the latest planting will also fail. The agency keeps no records of how fast its plantations are growing, or how robust they are. "The agency doesn't want to know what's happening out there," says Julie Norman, who is president of the board of Headwaters, an Oregon group dedicated to promoting sustainable forestry, and who is an expert on the Forest Service's computer-modeling program.

Forest Service officials often assure the public that the forests of the future will consist of genetically superior trees—vigorous, large, and straight-trunked. But the agency does not breed improved varieties. Rather, it reforests with seeds taken from trees with desirable qualities, and hopes that those qualities will be passed on. It is, of course, impossible to know in advance whether a given trait is genetic or merely the result of circumstances. Intensive management of the national forests did not begin until the nineteen-seventies, and specially selected seeds have been planted on a large scale for just over ten years. The Forest Service has estimated that areas replanted with these seeds will produce ten per cent more timber than ordinary sites. The agency's calculations are based not on data on tree growth from on-the-ground surveys but on assumptions and computer projections. Some foresters have raised questions about the reliability of this estimate, especially since the agency is not attempting to insure that a site is reforested with seeds collected from the locality. Plants adapted to one site may not do well in another whose soil, moisture level, and exposure to sun and shade are different, according to Barry Flamm, who was formerly the supervisor of the Shoshone National Forest, in Idaho, and is now the chief forester for the Wilderness Society. "The jury isn't in yet on whether a lot of these so-called improved trees are really improved in terms of timber quality and in terms of survivability over a long period," Flamm says.

The Forest Service's expectation that growth rates will increase is based on two assumptions: not only that intensive management will raise productivity but also that intensive management will be able to continue. Critics charge that since the latter assumption, at least, has not always been justified it makes a mockery of the agency's growth predictions. Herbicide spraying to keep down competing vegetation, for example, has been banned in national forests in Oregon and Washington since 1984. "The agency assumed that using herbicides would boost the cut by as much as thirty-seven per cent, but the cut hasn't dropped to make up for the fact that they're not spraying—and that they're not meeting their targets for clearing the brush by hand, either," Julie Norman says. In another case, analysts at the Siskiyou National Forest, responding to a request from Oregon's Governor Neil Goldschmidt, raised their estimate of the forest's sustainable harvest level by four million board feet a year on the expectation—which they had previously felt was unjustified—that Congress would give them money for fertilizers.

"It's voodoo forestry," Richard Brown, a resource specialist with the National Wildlife Federation in Portland, says. "Shorter rotations, better seeds—they conjure up all these intangibles that are supposed to enhance future growth. They don't really care if it works. The point is that it provides them with an excuse to cut more big old trees now."

Intensive forestry in the United States has a very short history. Only a few managed forests predate the Second World War. The forest ecologist Chris Maser has written, "I know of no nation and no people that have maintained on a sustainable basis, plantation-managed trees beyond three rotations. The famous Black Forest in

Europe is a plantation; it and other forests are dying at the end of the third rotation. The eastern pine plantations are dying. It's the end of their third rotation." Barry Flamm says, "It's a justifiable worry that forest productivity will decline."

Up to half the trees in the German and Scandinavian forest plantations are dying. In the mid-nineteen-eighties, the Forest Service detected a twenty-five-per-cent decrease in annual growth rates and a sharp increase in mortality rates in the plantations of the southeastern United States. The damage in both the American and the European plantations has been attributed to acid rain, but Maser hypothesizes that it is partly the consequence of several centuries of intensive management. By deliberately removing "extraneous" material, such as dead logs, from the forest floor, foresters interfere with the "dead-wood" cycle that produces the mycorrhizal fungi without which many trees cannot survive.

Though foresters like to apply agricultural metaphors to their trade, they face a much more difficult and uncertain task than do farmers whose crops mature in six months. First, trees must survive in a world of predators and environmental stresses for decades rather than for months. Second, the nature of the stresses is hard to predict or to guard against. "There are so many variables in the future—climate, insects, acid rain—that it's hard to say whether the second growth will live up to our expectations," Karl Bergsvik, of the Forest Service, says. Jerry Franklin adds, "We just don't know if we can do repeated croppings without serious problems. I think even some of the industrial-oriented people would agree on that when you backed them into a corner."

Research suggests that one solution is to mimic the natural variety and complexity of the forest—to try to grow forests rather than just trees. "What forestry has traditionally done is make the forest simple," Franklin says. "What we have to learn to do is make the forest diverse." The first step is to change the way we log. "Instead of working all over the forest, concentrate your activity for a decade or two at a time on smaller areas. Cut more of it in terms of per centage of landscape, but then get out, pull out the road system, and leave it alone. And in the cutting itself leave behind a lot of structure—green trees, dead trees, and downed wood." Such an approach would result in man-made clearings that are more like the clearings made by wind and fire, which leave behind "legacies," such as large living and dead trees, rotting logs, organic litter, spores of mycorrhizal fungi, and areas of undisturbed soil, that enable the forest to renew itself. "A diverse forest is more resistant to various kinds of perturbations, less susceptible to insects and diseases," Franklin argues. "It's likely to be more capable of responding to global climate changes, dealing with environmental stresses of one kind or another. So that simply by having a more diverse forest you increase its ability to resist—and if not to resist, then to recover from—these disturbances, and that also contributes to this idea of sustainable productivity."

The Forest Service is often criticized for selling timber from national forests at a loss, but the agency points out that, over all, its timber-sales program makes money; it made two hundred and sixty-seven million dollars in 1987. The profitability is largely due to the twelve old-growth forests in Washington, Oregon, and Northern California. Though the cost to the agency of doing surveys and building roads is just as high in the Pacific forests as in the other national forests, the volume of timber per acre in these old-growth forests is so much higher than it is in the rest of the country that sales of their timber are immensely profitable, even at low Forest Service prices. Ninety per cent of the Forest Service's 1987 net timber receipts came from sales in these twelve forests, though two-thirds of the timber came from the other hundred and forty-four forests.

Because of a unique arrangement, the Tongass National Forest is the only one of the old-growth forests to lose money on its timber sales. When the Tongass was designated a national forest, in 1907, it was seen as the key to the economic development of southeastern Alaska, but then Forest Service officials labored vainly for decades to get a local pulp industry started. The aftermath of the Second World War revitalized the agency's dreams. In ceding Manchuria to China and Sakhalin Island to the Soviet Union, in 1945, Japan lost almost half its timber resources. Japanese businesses sought to have Alaska make up for those losses, and they were supported by the American military administration that ruled postwar Japan and was looking for ways to rebuild its economy. In 1953, the Japanese agreed to build a pulp mill in Alaska instead of simply taking the raw logs back to Japan for processing.

The mill is operated by the Alaska Pulp Corporation, which is a consortium of virtually all the leading Japanese companies that have interests in any aspect of wood processing and trading. At around the same time, the United States government signed a contract to build a mill with the newly formed Ketchikan Pulp Company, which is now owned by Louisiana-Pacific.

In exchange for building the mills, the two companies received fifty-year contracts guaranteeing them timber supplies at extremely low prices. The contracts established what has been called a "duopoly" over two-thirds of the Tongass National Forest's commercial forestland. There is no competitive bidding for this timber; prices are subject to review every five years but can be raised only by agreement between the United States government and the mills. Almost all the timber from the Tongass goes to Japan and other Pacific Rim countries. Sitka spruce, which, along with Western hemlock, dominates the Tongass, is valued by the United States Customs Service at more than seven hundred dollars per thousand board feet. Alaska Pulp currently pays two dollars and twenty-six cents for a thousand board feet of Sitka spruce, and a dollar and twenty-two cents for a thousand board feet of prized Alaskan cedar. On the average, the company pays a dollar and forty-seven cents for a thousand board feet of Tongass timber. The Forest Service charges more than that for a road map of the Tongass. Ketchikan Pulp's prices are higher: they average just over forty-nine dollars per thousand board feet. Native Alaskans, who control about half a million acres of southeastern Alaska's forest, sell their timber abroad, because they cannot compete with the Forest Service's low prices.

In 1980, Congress set aside about a third of the Tongass as wilderness. The vast majority of the wilderness sites were mountainous areas, mostly rock and ice. Only nine per cent of the high-volume forest was designated wilderness, and the pulp companies were still guaranteed their contractual timber supplies. Nonetheless, Senator Ted Stevens, of Alaska, insisted on an addition to the Alaska National Interest Lands Conservation Act, or ANILCA. Section 705(a) of the act requires the Forest Service to make four hundred and fifty million board feet of Tongass timber available for sale each year, and to spend at least forty million dollars a year building logging roads and preparing timber sales, whether or not anyone wants to buy the timber. A Government Accounting Office report found that between 1980 and 1986 the agency spent a hundred and thirty-one million dollars building roads and preparing timber for sales that never materialized.

The Tongass is the biggest money loser of all the national forests. In some years, the government has lost ninety-nine cents for every dollar it spent on timber programs in the Tongass. Between 1982 and 1988, Tongass timber sales cost the government more than three hundred and fifty million dollars. Though the point of the fifty-year contracts and of ANILCA's Section 705(a) is to create and maintain local jobs, the number of timber jobs in southeastern Alaska has dropped to eighteen hundred from twenty-seven hundred in 1980, largely because of automation and a decline in the Japanese timber market. The Wilderness Society estimates that each remaining job costs American taxpayers thirty-six thousand dollars a year in subsidies. Southeastern Alaska's main industry is now fishing, which employs twenty-six hundred people directly; recreation-tourism, which employs around two thousand people, is its fastest-growing industry. Both are threatened by the continued logging of the old-growth forest.

In 1981, an independent Alaskan logging company won a suit in federal district court in Seattle, and Ketchikan Pulp and Alaska Pulp were found guilty of conspiracy and restraint of trade. The judge ruled that they had used the advantages their contracts gave them "to control the Alaska timber market, to eliminate competition, and to maintain and exercise monopoly power." A Forest Service review of the case concluded that the agency had lost as much as eighty-three million dollars in its dealings with the two companies. The Forest Service claimed damages against the two companies, and the case was referred to the Justice Department. Ketchikan Pulp settled the claim against it by making minor modifications in its long-term contract and agreeing to pay a million dollars. Alaska Pulp decided to fight the claim, and in 1987 made a counterclaim, that the Forest Service owed it eighty-three million dollars, because the agency had failed to fulfill a contractual obligation to provide the company with profitable timber. The company had taken exception to recent efforts by the Forest Service to direct logging to areas other than the richest, high-volume parts of the forest, which had borne the brunt of the logging so far. By the time both sides were ready to argue the case, the Justice Department announced that the statute of limitations had run out.

Both companies say that they need the contracts and the low timber prices to stay in business. Environmentalists say that the contracts and the provisions of Section 705(a) that force the Forest Service to build unneeded roads are tearing the heart out of the forest. Bart Koehler, the executive director of the Southeast Alaska Conservation Council, says, "Conservation groups around the country are fighting the Forest Service's multiple-use system. They groan when I tell them that our ambition in Alaska is just to get to that point—to get the contracts off our back so we can just deal with the same problems that are driving them crazy." The House of Representatives has passed a bill that would terminate the contracts, open Tongass timber sales to competitive bidding, give protection to a million eight hundred thousand acres of important fish-and-wildlife habitat, and stop construction of the Tenakee Springs road. It would also repeal Section 705(a), making the timber harvest and the Forest Service's budget subject to review, as is the case in respect to all the other national forests. The Senate is considering a bill that is much weaker from an environmental viewpoint. The Forest Service opposes the bills, on the ground that contracts with the federal government should be inviolable. The pulp companies say they will sue the government for several billion dollars on a charge of breach of contract if either version of the Tongass Timber Reform Act is enacted.

Even in the lower forty-eight states, where there are no long-term contracts, the Forest Service does not attempt to charge for its timber what it costs to produce it or will cost to replace it; instead, the agency charges what it estimates the buyer can afford to pay. It calculates the selling price for the finished product—lumber, plywood, or pulp—subtracts the cutting, transporting, and manufacturing costs, and then takes off a ten-per-cent profit margin. The remainder is what the Forest Service charges. If there are several prospective buyers, the price may be bid up, but often there is only one bidder. Because the Forest Service is such an important source of timber on the domestic market, private companies are forced to charge lower prices, too. Many small-woodlot owners choose to leave their timber standing rather than sell it so cheap, and their decision further restricts the amount of timber available to domestic mills.

In the past seven years, civil disobedience has become increasingly common as a way of protesting threats to the forest. Protesters have blockaded logging roads with fallen trees, boulders, and their own bodies; buried themselves up to their necks in the paths of advancing bulldozers, and suspended themselves from trees, dangling a hundred feet off the ground for days at a time. Less frequently, they have engaged in controversial acts of sabotage, ranging from pouring sugar into the gasoline tanks of logging trucks, to disabling bulldozers, to rendering trees worthless—and dangerous—for milling by driving six-inch-long iron spikes into them. In most cases, however, protesters have been able only to delay or publicize the objects of their protests.

It is in British Columbia, where critics of the province's forest management have little access to information, no right of administrative appeal, and no recourse to the courts, that civil disobedience has been most effective. One reason is the alliance between environmentalists and the province's native groups, most of whom, never having signed treaties with the government, maintain claims to their traditional lands, which compose the bulk of the province. In 1987, Canada designated over three hundred and fifty thousand forested acres of South Moresby, the southern fifteen per cent of the Queen Charlotte Islands, as a national-park reserve. The declaration capped a thirteen-year struggle to stop Western Forest Products from logging South Moresby. The effort had gained national attention in 1985, when seventy-two Haida Indians were arrested for blockading a logging road. Hundreds of thousands of people wrote to the federal government in support of a national park. When William Vander Zalm, the premier of British Columbia, turned down a federal offer to pay the province a hundred and six million dollars in compensation for the land, he received almost thirty thousand telegrams in one week.

Meares Island, in Clayoquot Sound, off the west coast of Vancouver Island, is small and still largely unlogged. Two mountains, cloaked by the ancient forest, dominate the island and the coastal landscape for miles around. Eagles nest in huge spruces; black bears hibernate in the cavities of dead cedars; otters and mink live along the tree-sheltered shoreline; cougars and wolves hunt in the island's forests; scores of species of ducks and other waterfowl search for food in one of western Canada's largest mud flats; and sea lions, harbor porpoises, and gray and killer whales feed and swim offshore. For centuries, this rich land has been home to the Clayoquot and the Ahousat people. Opitsaht, a village on the island, has been continuously inhabited for more than five thousand years. The native people have challenged the legitimacy of the tree-farm licenses under which MacMillan Bloedel and another logging company, Fletcher Challenge, control virtually the whole island. In April of 1984, the Clayoquots proclaimed Meares Island a tribal park. In the autumn of that year, when a boatload of MacMillan Bloedel loggers came to Meares to begin cutting, they were met by a flotilla of boats and crowds of protesters on the beaches. The loggers departed and the dispute went to the courts. "We stood guard on the island for six months, taking turns according to who could take time off from work or be away from their family," Steve Lawson, a commercial fisherman and tour-boat operator who lives on a neighboring island, says. "We were out in the water at dawn every day. At least twenty people, and sometimes as many as three hundred." The following spring, British Columbia's Court of Appeal enjoined logging on the island until the native island claim is settled.

Lou Gold once taught political science at Oberlin College and at the University of Illinois. Now he is a part-time hermit and a full-time advocate for an ancient-forest national park. Gold went to southwestern Oregon in 1982 to visit friends who live near the Siskiyou National Forest. By the following spring, he had been jailed for taking part in a protest against a logging road being built to Bald Mountain, a place Gold had never seen. Environmentalists objected to the road because it would break up the largest unprotected area of virgin forest in the continental United States—an area that they believe should be a national park.

Gold now spends four months of each year living on Bald Mountain, clearing up the considerable mess that fire-lookout stations have left behind. The rest of the year he travels around the United States giving slide shows about Bald Mountain and the Siskiyou Mountains and gathering support for ancient forests and for the plan to turn most of the Siskiyou National Forest into a national park. Forest Service officials have remarked that they can follow Gold's progress across the country by the postmarks on the letters they receive from citizens complaining about their plans to log the Siskiyous and to build almost five hundred miles of roads in an area fifty miles long and twenty-five miles wide.

The Siskiyou Mountains are the northern extension of what the writer David Rains Wallace calls the Klamath Knot, a complex of ranges which straddles the California-Oregon border and includes the Trinity Alps and the Marble Mountains. The Siskiyou is the oldest range west of the Rockies—two hundred million years old in some parts. Unlike most of this continent's mountain ranges, the Siskiyou has an east-west orientation. It links the coastal mountains with the Cascades and the Sierra Nevadas, to the east. The links with so many different ecological communities make the Siskiyou a center for diversity and a source of adaptation for future changes. "It's an area where there's a lot of evolution going on, because there's so much material able to come in and migrate out," Tom Atzet, the Forest Service's ecologist for the area, says. In botanical wealth and diversity, it is rivalled in North America only by the Great Smoky Mountains. The Siskiyou is the major center of plant evolution west of the Mississippi; it contains more than a hundred plant species listed as rare or sensitive by the Forest Service, and is the only meeting point for southern species such as redwoods, and northern species such as Alaska yellow cedar. Dave Willis, a moving force in the national-park campaign, says, "If there is any place in the country that deserves to be a national park, and that needs the protection of being a national park, this is it." Last summer, I accompanied Willis to the Siskiyou.

The botanical richness was evident everywhere as Willis and I made our way on horseback to Bald Mountain. I was on horseback because of my deep aversion to carrying heavy packs up steep mountain slopes. Willis rode because thirteen years ago, while climbing Mt. McKinley, he lost his hands and feet to frostbite. The injury makes it difficult for him to walk more than a few hundred feet at a time, though he still manages to ride, rock-climb, and lead wilderness treks for a living. The forest changed as we moved uphill. We started off in a riparian forest that is home to one of the rarest and most valuable trees in the world, the Port Orford cedar. As we began to climb, we entered a strange forest of stunted pines and hardwoods, and towering Douglas firs, a combination unique to the Siskiyou area. Farther on, we passed through a lovely tan-oak-and-madrona forest whose slender trunks and dappled shade remind one of an English beech forest; finally, we reached the great Douglas-fir forest that crowns Bald Mountain. The mountain itself is the high point of a forested ridge, three thousand feet above the Illinois River, that is dotted with lovely meadows—"prairies" in the local argot. These prairies are among the most beautiful spots on earth, surrounded by gracefully drooping Douglas firs whose lower branches gently brush the deep-green grasses. In these islands of sunlight, flowers bloom in a profusion that I haven't seen in almost twenty years of botanizing here and abroad: bearded mariposa lilies; orange-spotted leopard lilies; blue irises; and scores of blue, yellow, and pink flowers that I couldn't name.

In the summer of 1987, a fierce lightning storm started dozens of fires all over the Klamath Mountains, including several that raged across almost a hundred thousand acres of Bald Mountain, destroying some groves, merely scorching the trunks of others, and completely bypassing still others. Fire is a part of the natural cycle in these forests, and two years later much of the burned area was beginning to recover. The blockades of the Bald Mountain logging road in which both Lou Gold and Dave Willis took part had succeeded in slowing construction, but by July of 1983, when a judge decided that the road was illegal, about half of it had been built. After the fires, the Forest Service announced plans to complete the road so that close to ten thousand acres of trees in fire-damaged areas could be logged. Environmentalists argued that the forest should be left to heal itself—that logging and road building would damage an already stressed ecosystem—but they succeeded only in reducing the planned eight-mile extension to a mile. The logging operation was proceeding at full steam last summer, using helicopters to winch trees, including a good proportion of healthy trees, out from roadless areas. "It's like mugging a burn victim," Gold said.

In the United States, the future of the ancient forest is now being decided largely in the courts, where a symbiotic relationship has developed between government scientists and critics of the government. "It was the advocacy groups' picking up on the science and using it in their lawsuits that really brought us out of the closet," Jerry Franklin said last year. "If it weren't for them, I suspect, we'd still be in our ivory tower, shouting out the window with nobody paying any attention."

These lawsuits, which focussed on establishing the ecological value or vulnerability of individual sites scheduled for logging or road building, had mixed success. But as the ancient forest continued to dwindle a new element entered the equation—the northern spotted owl, whose habitat is the old-growth forest. In the early eighties, researchers in the Forest Service, the Fish and Wildlife Service, and academic institutions established that the northern spotted owl was nearing extinction, and that further destruction of its habitat posed a threat to its survival. In 1987, environmentalists filed the first of three spotted-owl lawsuits. Those suits dramatically changed the clash over forest resources. For the first time, the courts were being asked to rule not on just one stand of trees but on large areas of old-growth, stretching across many national forests. The Sierra Club Legal Defense Fund filed the suits for various coalitions of plaintiffs, including *Strix occidentalis caurina,* the northern spotted owl itself.

In Northern Spotted Owl v. Hodel, twenty-five environmental groups joined the owl in challenging the Fish and Wildlife Service's refusal to list it as threatened or endangered under the Endangered Species Act. In 1988, the federal district court in Seattle ordered Fish and Wildlife to reconsider its decision that the owl was not threatened or endangered, saying that "expert opinion is to the contrary." The environmentalists won their point in the spring of 1989, when the Fish and Wildlife Service proposed to list the spotted owl as a threatened species—a category that requires special protection of its habitat. As yet, the spotted owl has not been listed; the Fish and Wildlife Service can take up to eighteen months to complete the process.

In the two related cases, environmentalists argued that the Bureau of Land Management in western Oregon and the Forest Service in Oregon and Washington had acted illegally in allowing timber to be cut from public forests without properly considering the impact that logging would have on the spotted owl. In the B.L.M. case, the judge found that the bureau's refusal to consider logging's impact on the owl was "arbitrary and capricious," but the case was dismissed as moot in December of 1989, because of a Congressional ban on judicial review of the bureau's timber-management plans. A series of injunctions issued in the case had prevented logging in western Oregon for nearly two years. In the Forest Service case, the federal district court in Seattle enjoined the disputed timber sales in March of 1989 until that case could be fully heard. That ruling halted about a billion board feet of timber sales, and a subsequent decision by the Forest Service to postpone for the same period all timber sales in spotted-owl habitat roughly doubled that amount. The injunction was lifted in November, after Congress placed further restrictions on judicial review of Forest Service and B.L.M. actions. Both of these cases are now on appeal by the environmentalists to the Ninth Circuit Court of Appeals, in San Francisco.

One company affected by the spotted-owl lawsuits is Dahlstrom Lumber, in Hoquiam, a once-thriving mill town on Washington's Olympic Peninsula. The mills in Hoquiam and the surrounding towns depend on old-growth trees from the Olympic National Forest—an important home for the northern spotted owl. Monte and Kirk Dahlstrom are a good-natured, easygoing pair of brothers. They built their mills—a lumber mill and a veneer mill—themselves, financed by a Small Business Administration loan and second mortgages. Dahlstrom Lumber began operating in 1980. When the business is running at full capacity, it employs nineteen people directly and thirty through logging and trucking contractors. In addition, several hundred jobs depend in part on the lumber that Dahlstrom supplies to other factories. The Dahlstroms' sawmill and veneer plants require seven million and three million board feet of timber a year, respectively. They use nothing but old-growth hemlock from the national forests. "We bid only on the biggest timber," Kirk says. Sixty per cent of the lumber they cut is shipped to other mills in the United States, to be made into high-quality window frames, doors, and moldings. Twenty per cent is sent to Japan, for use in construction work. And twenty per cent is barely processed—just squared off into what are known in the industry as "cants"—and sent to Japan to be made into veneers, glued onto a plywood backing that originated as tropical hardwoods in Indonesia, and sent back to the United States as flooring. The veneer that the Dahlstroms make goes to a box factory in the United States and is applied to boxes for fruit, mostly kiwis and grapes. Old-growth veneer is used for this mundane purpose because it can stand up to the extended cold conditions under which the fruit is stored and shipped.

The moves to increase protection of the spotted owl have seriously threatened the Dahlstroms' timber supply. In January of 1989, the Forest Service announced that because certain lands were to be set aside as spotted-owl habitat, timber sales in the Olympic National Forest's Quinault Ranger District, which supplies the local mills, would be reduced to forty-two million board feet in 1989—less than half of what the service had been selling—and that future sales would drop to thirty million board feet a year. Despite that squeeze, the Dahlstroms felt that they could go on, though they would have to close the veneer plant to do so. They had a year's stockpile of timber, and they were high bidders on a timber sale, called the Canyon sale, that would keep them in business for a second year. But the Canyon sale was in spotted-owl habitat, so it was halted by the Forest Service-case injunction in the spring of 1989, as was virtually every other timber sale in the Quinault Ranger District. I visited the Dahlstrom brothers shortly after they learned that the Canyon sale had been cancelled, and they were still in a state of shock.

"All the value that we thought we were adding in expanding the mill—they just took it away with those injunctions," Kirk said. "But the point is, they're trying to take my way of life away. This is more than a business; it's my life." Both brothers contend that preservationists—as environmentalists are called around here—are outsiders who are toying with important local resources. "It's a living to me; it's a hobby to them," Kirk said. "My fight is supported by people in my community who know the situation. Theirs is supported by people in Boston, New York, Los Angeles, and Seattle, who don't understand. They want to live in a city, have all the advantages of living and working in the city, and play where I work, where I live." Casting a derisive eye at my notebook, he went on, "You know, this country can't survive on writers and computer punchers. It needs to use our natural resources, use them productively."

One of the Dahlstroms' biggest worries was having to fire workers. Closing the veneer plant meant laying off five people. "I have a good crew," Monte said. "I've got great guys. But a lot of them can hardly read and write. If we close, and the other local mills do, there's no place for these guys. Kirk and I won't starve—we'll be able to do something else—but what are they going to do?"

Kirk said that his worries about the business and the men who depended on him were putting him through "a mental anguish you can't believe." The idea, often proposed by environmentalists, of retraining for loggers and other workers in the old-growth-timber industry was met with contempt by both brothers.

"Don't insult me with low-interest loans," Monte said. "I don't want welfare. Just give me a timber supply."

Senator Mark Hatfield, of Oregon, came to the rescue of the Dahlstroms and the rest of the Northwest timber industry by inserting a clause in the 1990 federal appropriations bill which overruled the court injunction on the sale of timber from spotted-owl habitat. The clause required the Forest Service to release more than a billion board feet of timber from spotted-owl habitat for sale. The Canyon sale was one of those released. "The Canyon sale will get us through 1990," Kirk Dahlstrom told me earlier this year. "After that, though, we're not confident. We no longer have any faith in the federal government's promises." Pressure on the lands that supply the Dahlstroms' timber will increase because of a federal interagency report released last month, which concluded that the northern spotted owl is "imperilled over significant portions of its range," and called for three million acres of federal forestland to be withdrawn from logging in order to protect the owl's habitat.

As far as loggers, millworkers, and others in the timber industry are concerned, the issue is a simple one: jobs versus owls. The anger and fear of the threatened workers are reflected in the black humor of bumper stickers saying "Save a Logger, Kill an Owl" and T-shirts emblazoned with the motto "I ♥ spotted owls... barbecued, fricasseed, baked, stir-fried." One mill-owner showed me a spotted-owl joke that had come through on his fax machine: "What's the difference between a spotted owl and a logger? A spotted owl can still make a small deposit on a new pickup."

The northern spotted owl lives only in Northern California, Oregon, and Washington, but it has become a symbol to timber workers everywhere who are fearful of losing their jobs. In imploring a Senate panel meeting in Sitka, Alaska, not to cancel the pulp mills' monopolies in the Tongass National Forest, John Parton, a logger for the Alaska Pulp Corporation, compared himself with the owl. "I, too, am an endangered species," he said. "I am . . . a Pacific Northwest logger. Will you give my mate and I thousands of acres of timberland, for that is what I, too, need to survive." All through the Pacific Northwest, loggers and others in the timber industry are holding rallies, marches, and "spotted-owl barbecues"—often with their employers footing the bill—to protest the threat to their jobs.

The timber industry in the Northwest has been suffering for years, however. Its problems predate public concern about ancient forests or the spotted owl. Throughout the region, mills—especially mills that depend on big, old trees—have been closing down. Some towns, such as Westfir, Oregon, that were founded on timber and until recently thrived on it have lost all their mills. Oregon's Department of Employment has reported that between 1977 and 1987 the state lost more than twelve thousand jobs in logging and wood processing, and that its timber industry now provides only about five per cent of Oregon's jobs. As other industries—notably tourism, now No. 3 in Oregon—pick up the slack, timber is losing some of its political clout in the region. Nevertheless, David Mumper, a timberlands resource manager at Weyerhaeuser, recently said of Washington State's growing population, "I look at it as twenty thousand people a year moving into the state that have no use for us, because our industry's not growing. Politically, the people in this state could kill us."

The reason for the job losses is not a shortage of timber from national forests; in fact, figures from Oregon's Departments of Employment and Forestry show that the amount of timber taken from the state's national forests has increased as jobs have disappeared. Oregon's fifteen-per-cent drop in logging and processing jobs accompanied a sixteen-per-cent increase in wood taken from the national forests. The main reason for the job decline is growing automation of the timber industry. In 1977, for example, it took 10.12 workers to process a million board feet of wood. Ten years later, only 8.2 workers were required to handle that amount—a rise of almost twenty per-cent in worker productivity. As automation has reduced the number of jobs, "management has been able to extract some pretty strong concessions, including twenty-five-per-cent pay cuts from union members," says Jeffrey Olson, a former economist for Boise Cascade who now works for the Wilderness Society. Instead of pinning responsibility for pay cuts and lost jobs on their own modernization programs or on overcutting of the industry's own lands, managers have encouraged the notion that those problems result from environmentalists' demands to "lock up the forest."

Unlike the United States Forest Service, British Columbia's forest service makes no pretense of managing its public forests equally for timber and for other uses. The single goal of its timber management is to create a prosperous timber economy. Instead, by allowing over-cutting, it has contributed to the destabilization of the timber industry. In the past decade, jobs in the province's timber industry have declined by twenty-five per cent, partly because of automation, partly because of a slump in the market, and partly because in some areas old-growth timber has run out. "It was a social contract," Cameron Young, the author of "The Forests of British Columbia," says. He explains, "The companies were given free access to public forestland. In return, they provided work and healthy economies. If there were no more fish in a stream, there was always another stream. If a forest was destroyed, there were always more forests. No one complained. But the social contract has been abrogated. Employment has declined even though they are cutting more and more wood."

Formerly prosperous mill towns in the province, such as Nanaimo and Chemainus, have turned to other sources of revenue, from sponsoring International Hell's Angels conventions and bathtub races to covering the town's walls with murals of the glory days of logging. The layoffs have come at the same time that timber companies have been making record profits. "Woodworkers accept that this is a cyclical industry, but this is the first time we've been losing jobs at the top of the cycle," Lyn Kistner, a union official, told the Toronto *Globe & Mail* a year ago. In the early nineteen-eighties, when timber companies were losing money because of a slump in the timber market, British Columbia's forest service adopted a policy known as sympathetic administration, under which standards for environmental protection, road engineering, timber wastage, and other such activities were lowered to save the companies money. "The focus was on turning a profit," Norm Godfrey says. "So the forest service set aside a lot of things they'd wanted us to do, to let us make a profit." It worked. A combination of sympathetic administration and a layoff of several thousand workers enabled MacMillan Bloedel, which had lost money from 1982 to 1985, to turn record profits, of two hundred and eighty-one million dollars in 1987 and three hundred and thirty million in 1988.

Many mills, like the Dahlstroms', are geared to process only trees at least two and a half feet in diameter, but those trees are almost gone. They are already gone from private lands, and once the public forests are cut down there will be no more big trees, ever. The hundred-and-fifty-to-two-hundred-year rotations needed to produce large-diameter trees are no longer economically feasible. Private companies, unable to afford long-term investments, are planning to cut their next generations of trees when they are only forty years old, or even only twenty-five, in the south. A few private timber companies—notably Medco, in Oregon; Plum Creek, in Washington; and California's Pacific Lumber, which owns the largest privately held virgin redwood forest—once tried to maintain long rotations by logging their lands slowly and selectively, but in today's market their large stocks of uncut trees are seen as underutilized assets, which should be cashed in. Two of these companies have recently been the subjects of leveraged buyouts by companies that plan to liquidate their timber resources as quickly as possible, in order to pay their debts, and the third is also getting rid of its timber, in an effort to prevent a takeover. Even the Forest Service, which originally planned rotations of a hundred and twenty to a hundred and fifty years in these forests, now plans to cut second-growth trees much earlier; according to the final management plans, some second-growth stands will be cut at sixty years in the Siuslaw National Forest and at seventy-five years in the Siskiyou. Shorter rotations are also planned in British Columbia. Older mills that do not retool will close; those which do install modern equipment will need fewer workers. Either way, the number of jobs in the timber industry will fall.

Right now, most old-growth wood is used wastefully: centuries-old Douglas firs are cut into two-by-fours and used to frame our houses; rare cedar planks are nailed into molds for poured concrete and then thrown away; ancient hemlocks are pulped and converted into rayon or cellophane, wrapping paper or disposable diapers. "That's just plain wrong," Bart Koehler, of the Southeast Alaska Conservation Council, says. "When a four-hundred-year-old tree ends up on some baby's ass, it's an insult to all that's good and right with the world."

Fast-growing, coarse-grained, knotty wood from plantations can do many of the jobs now being done by wood from the ancient forests. But products that require high-quality wood—fine furniture, wooden boats, musical instruments, and more plebeian objects, like door and window frames—will become luxury items or disappear altogether. "Composite materials will take the place of solid wood," William Banzhaf, of the Society of American Foresters, says.

Environmentalists argue that the public forests are being exhausted to compensate for the industry's abuse of its own lands and its abandonment of domestic mills in favor of more profitable deals overseas. Less and less timber is coming from private lands, which have been crippled by overcutting. Thus more and more of the burden of supplying industry with timber is falling on public lands. Between 1977 and 1987, the amount of timber coming from private land in Oregon declined by almost nine per cent. In an effort to make up the shortfall, the timber harvest from public lands in the state was increased by thirteen per cent during that period. In 1987, public lands supplied sixty per cent of Oregon's timber cut, compared with fifty-four per cent ten years earlier.

Much of the Northwest's private forestlands are in the hands of a few large, integrated companies, such as Weyerhaeuser, Simpson Timber, and Boise Cascade. As mills are shutting—and mill towns are dying—for lack of timber, the giant companies are sending much of their timber overseas without processing it. Many are selling or closing their own mills to concentrate on the export market, where prices are fifteen to forty per cent higher than they are in the domestic market. Thus Japan, Korea, and Taiwan, rather than local economies, get the jobs, and the added value when the processed wood is sold, often back to the United States.

In 1988, three billion seven hundred million board feet of raw logs were exported from Oregon and Washington—a quarter of the total cut in those two states. Some of the exported logs are from national forests, even though federal regulations forbid exports of unprocessed wood from national forests or from land controlled by the Bureau of Land Management. The ban was imposed in 1968 to insure that federal forests provide raw materials for local companies, not foreign ones, but loopholes in the ban allow some large landowners to ship timber from their own lands overseas and feed their sawmills with federal timber—a process called substitution.

The Senate has passed a bill introduced by Robert Packwood, of Oregon, that would make the ban on federal log exports permanent and close the loopholes that allow substitution. The Bush Administration, on the other hand, has proposed to end the ban on the export of raw logs from federal lands. No other major wood-producing country allows the unrestricted export of unprocessed wood. Even Third World countries such as Indonesia, Thailand, Malaysia, and the Philippines set strict limits. Canada has virtually halted exports of unprocessed logs, by imposing a heavy tariff on them and requiring that the exporters prove that the logs are not needed in Canada. "We are the last nation on earth that allows the unfettered export of raw logs," says Oregon's Representative Peter DeFazio, who has introduced a bill to allow states to ban the export of logs from their lands. "The Weyerhaeuser Company and others are getting very rich by selling our heritage to the Japanese, and they don't want things to change. It's easy money for them. It's very profitable and much simpler than running a mill, and, in fact, their recent pattern of mill closures shows that in many cases they'd prefer to close mills and continue exporting logs than make the capital investment to update the mills."

The guidelines set forth in the 1976 National Forest Management Act were supposed to enable the Forest Service to resolve conflicting demands on the nation's forests. The conflicts have only intensified, however, and the courts have become the main arbiters of forest policy. Environmentalists, the timber industry, scientists, and politicians are all saying that Congress must step in. "The prospect is of the courts' essentially dictating and managing the forests," Peter DeFazio says. "I think we're close to the point where the policy makers are going to have to roll up their sleeves and get back into the middle of this debate."

Andy Kerr, of the Oregon Natural Resources Council, agrees. "In 1976, when Congress confronted the fact that our forest policy was out of synch with public feelings, it lateraled," he says. "It just handed off to the Forest Service. It passed a law that let the Forest Service make all the tough choices. So it's telling the Forest Service, 'Cut a lot of timber and have a lot of everything else, too.' We are now at a point where there are conflicts that Congress alone can resolve."

Many in the Forest Service would welcome a clearer directive from Congress. "We'll manage the national forests of the United States however the citizens of the United States want us to," Douglas MacWilliams, the forest supervisor of the Mt. Baker–Snoqualmie National Forest, says. "We don't own them. We're managing them in trust for the people of the United States, but the people of the United States are giving us conflicting advice about how they want them managed."

Probably the strongest congressional supporter of continued high levels of cutting from public forests is Oregon's Senator Hatfield, a liberal Republican with an excellent record on all environmental issues except those which intersect with forest policy. Hatfield is certainly the politician most feared and detested by ancient-forest advocates. Since 1980, Hatfield, the ranking minority member of the Appropriations Committee, and Republican Senator James McClure, of Idaho, another influential member of the committee from a big timber state, have succeeded in getting Congress to direct the Forest Service to cut more timber than it had planned to.

Hatfield has also unsheathed a new, powerful, and highly controversial weapon to prevent environmentalists from challenging the Forest Service in court. Since 1985, he has loaded appropriations bills and numerous riders that restrict citizens' ability to appeal to the courts. The first such rider concerned the Mapleton Ranger District, in the Siuslaw National Forest. In response to a lawsuit charging that logging had destroyed half the salmon and steelhead habitat in the district, a judge had enjoined all timber sales there until the Forest Service completed the management plan required by the National Forest Management Act. Hatfield attached a rider to the fiscal-year-1986 appropriations bill which allowed some timber sales to go ahead. A subsequent rider, extending the exemptions from the judge's decree, stated that the draft forest plan "shall be treated as satisfying all requirements of the National Environmental Policy Act . . . and the Forest and Rangeland Renewable Resources Planning Act of 1974, as amended by the National Forest Management Act . . . and shall not be subject to administrative or judicial review for compliance with such acts."

The right to appeal federal land-management decisions is not a constitutional right but one created by Congress. Measures to limit judicial review have been used mainly to protect the national security. Increasingly, however, they are being used to override the laws designed to protect the environment. In a letter to his constituents Hatfield explained that his riders "are intended to mitigate the unacceptable economic disruption that would result if entire areas of the state were denied access to national-forest timber." The American Civil Liberties Union has joined environmentalists in protesting the use of riders to limit a citizen's ability to appeal to the courts.

Because the riders are attached to appropriations bills, which expire after a year, they must be renewed annually. So far, all of them have been, partly because few members of Congress or their staffs are aware of these brief amendments to appropriations bills that are several hundred pages long, and partly because Congress is a great respecter of local interests. Until recently, national-forest matters have been considered local issues, and in local issues Congress generally goes along with the representatives of the state or the region concerned. Gradually, however, national forests are becoming a national issue. "The old-growth forests are like Yellowstone or the Everglades or the Grand Canyon," representative Jim Jontz, of Indiana, says. "Nobody would argue that just the people in Arizona should have something to say about the Grand Canyon."

Environmentalists argue that the prospect of economic dislocation should not hinder attempts to reform the timber industry and the management of the national forests. "When you have a war between nations, you don't refuse peace just because it might cause unemployment among soldiers," Lou Gold says. "And that's what we've got. We've been waging war on nature for a long time.

It's time to declare peace with nature. We're going to have problems making the transition, but it's ridiculous not to end a bad practice because doing so would cause unemployment."

The "bad practice"—liquidating the ancient forest—will end when the forest is gone. And when it has ended, a large part of the timber industry will suffer and will need help in adjusting to the new reality. The shortages and the suffering have already begun. The fate of the whales and of the whaling industry presented the world with a similar problem. The question was a simple one: Should a species be exterminated to postpone the inevitable collapse of the whaling industry? The choice we now face is less extreme. Unlike the whaling industry, the timber industry is not doomed; change, not death, is inevitable. The question for us now is: Shall we destroy our ancient forests to postpone this change for a few years?

The battle to preserve what remains of our ancient forests is not driven by science or economics or an abstract respect for natural systems, though all those do play a role. It is driven primarily by passion for a place. Across the Pacific region, people have fought to save their patch of forest—the one they live near, the one they know, the one they walk in or camp in, the one that overlooks their town, the one they see every day. What has now come to be referred to as "the ancient-forest movement" was not started by professional environmentalists in Washington, D.C., for some theoretical or bureaucratic reason. It was started and is being carried on by scores of local groups, such as the Friends of Clayoquot Sound, the Cathedral Forest Action Group, the Save Opal Creek Council, the Northcoast Environmental Center, and the Quilcene Ancient Forest Coalition. Behind the groups are people who live in towns like Tenakee Springs, Alaska; Tofino, British Columbia; Arcata, California; Galice, Oregon; and Bellingham, Washington. They are people with jobs and children, with ordinary lives.

"Most people are shocked to find that this is going on—to find that there's *any* cutting in national forests, much less clear-cutting," Lou Gold has said. "If you look at any road map, you're gonna see these big green areas all over the West—national forest this, national forest that. People think that means these are protected forests, like national parks. And if you come out and drive through these forests it's still not likely you're going to find out what's going on, because of the 'scenic protection'—a fringe of trees along the highway, so that drivers don't have to see anything ugly. Ask yourself who that scenic protection is for—you or the Forest Service. They're hiding what they're doing, and that's because they know that the American people would be furious if they learned what was happening back there."

Peter Matthiessen

From *Indian Country*

Coming up from Pecwan, on the Klamath River, to Low Gap, we could see across the whole wild reach of upper Blue Creek and its forks to the remote High Siskiyous, where we were going. There are no roads into Blue Creek, only rough cat tracks for the loggers, and on this dry summer afternoon, the truck raised a long column of hot dust as it descended the raw eroding zigzag scars down the steep mountainside. Where the trees were stripped off, the stumps, torn earth, and littered deadwood evoked the desolate, blasted hills of war, and the effect was especially depressing where the defoliant called 2,4,5-T had been used by the Simpson Timber Company to "inhibit" broad-leaf growth in favor of the conifers; in these seared areas, there was no life of any kind, no birds or flowers or berries, and the streams were poisoned. "Some people make the mistake of boiling their camp water, to purify it—that just concentrates the poison," John Trull said, glaring out the window. Trull, a big man with a boyish grin, had been a logger and a cat skinner for many years, but as a woodsman and an Indian—though he looks white, he has Cherokee blood and is married to a Yurok woman—he was troubled by the scope of the destruction. His stepson, Richard Myers, sitting beside him, shared his opinion that these poisons being dumped onto the landscape by timber companies and federal agencies were cheap surplus stocks of the notorious Agent Orange that was used by the federal government in Vietnam, and that the use of this 2,4,5-T (its by-product, dioxin, is the most toxic substance, after nerve gas, ever made by man) was excessive and very careless; at one point, ten children were sent home pale and vomiting from the school at Weitchpec as a consequence of wind drift from spraying by the Bureau of Indian Affairs on the Hupa Valley Indian Reservation. Up the river a few miles, at Orleans, a number of dead or deformed babies had been reported.

Where the track descended toward Blue Creek, Dick Myers saw a young black bear in a thicket, but otherwise the summer trees were still. We parked the truck where the cat track ended, in alders by the stream. Five miles downstream from this place, Blue Creek joins the Klamath River, which flows north and west perhaps fifteen miles to the Pacific. Until the great logging boom came to this part of far northern California after World War II, lower Blue Creek was forested by great coast redwoods; the few that remain stand like mourners for the many that are gone. Having logged out the redwoods, Simpson Timber was now seeking access to the old-stand Douglas fir and other valuable timber trees in the inner reaches of Blue Creek and its eastern forks, which lie entirely within the Six Rivers National Forest. For a variety of excellent reasons, the Indians and the environmentalists, the scientists and fishermen, were trying to stop it. Even those local people like John Trull whose livelihood depended on the lumber industry had strong mixed feelings about the imminent destruction of Blue Creek, which is one of the last clear streams and wildernesses in the country.

In recent years, Blue Creek has become a symbol for the fight to save the Siskiyous, which rise seven thousand feet and more above the Klamath. One group of isolated peaks and rocks, traditionally approached through the ascent of the forks of Blue Creek, is a sacred "High Country" for the Indians—the Yurok; the Karuk, farther upriver to the east; the Tolowa, of the northern coast and southern Oregon; and occasionally the Hupa from the Trinity River, which flows into the Klamath at Weitchpec. "Yurok," or "downriver people," seems to be a Karuk ("up to the east" or "upriver people") term for these small, scattered bands of the lower Klamath, from Bluff Creek to Requa, at the river's mouth, and a short distance north and south along the sea. Though all tribes of the region are now quite similar in customs and beliefs, they are very different in origin; the indigenous Karuk are of Hokan linguistic stock, the more recent Hupa and Tolowa are Athapaskans from the Canadian Northwest, and the Yurok are Algonkin, a small western offshoot of those woodland tribes that once occupied almost all of eastern North America.[1]

In addition to its traditional role in Indian life, Blue Creek is a superb spawning stream for both steelhead and salmon—one of the finest in the Siskiyous, which are the most productive watershed in California—and the people knew that logging would hasten the end of the dying salmon fishery so crucial to both whites and Indians in the depressed economy of this region. As Dick Myers says, "Poor logging practices make these creeks run too fast in winter and spring so that they dry up much too soon during the summer. It spoils the rivers, and it spoils the fishing." Botanically, these mountains are one of the most varied regions on the continent, and a reservoir of rare animals and relict plants such as the Brewer's spruce, whose closest relation is found in northeast Asia. For all these reasons, very suddenly, this little-known wilderness has become one of the most controversial in the country.

The traditional way into the High Country is one of a network of old Indian paths known to the Indians of the lower Klamath as *thkla-mah,* meaning ladder or steps (the stepping-stones for ascent into the sky world); the term is transcribed by sentimental bureaucrats as the "Golden Stairs." This path begins just above the confluence of Blue Creek with its Crescent City Fork and climbs the ridge between those streams in a northerly direction to a point off to the east of a huge dark boulder. Perhaps one hundred feet in height, the boulder is poised on the bare saddle of a rocky ridge as if it had descended from the sky. This is *Ha-ay-klok,* Rock Set upon a Rock, known as Medicine Rock in the nineteenth century and now called Doctor Rock. It was and is an important site for medicine training, of which healing is only one part, practiced mostly by women; the men who went to the High Country to "make medicine" were on a vision quest, in pursuit of spiritual power. In recent decades, with the demoralization and acculturation of the tribes that the logging boom served to accelerate, Doctor Rock and other sacred sites have been little visited except by hunters. Dick Myers, who had never visited the High Country, was delighted to be going by the Steps, in case the fight to save Blue Creek was lost. "Nine tenths of the people have never been to Doctor Rock," he said, "and the rest of 'em went up most of the way by truck."

Dick Myers is one of the young Yurok of the Klamath region who are seeking a way back toward traditional Indian life. At Pecwan Creek he was engaged in the unearthing and reconstruction of the Yurok sweat house, last used in 1939, that was silted in, then buried, in the big floods of 1955 and 1964. He was also trying to reconstruct a house for the Jump Dance, a traditional ceremony used by Karuk and Hupa as well as his own Yurok people to "renew the world." A humorous, handsome, easygoing man who does not try to hide his people's ignorance, neglect, and loss of their own traditions, he had finally resorted to turn to a white authority, the great anthropologist Alfred Kroeber, for certain details of the ceremonies. When Kroeber worked along the Klamath just after the turn of the century, Myers' Aunt Queen James, aged ninety-three, was already in her twenties. The last elders, increasingly cut off from one another in the small and remote settlements of the Klamath Mountains, felt that the old ways were lost forever, and when I suggested that bringing these old people together for a few days might exhilarate them and refresh their common memory, thereby preserving at least a part of the old knowledge, Dick politely agreed, but in a way that indicated he would not do much about it. This was not so much apathy or low morale as resignation; Indians, even in these desperate times, are reluctant to share family "songs" or knowledge. For example, Aunt Queen had forbidden Dick to lend the family's ceremonial headdresses (made from the scarlet crests of pileated woodpeckers) to an old Indian down on the coast who was trying to reconstruct the Jump Dance; she declared that this man had failed to learn the traditional Jump Dance medicine from his father. "That old man is only interested in making money," Dick laughed, shaking his head. "Last time we danced, he never even gave us a piece of watermelon and a box of Cokes—'Here, boys, have a good time while you're cleaning up!'"

We shouldered our packs and forged across the torrent, hip-deep and still swift and cold here in early July, to the wooded bench or "flat" on the far side, where we headed upstream. On the east bank, Slide Creek comes swiftly down from Blue Creek Mountain. The huge dead trees that choke its mouth are not the consequence of wasteful logging practice but of the frequent slides that give this creek its name. Natural landslides are common in this region, where the most recent uplifting of two million years ago did not turn the old rivers from their courses but only deepened them, so that the steep mountainsides may fall away even without excessive rain or snow. The soil itself, shot through with intrusions of the beautiful weak slaty jade called serpentine, is poor and shallow, and those slopes that are marginally stable when bound up by forest roots collapse quickly in the first rainfall and erosion that follows road-building and the removal of the trees. This is the main reason environmentalists insist that the Siskiyous should not be logged at all. This situation is worsened by the winter and spring floods that undercut the slopes, causing whole tracts to fall away into the torrent. The Christmas flood of 1964 scoured all rivers in the region and changed the whole appearance of Blue Creek, washing out the forest banks and leaving broad gravel bars that emerge in summer.

We forded the river once again and ascended the eastern bank to Bear Pen Flat, where the mouth of Nickowitz Creek comes into view. John Trull said that in the lower Klamath tongue, what the white man writes as "Nickowitz" is actually *nik-wich,* the grizzly bear, a creature now officially extinct in California. There is an account of an eight-hundred-pound grizzly killed down toward the coast in the 1890's, and on my first visit to the Klamath region, in 1975, I was told that five grizzlies still survived in the Blue Creek drainage. The authority cited was an ecologist at Humboldt State University at Arcata, who wished the news kept quiet, it was said, lest hunters flock into Blue Creek to destroy them. I did not take the report seriously; the source was suspect, and anyway, the grizzly is an open-country species. I was therefore surprised to hear Trull say that about 1952, under Low Gap on the south slope of Blue Creek Mountain Ridge, he saw a huge dark-brown grizzled animal move out of some high grass and cross a mountain meadow or "prairie." "It was so big, y'know, and that damn hump on it—for a minute there, I thought I was lookin' at a buffalo!" John is a logger and a lifelong hunter—one of that old breed, now nearly extinct, who are true woodsmen as well. He had seen hundreds of black bears in the wild and was not likely to mistake one for a grizzly, and the least plausible word in his description, "buffalo," is just the one that made his story hard to discount. Some years ago, I made my way to the main garbage dump in Yellowstone National Park, where I had been told that grizzlies came in numbers every evening (the Yellowstone grizzlies, unlike the black bears, are still wild and stay far from the main roads). When, at dusk, the great bears appeared, rolling through the high brush of an open plain as the nervous black bears loped away in all directions, a young park ranger who accompanied me cried out, "Look! Look! Buffaloes!" before he realized his mistake.

According to Forest Service personnel, the Siskiyous, with no ranches and few visitors, is the only wild region left in California to which restoration of the grizzly has been considered. Blue Creek is still a haunt of the fierce wolverine, one of California's rarest mammals, and also of its scarce mustelid cousins, the marten and the arboreal fisher. An uncommon creature of these streams called the sewellel, or mountain beaver, is considered a "pest" by foresters, who would like to eliminate it. (They are also anxious to eliminate the corn lily on the grounds that it may cause fetuses to be aborted if it is eaten by cows on the nineteenth day of pregnancy. That there are no cows here is a technicality.) The shy cougar comes and goes, and the rare spotted owl frequents the stands of old-growth timber near the creeks.

It was just this primordial forest of immense fir and cedar, concentrated on the shady and well-watered deposits of good soil nearest the streams, that was most coveted by Simpson Timber Company and the sawmills of the coast, which were fighting hard against all efforts to have it protected by the National Wilderness Act, passed by Congress in 1964. As in the Olympic National Forest in Washington, where Simpson and the Forest Service had a special understanding, the industry counted on assistance from this cumbersome and conservative bureaucracy, which tended to oppose the protection of national forest land in favor of commercial possibilities, even where—as in the Siskiyous—other values far outweigh the worth of what will almost certainly be a single "crop" of timber; once that crop has been harvested, this fragile region may not recover for a thousand years.

Both sides of lower Nic-Wich lay on a Simpson holding that penetrated the national forest from the west, and the access road that came down through the national forest from Lonesome Ridge was the only lumber road in the Blue Creek drainage east of the Crescent City Fork. In this lower stretch, at least, Nic-Wich was ruined. The ugly detritus of deadwood and shale pitched all the way down from the clear-cuts high above gave a vivid idea of what Blue Creek would look like if the Forest Service management plan were carried out. Much of the land slope in these dark

V-shaped canyons lies at a sixty-to-seventy-degree angle—as steep as the steepest staircase, as anyone will learn who cares to try it, either up or down—and a Forest Service study acknowledges that eighty-three percent of the land area in the Blue Creek Management Unit and the contiguous Eightmile Unit to the north is "moderately unstable or worse." In one region of the Siskiyous, another study shows, the soil loss from new clear-cuts may reach twenty-two tons per acre every year, most of which descends to spoil the streams. (Both of these studies are considered optimistic by outside observers.) Since productivity may be reduced eighty percent with the loss of just one inch of the thin topsoil, and since in the Coast Range thousands of years may be required for a new topsoil to form, the prospects for reforestation here are dismal. Yet despite accumulating warnings (many from its own personnel or from experts hired under Forest Service contract) that the High Siskiyous are too steep, fragile, and unstable to support intensive logging—that owing to the loss of soil, it would not in fact be possible to observe the agency's own legal obligation to manage its forests with a perpetual and sustained yield, and that the inevitable "mismanagement" would therefore be illegal—the Forest Service has held stubbornly to plans to sell 929 million board feet of timber out of Blue Creek alone. The access roads planned for Blue Creek and Eightmile totaled 265 miles, far more than enough to undercut all of these steep mountainsides and bring down a whole rare world into the creeks.

Everywhere else in the Northwest the result of logging (and eroding logging roads) has been the extensive siltation of the waters, the muddying of the clear gravel beds used by the salmon species and the beautiful anadromous rainbow trout that are called "steelhead." The fish must cover their fertilized eggs with stream gravel to protect them, and the gravel must be clean and porous so that cold water providing crucial oxygen can circulate at the constant temperature necessary for embryo development. Logging drastically increases erosion and sedimentation that may smother the gravel beds, and in addition, the clearing of the land, by increasing sunlight, raises the temperature of the water to a degree that may prove fatal to the young. In many places, logjams resulting from erosion slides or wasteful cutting can prevent access to a spawning stream for years.

The sudden and drastic decline in the Klamath fisheries is precisely coincidental with the advent of heavy logging in the region. Already, all commercial fishing has been stopped in the Klamath delta, between the coastal highway bridge and the mouth of the river, which is the traditional gill-netting grounds of the Yurok Indians at Requa. (The Yurok, like the Puyallup-Nisqually and many other coastal peoples from northern California to British Columbia, have been blamed increasingly for fisheries depletion caused by dams, logging, and industrial pollution; where no Indians are handy, sea lions and cormorants will do. When I was in south Alaska's Kenai Peninsula in 1957, the depletion of the salmon fisheries by overfishing was being blamed on the greed of the Kodiak bears.) And so a renewable resource that provides many jobs, not only in commercial fishing but in the tourist-attracting sports fishery as well, may be wiped out by a self-devouring industry that will devastate the mountainsides before moving on.

Since it is generally agreed that artificial reforestation of this region, with a sustained yield, is unrealistic, and since the Klamath sports and commercial fisheries, though much depleted, are worth millions of dollars annually, one wonders at the willingness of the Forest Service to abet the destruction of a natural resource of such long-term benefit to many in order to further the short-term profits of a few. And this is true not only of Blue Creek but throughout the whole Siskiyou wilderness, which is presently threatened with irretrievable destruction despite the warnings of geologists, foresters, biologists, and anthropologists alike that the potential loss, not only to the Indians but to the whole nation, far exceeds the value of its wood.

In recent years, the excuse that has been trotted out for the proposed "multiple-use management" of the Siskiyous is the alleged loss of jobs in the timber and sawmill industries in Humboldt and Del Norte counties caused by government expropriation of coastal forests for the Redwood National Park. But the decline of the vast private timber reserves started more than twenty years ago in Humboldt County, long before the Redwood National Park came into being. As early as 1952, when the lumber boom had just begun, Humboldt County farm adviser W.D. Pine predicted that unless the lumber companies brought their wasteful practices under control, the county would suffer the same boom and bust that had occurred in other timber regions, forcing the companies to intensify their operations here in northern California.

Despite strenuous public propaganda to the contrary (one thinks of all those phony ads in which happy deer and chipmunks gambol merrily among the noble stumps of managed forests), there was no serious attempt at sustained yield. Overcutting, waste, and the wholesale export of unmilled logs to other countries, in particular Japan, accompanied the scare campaigns that threatened America with a lumber shortage, as the companies proceeded with the rapid despoliation of this great conifer forest that is widely regarded as the finest in the world. Increasingly, as private holdings dwindled, and the sawmills replaced the precious redwoods with former "weed trees" such as the Douglas fir and hemlocks, pines, and cedars, the industry sought leases on the national forest lands that lay just inland from the private holdings. That part of lower Blue Creek that lay west of the national forest was already logged, and so was its once beautiful West Fork; the west bank of the Crescent City Fork was under lease and going fast. But its eastern slope was still intact, and so were upper Blue Creek and the whole East Fork, which together constitute the heart of the Blue Creek drainage.

Note

---

1. For general background, see A.L. Kroeber, *Handbook of the Indians of California* (Washington D.C.: Bureau of American Ethnology Bulletin 78, 1925). "The Gasquet–Orleans Road, Chimney Rock Section, Draft Environmental Statement," Six Rivers National Forest, November 1977, and succeeding documents, include much ecological as well as anthropological information.

Richard Nelson

The Forest of Eyes

A seal drifts in the reflection of Kluksa Mountain, watching the boat idle into Deadfall Bay. Our wake shimmers through the mirror, distorting images of the surrounding hills, the forested shore, and the sallow disk of sun anchored in a thin, racing overcast. Falling tide leaves a line like a bathtub ring around the bay's shore, with snow-covered rocks above the water's reach and shiny black ones below.

I shut down the outboard and let the skiff glide, matching stares with the curious seal and enjoying the silence after a long ride from home. As I paddle toward the rocks, each clunk and plash echoes through the hollows of the bay. Impatient Shungnak jumps ashore to sniff the area while I unload. My raingear is soaked from rough water in the strait, but everything else is dry. The forward two-thirds of the skiff is protected by a canvas dome stretched over a metal frame, like a streamlined covered wagon. Only the captain, who stands in the stern, is exposed to the full brunt of wind and spray.

A pleasant, excited anticipation warms my insides as I spot the old logging road that runs across the island. I hiked the road once before, and during the few hours I spent at Roller Bay I was struck by the peace and beauty of the place. Along one side of the bay was a series of rocky headlands, and I've yearned to explore the isolated beaches and crannies between them. I've also hoped to see how ocean swells break along the shore, to learn if they might nurture the passion for surfing that draws me to this island in a special way. There is also a darker question: in the nearby hills and valleys are sprawling clearcuts, and I've wanted to experience them more closely, to learn how logging has affected this part of the otherwise pristine island.

Once the bicycle and backpack are ashore, I heft three watermelon-sized rocks inside the boat and paddle out to deep water.

Then I lay the rocks on a piece of heavy trawl net, pull it up around them to make a pouch, and lace the whole thing shut with one end of a coiled half-inch rope. After making sure the rope is long enough to reach the bottom and allowing for a twenty-foot tide range, I tie a loop in the free end and fasten a small float onto it. This done, I push the netted rocks overboard and tether the skiff's bow line onto the floating loop. It's taken only fifteen minutes to make a secure mooring buoy for the skiff, using materials picked up from the island's beaches.

As I paddle the punt back to shore, Shungnak enjoys a frolic in the snow. It's only an inch deep here, but I wonder about the hills farther inland. This mid-February afternoon will pass quickly, and if there's too much snow to ride the bicycle we might not get to Roller Bay before dark. I inspect the vintage three-speed bike, then hoist up my backpack, with a final lament about bringing too much stuff. But there would be a lot more complaining if I found good waves and hadn't been willing to carry the extra weight of wetsuit gear and a small belly-rider surfboard.

The first section of road follows the bay's edge, behind a strip of tall, leafless alders. When we're about halfway around, a bald eagle in dark, youthful plumage sails down to a fish carcass on the beach just ahead. He seems careless or unafraid—quite different from the timid, sharp-eyed elders—so I leash Shungnak to the bike, drop my pack, and try to sneak in for a closer look. Using a driftwood pile as a screen, I stalk within fifty feet of the bird, but he spots me peering out between the logs. He flaps out over the water, turns for another look, and then lands forty feet up in a beachside spruce.

There's nothing to lose now, so I walk very slowly toward the eagle, looking away and acting uninterested. He seems content to watch me, or perhaps doesn't care now that he's beyond my reach. Foolish bird: nearly all dead or wounded eagles found in this part of the world have bullets in them. Finally, I stand almost beneath him, gazing up at the eagle as he looks back down at me.

The bird's placid demeanor gives rise to an idea. A gray skeleton of a tree leans beneath his perch, making a ramp I can climb to get closer. His eyes fix on me as I ease to the leaning trunk's base; but he holds fast to the branch. I've never been this close to a wild, free eagle. I think of the ancient hunters, lying hidden in loosely covered pits with bait fastened above, waiting to grab the descending talons. But I seek no blood, no torn sacred feather. Closeness is my talisman, the sharing of eyes, scents twisted together in the same eddy of wind, the soft sound of a wheezing breath, quills ticking in the breeze, feet scuttling on dry bark, and the rush of air beneath a downswept wing.

I inch slowly...slowly up the bare trunk, twist myself around the stubs of broken limbs, until I'm twenty feet from the bird and can't come closer. Nothing is left except to be here—two intense, predatory animals, given to great suddenness, for these moments brought within whatever unknowable circle surrounds us. Perhaps neither of us will ever be so near another of our respective kinds again. I don't need to believe that we communicate anything more than a shared interest and regard, as we blink across the distances that separate our minds.

When the eagle moves or teeters, I can see his feet clutch the branch more tightly, and the needled tips of his talons pierce more deeply through the brittle, flaking bark into the wood beneath. Two loose, downy feathers hang incongruously from his breast, out-of-place feathers that quiver in the gentle current of air. I think how strange it is that I expect an eagle to look groomed and perfect, like the ones in books.

The bird cranes his head down to watch me, so the plumage on his neck fluffs out. His head is narrow, pinched, tightly feathered; his eyes are silver-gold, astringent, and stare forward along the curved scythe of his beak. Burned into each eye is a constricted black pupil, like the tightly strung arrow of a crossbow aimed straight toward me. What does the eagle see when he looks at me, this bird who can spot a herring's flash in the water a quarter-mile away? I suppose every stub of whisker on my face, every mole and freckle, every eyelash, the pink flesh on the edge of my eyelid, the red network of vessels on the white of my eye, the radiating colors of my iris, his own reflection on my pupil, or beneath the reflection, his inverted image on my retina. I see only the eagle's eye, but wonder if he sees down inside mine. Or inside *me,* perhaps.

I take a few more steps, until I stand directly beneath him, where for the first time he can't see me. This is too much. He leans forward, opens his wings and leaps out over my head, still staring down. He strains heavily, like a swimmer stroking up for air. One of the loose feathers shakes free and floats down toward the thicket. I've always told Ethan that a falling eagle's feather, caught before it reaches the ground, might have special power. I wish I could run and catch this one; but the bird has shared power enough already.

As I watch the eagle rise above the bay, I let myself drift out beyond an edge, as though I were moving across the edge of sleep. I feel his quickened heartbeat in my temples, stare up through his eyes at the easy invitation of the sky, turn and look back at the figure of myself, cringed against the leaning snag below. I am filled with the same disdainful surge that releases him from his perch, feel the strain of air trapped in the hollows of his wings.

Fixed within the eagle, I see the bay slowly dilating below, and the long black line of the island's border, stretched out for ten miles against the gray waters of Haida Strait and ending in the distant finger of Tsandaku Point. The island is a variegated pattern of dark forest and snow-covered muskeg, splayed out beneath the slopes of Kluksa Mountain and neighboring Crescent Peak. As the eagle lifts on currents of air, his eye traces the ribbon of road to the island's far side, where it meets the bight of Roller Bay. I try to imagine his view of the other shore, to satisfy the hope that brings me here. But I see only myself, a fleck at the timber's edge, like an insect crawling through feathers of moss—an irrelevant fleck on the island's face.

The eagle sweeps away in great, lazy arcs, drifts against the corniced peaks, and soars up toward the smooth layer of cloud. From this height the island looks like an enormous, oblong cloth, pulled up at its center, curving symmetrically down to its timbered edges, its fringe of contorted rocks, wide bays, and crescent beaches, then plunging through the lace of whitewater and tortured reefs, to root itself beneath the sea.

At three thousand feet, the feathered sails flex and shake against a torrent of wind. Kluksa Mountain stands like a rock in a swift river; the wind whirls and eddies in its lee, rolls over its summit, and tumbles in breaking waves. I can feel the lash of gusts as the eagle planes above the mountain, gaze through his eyes at the fissured, snow-laden peak, and share the craving that draws him more deeply into the island's loneliness.

Nearly lost in the bottom edge of clouds, the bird has risen until his eyes take in the whole encircling horizon. He looks out over the island's whitened mass, beyond its western shore, where the Pacific lies out to the hard seam of sky. A banking turn brings him back toward the strait and a view of the mainland's mountain spine. Toward the north it rises to a frozen massif; toward the south it falls away and sinks like an otter's tail beneath the sea. For the eagle, the crest of land is a ridge to glide across, a spangle of streams that brings the feast of salmon each year, and gray tiers of ranges that fade into the interior beyond.

I am lost in a dream of eagles, balanced on the precipice of sky, peering into the waters below, waiting for the flicker of prey to be revealed. Prey? The thought awakens me. I have flown, however artificially, and have looked down over the island and the strait. But I can never know what the eagle sees with those blazing eyes, what are the shapes of mountains and shores amid the maze of detail that leaps into his brain.

There is the eagle's world, and there is mine, sealed beyond reach within our selves. But despite these insuperable differences, we are also one, caught in the same fixed gaze that contains us. We see the earth differently, but we see the same earth. We breathe the same air and feel the same wind, drink the same water and eat the same meat. We share common membership in the same community and are subject to the same absolutes. In this sense, the way we perceive what surrounds us is irrelevant: I have the eagle's eyes and the eagle has mine.

Shungnak prances and wags her tail when I return, then she sets a lively pace beside the bicycle. The road bends inland, crosses several forested hills, and gives way to swales with a mix of muskeg and open woods on either side. Recorded in the snow are many red squirrel crossings, the meanders of a few marten, and the place where a raven landed, hopped around without apparent purpose, then took off again. Tracks of large, solitary deer cross the road in a few places, and a mixed scuffle of four or five smaller ones follows it for half a mile. Like their human counterparts, adolescent deer seem to prefer going around in bunches. I'd hoped to see at least one or two deer along the way, but apparently they've all found resting places in the woods.

The road opens to a stretch of logged-over hills that look like a war zone, partly screened from view by alders pushing in from either side so they only leave a narrow pathway. In some places, we glide through a tunnel of silver trunks with laceworks of branches arching overhead—the beauty that shelters us from jarring ugliness. Along its whole length, the road is covered with one or two inches of snow, which helps to cushion the eroded gravel underneath. The snow makes peddling uphill a real sweat, but on level stretches and downhill runs the bike seems to float on a bed of feathers. I think of Ethan's enthusiasm for bicycles, and how he would love to share this ride. But even if there were no school, he'd probably choose to stay behind with his friends.

Shungnak lolls her tongue, bites snow to refresh herself, and occasionally lags behind. I remember her as a young lead dog up north—the effortless way she danced at the head of the team, looking back at the other dogs to beg more speed out of them. She still has some of the boundless, rollicking, contagious energy that mushers love to see in their dogs, but at eleven years old, she's begun to ration it more carefully.

Atop the last rise, I can see Roller Bay and the open Pacific through a space between overlapping hills. My back aches from the heavy pack and my legs are tired, but then the road tilts into a mile-long downhill, levels out, and dead-ends beside the grassy expanse of Deer Meadow. A river wanders down the valley and enters the ocean at Roller Bay. Usually the stream is only a few feet deep, but with a strong high tide this evening, sea water has pushed up into it, swelled over the banks, and turned much of the meadow into a brackish swamp.

Shungnak sprawls on the snow to cool off, while I consider the options. We're only a mile from the beach at Roller Bay. But the trail crosses the flooded meadow, so we'd have to find a different route on higher ground. Sunset glows through the overcast and steep hills loom dark beside the valley. I'm drawn toward the sound of surf beyond the distant line of forest, but it will soon be night under those trees. We're not far from an abandoned settler's cabin in a grove of spruce at the meadow's edge. My tired body registers a vote to sleep there, and I take Shungnak's interest in the fresh deer tracks headed that way as a vote of agreement.

Deer Meadow is well named, but it's also the favorite haunt of a more formidable animal. During the salmon runs, this road is so littered with bear droppings that it looks like a cow path; but in midwinter, only the most eccentric bear would be away from its hibernation den in the high country. This is the one season when I can feel comfortable on the island without carrying a rifle and keeping a close watch for trouble. Though I've never had a frightening encounter with a brown bear, the possibility is real enough. Every year there are close calls or worse; not long ago a hunter was badly mauled on this island.

The deer tracks are as wet and fresh as Shungnak's, so I suspect their maker is in the brush somewhere nearby. After a short hike we reach the sagging, saturated cabin where we'll spend the night. It's a simple frame of split logs, covered with cedar shakes. The roof supports a fair growth of moss, matted grass, and sapling spruce, giving it a distinctly organic touch. I peer through the gaping hole once occupied by a door and part of a corner. The inside is a chaotic mess of rusted cans, broken bottles, shredded blankets, and assorted debris left over the years by trappers, hunters, and other itinerants like myself. But it does have a roof of sorts, a tiny window with glass intact, a wooden bunk along one wall, and a punctured barrel stove. The stove is an unexpected gift, though a little work is needed to make it functional.

Working by candlelight, I pile the rubble outside the door, then cut open a few cans for stove patches, and finally scrounge nails to hang a chunk of soggy cloth over the missing corner. It takes some patience to start a fire, which hisses indifferently in the stove, but eventually the place warms enough to seem almost cozy. I spread out my sleeping bag, eat voraciously, drink icy water, and then eat some more. Shungnak curls up in a corner while I lie down to rest. A breeze sifts in through cracks in the wall. I think of ways to patch the perforated roof, but only have enough energy to hope it doesn't rain.

Everything is quiet, except for distant fulminations from the shore. I can hardly wait for morning, when I'll hurry down to see the shape of those waves. But for now, I savor a contentment that comes only with exhaustion and in the most basic of circumstances. I wonder how much longer it will be until a storm gust or heavy snow collapses this old shack. And then the bears will take full possession of the meadow once again.

Candle out. Pitch dark. And I think, if this were summer I

would spend the whole night watching that flimsy rag door.

I'm awakened at dawn by the demented chattering of a red squirrel outside the cabin wall. Shungnak slips under the curtain door, chases the squirrel up a tree, and waits for it to come down the whole time I'm getting ready to go. The bulging pack feels like a sumo wrestler riding piggyback on my shoulders. But now that the tide's drained out it's easy walking along the trail. I can see the entire length of Deer Meadow, stretching flat and dead brown for three miles up the valley behind us, gradually narrowing between mountain walls. Filaments of cloud hover along the slopes and wreathe the high peaks. Except for the whiteness above timberline, this might be a hidden defile in Borneo or New Guinea. The overcast is jammed together like an ice floe and drifts on the same southeast wind that shivers through the trees. The ocean's sound has not diminished and the breeze will blow offshore—ideal conditions for surfing, if only the waves are right.

Our path cuts through a peninsula of forest and comes out on the riverbank. While we're taking a rest, a pair of red-breasted mergansers works toward us along the shore, diving for feed, unaware that they're being watched. Long bodies, narrow bills, and crested heads give them a rakish, streamlined appearance. The female is a fairly nondescript cinnamon and gray, but the male is striking and gaudy. His body is marked with an intricate, geometrical pattern of black and white spikes, chevrons, and fine hatchwork. A speckled, burnished glaze saturates his chest, like the color of old porcelain, and an ivory collar encircles his neck. Mounted atop this ornate body is a head that looks almost imaginary—high-browed, flaring back to a shaggy, double-pointed crest suffused with emerald iridescence like a hummingbird's back, and set off by a flaming red eye.

He looks like an exotic bird from the mangroves of Asia, not a common duck of these northern waters. Perhaps because I see mergansers so often, I'd forgotten to appreciate them. This is especially ironic in a place where few animals show the colorful extravagance so common in the latitudes of parrots, toucans, and birds of paradise. Of course, our animals have their own kind of loveliness, but there is a plain, businesslike, almost protestant flavor to it. In such a community, the merganser is all the more stunning. Chief Abraham, an old Koyukon hunter, once told me that in the Distant Time, when animals were people, Merganser's wife was known for her fancy sewing. She made her husband an elaborately decorated set of clothes, and when he was transformed into a bird his feathers took on the same color and pattern. Chief Abraham kept a merganser's stuffed skin inside his house so he could have the pleasure of looking at it, the way someone might admire a painting.

The muffled throb of surf becomes clearer and more rhythmic as we weave through the last stretch of forest. I hurry along the trail behind Shungnak, forgetting the weight of my pack, looking anxiously for streaks of light that mark the woods' edge. When we get close, Shungnak whisks off and disappears. I'm afraid she's following a deer scent, but I find her standing above the beach, taking in the view like a tourist.

The smooth crescent of black sand slopes gently toward lines of onrushing surf. At one end, the beach gives way to cliffs and cobbled coves, with mountains rising sheer above them. At the other is the rivermouth, channeled against a point of bare white rock that thrusts into the breakers. Beyond the rock is more beach and several headlands, along a shore that curves out for a mile and slopes down to a storm-battered point. The opening of Roller Bay is several miles wide and faces directly into the Pacific. Barren rocks and timbered islets stand off from either side, and there is one fair-sized island near the middle, covered with tall, flagged spruce. Those trees must be wedged into bedrock to survive the winds that thrash in from the sea beyond. In the peak of the highest one is a bald eagle, silhouetted against the tarnished clouds, gazing over its stormy domain.

Before getting on with the exploration I find a place to make camp. The beachside forest is an open, shaded gallery of tree trunks, like a park with cushiony moss instead of grass; all that's necessary is a flat place away from any dead trees that could guillotine the tent in a heavy wind. In case we get back near dark, I put up the tent, get everything set for cooking and sleeping, and find good water in a tiny creek nearby. Then I cram the surfing gear into a small pack and head off toward the beach.

Shungnak lopes out across the hard-packed sand, stopping to sniff at stranded jellyfish, razor clam shells, fragments of crab, and hawsers of bull kelp. My rubber boots are barely high enough to cross the river's mouth where it splays out over the beach, so there could be problems if we come back at a higher tide. We climb up onto a rock point and I sit for a while watching the surf. Each swell rises in a long, even wall, bends to the curvature of the beach, crests against the wind, and breaks almost simultaneously along its entire quarter-mile length.

Three harlequin ducks bob up in the froth behind each wave, then dive just before the next crashes on them. Occasionally, they ride partway up a wave's face and plunge into the vertical mass of water at the last instant before it breaks. I'm amazed by the boldness and timing of these birds, and wonder what food is rich or delicious enough to entice them into the impact zone. Beautiful as the waves are, I feel a twinge of selfish disappointment that the sudden, explosive way they break makes surfing impossible. But it's near low tide, and a rise of water level could change the surf considerably.

In the meantime, I wonder what lies beyond the next point. Shungnak scrambles across the rock and down onto another long beach, where she inscribes her tracks among those of deer and otter, the little prints of mink, and the odd scratchings of eagles. At its lower edge, the beach is covered with a sheen of water, but higher up it darkens and dulls, then becomes dry sand with clumps of dead grass. They bring to mind one of the riddles that Koyukon people use to entertain themselves and test each other's eye for nature:

> *Wait, I see something: My end sweeps this way and that way*
> *and this way, all around me.*
> *Answer: Long tassels of winter grass, bent down so their tips*
> *have drawn little tracks around themselves in the breeze.*

At the end of the sand, we climb a headland covered with timber and laced with deer trails trodden down to bare dirt. I stick to the trails, knowing they're always the best routes along slopes and through tangles of brush or fallen trees. On the point's far side is another beach with pounding waves much like those at the harlequin place. Littering the strand are dozens of sand dollars, and down near the tide I find several still alive, covered with fine, stiff bristles that must rub off soon after they die. The bristles undulate like wind blowing in slow motion through a field of grass. These animals live half buried on edge in the sand offshore, but heavy surf must have gouged them up and deposited them here to die. I pitch them as far out as possible, with a warning that months could pass before another rescuer comes along. Then I put a dozen bleached, unbroken ones in my pack, thinking Ethan might enjoy giving them to friends.

Beyond the next point we find a magical little cove, nearly enclosed except for a narrow entrance, with an apron of white sand along its inner shore. The water grades from pearl to turquoise to vibrant tropical blue. A crystal stream rushes out from the forest, tumbles over white rocks and down across the beach. Tiny waves wash up and slip back, rolling pebbles and shells. At the far end, a deer stands in the grass, waits until we come close, then turns and struts into the woods. For a moment I wish I'd found this idyllic cove on some equatorial island, but then admonish myself to appreciate things as they are given. There are perfect places everywhere on earth, and a part of their perfection is in belonging exactly where they are. This thought is punctuated with a gift partway down the beach—a softball-sized net float made of green glass, lying like a pearl on the sand. I wonder if wind and current brought it all the way from Japan, or if it was lost from a fishing boat nearer this coast.

On our way back, we come across two ravens on the sand dollar beach, pulling ribbons of flesh from a dead lingcod awash in the surge. A seagull stands to one side, clucking incessantly, pointing its beak this way and that, waiting for a turn. Along this coast, there are always plenty of scavengers to welcome any death. Greedy and tugging, but ever watchful, the ravens wait until Shungnak bounces playfully toward them, then lift on a gust and circle above us. The wind has strengthened to a fair southeaster and a few drops of cold rain prickle against my face. There could be a blow tonight, but the skiff is well moored and we have a snug camp waiting.

Partway down the next beach, I notice something different in the pattern of the surf ahead. Straight off the jetty of bare rock, where the harlequins were feeding, rip currents have dredged a channel in the sand underwater, and waves breaking along either side of it look ideal for surfing. I run down the hard, wet beach, my heart pounding with excitement. Shungnak's happiness is in the running itself, as she darts back and forth in front of me. The closer we get, the better it looks.

I was thirty years old when I first encountered surfing, and I've pursued it intensely ever since, not only as a sport but as a way of engaging myself with a superbly beautiful part of the natural world. Places where swells break at the right angle and speed for surfing are a rarity, and searching for them amid the island's wildness and solitude has given me tremendous pleasure. Only a few times have I experienced a moment like this—standing on a remote shore, watching nearly perfect waves that may never have been ridden before. And now I can reward myself for carrying this heavy gear across the island. Up under the trees, sheltered from the rain and wind, I shiver into my wetsuit, gloves, boots, and hood. With the winter Pacific at forty-two degrees and the air a breezy thirty-five, I could hardly touch this water without protection . . . and even this way it isn't easy. Shungnak finds a comfortable place to lie down as I dash toward the water.

Carried out by the rip current, I push through a series of broken waves and finally reach the spot where they first begin to peak. After a few minutes a large swell approaches. Moving onto the sandbar, it grows higher and steeper, and its face hollows against the offshore wind. Then the crest pitches out to make a flawless, almond-shaped tube, and exploding water flails down the length of the wave like a zipper closing a cleft at the ocean's edge. I stroke toward the elevating face of the next swell, turn around just when it begins to break, paddle with all my strength, and feel it pick me up like a pebble in a cupped hand. There is an electrifying sense of weightlessness and acceleration as I drop toward the bottom and twist the board into a hard turn that sets me skimming along parallel to the wave's crest, like a skier traversing the slope of a liquid mountain. The reticulated wall of water stretches out ahead of me, lifting and feathering, gleaming and shattering, changing shape as it moves toward the shallows. I strain forward to outrace the whitewater cascading at my heels, and feel like a molecule hitching a ride on a meteor.

Suddenly the wave steepens, its crest throws out over my body, and I careen beneath a translucent waterfall that pounds down beside my shoulder, surrounded by the noise of erupting whitewater, barely able to stay ahead of the collapsing tunnel. An instant later I shoot out into the wind, turn straight up the wave's face, and fling myself over it toward the open sea. Spindrift blown from the wave spatters against my back. Surprised, ecstatic, hooting breathlessly, I thank the ocean and the island for this gift. And I wonder, does the sea that bends down across half the earth's surface care that I've flecked its edge and given back the token of a grateful voice? Does it matter, this acknowledgment amid the immensity and power and fecundity of an ocean? I can only trust the rightness of what Koyukon elders teach—that no one is ever alone, unseen, or unheard, and that gratitude kindles the very heat of life.

Looking at the swells as I paddle back out almost equals the exhilaration of riding them. Breaking waves pour against the sandbar, leap and spin like fire as they roll shoreward, then climb the rocks and thunder against the sand. I could spend whole days watching them, and the last would be as hypnotic and fascinating as the first. Each wave is unique, and the surf breaking at every beach or reef has qualities found nowhere else, subtle differences that take much practice even to see. I've never watched breaking surf without also studying it, trying to understand what tricks of tide and reef and wind have shaped. But still, I've only begun to learn. Perhaps there is too much difference between the human mind and the mind of water.

Or perhaps I haven't watched long enough. I think of Koyukon elders, who have spent their lifetimes studying every detail of their natural surroundings, and have combined this with knowledge passed down from generations of elders before them. The more people experience the repetitions of events in nature, the more they see in them and the more they know, but the more they realize the limitations of their understanding. I believe this is why Koyukon people are so humble and self-effacing about their knowledge. And I believe that Koyukon people's extraordinary relationship to their natural community has emerged through this careful watching of the *same* events in the *same* place, endlessly repeated over lifetimes and generations and millennia. There may be more to learn by climbing the same mountain a hundred times than by climbing a hundred different mountains.

For the next hour, I lose myself at play in the breaking waves, ignoring my numb hands and feet, paddling as hard as I can to delay the onset of shivering. At one point a bull sea lion breaks the surface nearby, snorts a few times, and dives. I think little of it, but then three sea lions appear, looming like an apparition in the translucent face of a swell as it begins to break—body surfing underwater. They disappear as the curtain of whitewater falls, and afterward I watch nervously, wondering what might happen next.

Although I'm somewhat prepared, my heart makes a terrific jump when a huge bull sea lion—easily ten feet long and weighing perhaps a ton—rolls up a dozen feet behind me, not the usual way but upside down, with his eyes underwater. I sit high on my board, staring into the blue-green murk, trying to make myself inconspicuous by some act of will, hoping the animal doesn't feel territorial, doesn't have protective urges about the two females, doesn't mistake my dangling legs for a plaything, doesn't feel vengeful because someone tried to shoot him for stealing fish from a net or line. Then I see his shape ghosting toward me. He hovers just under my feet, apparently checking me out, but showing no inclination to be playful or aggressive. After he leaves I consider going ashore, but then glimpse all three of them heading away, perhaps to surf in a less crowded place.

The swells become larger near high tide, and I feel uneasy about staying out alone. Then a series of ponderous waves mounds on the outer shoals. I paddle desperately and manage to escape the first, then plunge into the sheer wall of the second like a harlequin duck, and surface just as it breaks behind me. Looking up at the third, I realize my luck has run out, so I take a deep breath and dive. Caught at the point of impact, I'm pushed down, thrashed around in the frigid, swirling water, and finally released to the surface, gasping for breath. Afterward, I wonder how those little harlequins kept from being torn apart and having every feather plucked from their bodies.

Shortly, an even larger series of swells approaches, but I'm far enough out to catch the biggest one and prudent enough to make it my last. As I wade ashore, I watch the energy of the wave die, rushing to the top of the beach and slipping back down again. And I remember its power rising to a crescendo around and under me during the final moments of its life, after traversing a thousand miles of ocean from its birthplace in a far Pacific storm. The motion that so exalted me was given freely by the wave, as the wave was given motion by the wind, as the wind was given motion by the storm, as the storm was given motion by the whirl of the atmosphere and the turning of the earth itself. Then I remember the sea lions, cradled by the same ocean and pleasured by the same waves. All of us here, partaking of a single motion. Together and alive.

Shungnak's greeting barks and wags are especially welcome after I've surfed this winter place alone. She makes good company when we're on the island together, and she lets me focus my attention on the surroundings without the need for conversation. I always miss Nita and Ethan, and I enjoy the companionship of friends who often come along to explore or surf together. The social part of these experiences is a special pleasure, but they are very different from times when I come only with Shungnak. The desire for company is so strong that it's often tempting to let the solitude in nature slip away. But when I do this, I eventually feel out of balance; my mind clutters with work and personal concerns, and only a good immersion into the island can cleanse it. I come back from the wild places feeling renewed.

When we reach the rivermouth, Shungnak takes one look and realizes her predicament. The tide has risen, and six feet of water cover the place we waded across this morning. So we have two choices: hike several miles back to the shallows in Deer Meadow or swim across right here. Part of Shungnak's sled dog heritage is a strong aversion to water. She cowers in the woods while I put my packful of clothes on the surfboard, then watches dejectedly as I swim across the stream, pushing it ahead of me.

When I paddle back, she knows it's her turn but has no intention of coming along voluntarily. After some struggling and impatient words, I carry her into the water and plant her on the teetering surfboard. She stands straddle-legged, shivering and terrified, and almost capsizes the board several times despite my efforts to keep her calm. Halfway across, I wonder what someone would think who chanced to witness this strange behavior in such an improbable place. Finally we reach shallow water and the reluctant surf-dog slips off. She scrambles ashore, shakes herself, then dashes around on the dry sand, elated. She even sprints out to me again, splashing happily in the water she so dreaded a few minutes ago.

Numb and shaking, I strip to bare skin outside the tent, dry off as quickly as possible, and blissfully experience the genius of human clothing. A brilliant blue Stellar's jay perches in the branches nearby, rasping the chill air with calls, apparently drawn by the spectacle of a creature that takes off one skin and puts on another.

We lavish ourselves with the rich comfort of food and warmth inside the tent after nightfall. Rain drives down through the trees, as they tilt and hiss in a gusty southeaster. I'm truly relieved to be in this tight little pod rather than in the dubious protection of the Deer Meadow cabin. Intensifying surf sets the earth trembling beneath the tent. During the quiet between squalls, heavy droplets thump without rhythm from the high boughs. These two sounds epitomize the twin personalities of water—gentle or powerful, peaceful or tempestuous, life sustaining or life threatening.

The rain envelops me, like a lover breathing in my ear through the black night. My heart finds sanctuary in this love, who will never slip away and leave the dawns empty.

By morning there is scarcely any breeze, but the ocean still rumbles. I peer out in the early light, and through the gaps between tree trunks I can see enormous swells rising along the horizon, first gray, then darker, then black in their hollows, then suddenly white as they break with a force that reverberates through the timber and the shore. I know immediately that the surf is only for watching. It looks like a good day to hike through the forest toward the distant clearcuts.

After breakfast, we walk down the shore in the opposite direction from the one we took yesterday, where there is no river to cross. Cooler air has sunk in behind last night's weather front, and a blue rift has opened amid high escarpments of cloud. For a few minutes, sunshine glistens on the windrows of gray and amber drift logs. Beyond the shore of Roller Bay, Kluksa Mountain is bright with new snow. A huge cornice purls down a thousand feet of fluted ridge beneath its crest. Radiating outward on the lower slopes are corrugated hills patterned with forest and muskeg, descending toward points of black rock that vanish beneath the sea.

We come to a broad pond less than an inch deep, covered with rippled islets of sand floating in the reflection of our surroundings. Standing at its edge, I suddenly feel adrift in midair as I gaze down at the whole sweep of Kluksa Mountain plunging into the earth and reaching toward the subterranean clouds. Then I look up to see the mountain soaring skyward and the clouds hovering high above. I step across an abalone shell at the bottom of the pool, and walk on, feeling like a man who has just been given sight.

We follow the beach until it ends abruptly against a rock-bound shore—cobbled coves separated by pillars and fists of stone, then impassable cliffs with timbered mountainsides above. After picking our way along the rocks just above the surge, we climb to a high, grassy overlook. The whole breadth of Roller Bay is laid out beneath us, like arms opened to embrace the sea. This side of the bay is scalloped into a sequence of three promontories: Black Point the closest in, then Ocean Point, and finally Ragged Point at the bay's outermost edge, five miles away. Towering waves sweep onto the reefs off Ragged Point, throwing off clouds of spindrift and roiling shoreward in bores of whitewater that must be huge to be visible from a distance. Closer at hand, a series of enormous swells moves toward us, ridges twenty feet high, extending across the mile between shores, building higher as the bight narrows and rises into shoals. Each swell bends like an enormous wing, as its middle slides ahead in deeper water and its tips drag behind in the shallows, careening across rocks and raking the cliffs on either side. There is a terrifying inexorability and slowness about these waves, sweeping in from the open sea, rising above the canyons of their own troughs, and making the island tremble with their explosions.

The entire bay is alive with leaping water, scrawled with thick streamers of spume, and stained by patches of half-decayed organic debris scoured up from the depths. An eagle looks down from its perch in a weathered snag on the cliff, then suddenly launches, planes out over the bay, and sets its eye on a glint amid the froth. A hundred yards from shore, its descent steepens, like the down-curved flight of an arrow. The eagle bends its head to look straight below, releases its grasp on the air, swings down its opened talons, and plunges bodily onto the water. For a moment it lies there, wings extended like pontoons. Then, with great effort and flailing, it strokes against the sea and rises, shaking streams from its feathers. A fish the size of a small cod swims helplessly in its grasp and stares uncomprehendingly at its lost element below.

The eagle labors back toward shore, water still trailing from its pinions. It circles at the timber's edge, drops down, then rises to the high bough it has chosen and grasps it with one foot, still holding its prey in the other. The slender treetop sways as the bird settles, shakes its head, ruffles the white feathers of its nape, and stares at the cold, shining fish.

I shrink away into the forest, mindful of the paradox that life sustains itself in the violence of that flensing beak, brought down beneath the closing shadow of wings.

Released from her boredom, Shungnak bounds ahead into the woods, weaving through faint webs of scent, exploring a rich world of odors that scarcely exists for me. We work back along the hillside, through tall timber with a fair undergrowth of blueberry and menziesia bushes. The gales of fall and winter are channeled along this exposed slope, yet the trees are not huddled or bent or gnarled. Apparently the straight-trunked forest creates its own wall and protects itself by shunting storms over its heights. But while the whole community stands, each tree must eventually succumb. A massive trunk blocks our way, sprawled across the ground, its fractured wood still bright and smelling of sap, its boughs green and supple. Because it looks so healthy, I surmise it was thrown down by a contrary gust, perhaps the only one to hit just this way in a hundred years, or five hundred. And I imagine the maelstrom that ripped through the forest as it fell, carrying two others with it and clouding the air with a mass of splintered debris.

Studies of coastal forests like this one reveal that exposure to wind is what most determines the age of trees. Whereas spruce trees in vulnerable stands live an average of two hundred years, those in sheltered, fertile areas like the Deer Meadow valley can live eight or nine hundred years. Yellow cedars, which are better able to resist wind, commonly survive for a thousand years. Small openings created by the fallen trees allow diversified plant communities to grow up, enriching the environment while the surrounding timber remains intact. The biomass in these forests—that is, the combined weight of their living material—is among the highest in the world, greater even than the biomass of tropical rain forests.

Farther on, two fallen giants with an uptorn mass of roots lean against a stone outcrop, half their length projecting over a cliff like bowsprits. They appear to have come down at least twenty or thirty years ago, perhaps even before I was born. Green algae coats the trunks, and the thick, branchless limbs are swaddled with patches of moss. Eventually these sodden hulks will snap and crash down the slope, then rot away to a lump in the forest floor. But they will not disappear until long after my every trace has vanished. Trees decay as slowly as they have lived and grown.

A sluggish stream runs along the base of the hill, with forest impinging closely on either side. We follow the bank looking for a place to cross. After a quarter-mile it opens to a long meadow bordered by alder patches and muskeg. I notice a few signs that plants have already begun to stir. Alder, salmonberry, and red-stemmed blueberry have swollen buds with tiny fissures of embryonic leaves. In the yard at home, some of our domesticated plants are much more adventuresome. The little, drooping snowdrops came up in mid-January and are now in full bloom. A few crocuses have put up blossoms, though most of them only show grassy bladelets. Daffodil sprouts are finger-high; and fleshy red domes show at the base of last year's crumpled rhubarb leaves.

The wild flowers stay dormant and hidden well after our yard is bright with blooming domesticates. Yet our carefully tended plants show no sign of spreading into the thicket beyond. Garden flowers can afford their springtime gambles and flashy moves only as long as we're around to hold back the competition. But someday the house will decay, the walled gardens will crumble, grass and sedge will strangle the flowers' roots, while cow parsnip and salmonberry rise above them. The garden plants have cast their lot with us; if we go, so will they.

As we wade across the stream, I notice the sky has darkened and gray haze has settled against the mountains. Shortly afterward, a mix of drizzle, sleet, and snow begins to fall. But when we slip back beneath the canopy of trees, there are no needling flakes, no icy droplets, and the chilling breeze is gone. I feel enveloped by the soft, wet hands of the forest. Moving in from the edge, I realize this is one of the purest stands of aged spruce and hemlocks I've found on the island. The forest unfolds like a lovely and complex symphony, heard for the first time. It has a dark, baritone richness, tinkled through with river sounds and chickadees. There are almost no shrubs or small trees, just an open maze of huge gray pillars. And everything is covered with a deep blanket of moss that mounds up over decaying stumps and fallen trunks like a shroud laid atop the furnishings in a great hall.

There must be few wetter places on earth. My rubber boots glisten each time I lift them from the swollen sponge underfoot. Stepping over a mossy windfall, I press my knees against it and instantly feel the water soak through. When I call Shungnak, the feathers of plushy moss deaden my voice, as if we were in a soundproof room.

The sense of *life* in this temperate jungle is as pervasive and palpable as its wetness. Even the air seems organic—rich and pungent like the moss itself. I breathe life into my lungs, feel life against my skin, move through a thick, primordial ooze of life, like a Paleozoic lungfish paddling up to gasp mouthfuls of air.

It seems that the rocks beneath this forest should lie under a thousand feet of soaked and decaying mulch. But the roots of a recently toppled spruce clutch small boulders torn up from only a foot or two below the moss. What has become of the trunks and boughs and branches that have fallen onto this earth for thousands of years? And the little showers of needles that have shaken down with every gust of wind for millennia? Digested by the forest itself, and dissolved into the tea-colored streams that run toward the island's shore. The thought makes me feel that I truly belong here—that I, too, hold membership in this community—because all of us share the same fate.

Looking carefully, I pick out the shapes of many fallen trees and their root masses. They are nearly hidden by robes of moss that reduce them to hillocks, and by the camouflage of trees that have grown up on top of them. Tendrils of living roots wind down through the lattice of older, decaying roots, straddle broken stumps, and wrap over prostrate trunks. Sometimes four or five large trees grow in a straight line, each supported by an elevated, empty cagework of roots. These roots once enclosed a fallen mother tree which has completely vanished. The whole impression is of a forest on contorted stilts, sheathed in moss, climbing up over its own decay, breathing and wet and alive.

Only a few raindrops and oversized snowflakes sift through the crown of trees as a squall passes over. I'm grateful for the shelter, and I sense a deeper kind of comfort here. These are living things I move among, immeasurably older and larger and more deeply affixed to their place on earth than I am, and imbued with vast experience of a kind entirely beyond my comprehension. I feel like a miniscule upstart in their presence, a supplicant awaiting the quiet counsel of venerable trees.

I've often thought of the forest as a living cathedral, but this might diminish what it truly is. If I have understood Koyukon teachings, the forest is not merely an expression or representation of sacredness, nor a place to invoke the sacred; the forest is sacredness itself. Nature is not merely created by God; nature *is* God. Whoever moves within the forest can partake directly of sacredness, experience sacredness with his entire body, breathe sacredness and contain it within himself, drink the sacred water as a living communion, bury his feet in sacredness, touch the living branch and feel the sacredness, open his eyes and witness the burning beauty of sacredness. And when he cuts a tree from the forest, he participates in a sacred interchange that brings separate lives together.

The dark boughs reach out above me and encircle me like arms. I feel the assurance of being recognized, as if something powerful and protective is aware of my presence, looks in another direction but always has me in the corner of its eye. I am cautious and self-protective here, as anywhere, yet I believe that a covenant of mutual regard and responsibility binds me together with the forest. We share in a common nurturing. Each of us serves as an amulet to protect the other from inordinate harm. I am never alone in this wild forest, this forest of elders, this forest of eyes.

After a long hike, taking the easy routes of deer trails, we move into a stand of shore pine that ends beside a half-overgrown logging road. This is the first sign of human activity since we left camp, and it indicates we're approaching the clearcut valley. The road follows a narrow bank of muskeg that has all the delicate loveliness of a Japanese garden, with reflecting ponds and twisted pines in bonsai shapes. Farther on, it cuts through an alder thicket and runs up a steep, forested slope. A dense flock of birds sprays into the high trees, twittering like canaries, hundreds of them, agitated and nervous, moving so quickly they're difficult to hold for long in the binoculars.

The birds are everywhere, hanging upside down from the twigs and working furiously on spruce cones. Each one plucks and twists at its cone, shaking loose the thin scales and letting them fall. The air is filled with a flutter of brown scales. I recognize the sparrow-sized pine siskins immediately, then identify the larger birds as white-winged crossbills. I've never had a good look at a crossbill before, but the hillside roadway gives an easy view into the tree crowns, where bright red males and olive females swarm through the boughs. With some patience, I can discern the tips of their beaks, which crisscross instead of fitting together like an ordinary bird's. This allows the crossbill to pry the scales apart and insert its tongue to extract seeds embedded deep within. Once again, I'm reminded that tropical animals aren't the only ones who have added a little adventure to their evolution. Suddenly the whole flock spills out from the trees and disappears, like bees following their queen.

After another half-mile, a slot appears in the road ahead. As we approach, it widens to a gateway out of the forest—a sudden, shorn edge where the trees and moss end, and where the dark, dour sky slumps down against a barren hillside strewn with slash and decay. Oversized snowflakes blotch against my face and neck, and the breeze chills through me. I look ahead, then look back toward the trees, breathless and anxious, almost wishing I hadn't come. It's the same foreboding I sometimes feel in the depths of sleep, when a blissful dream slowly degenerates into a nightmare; I am carried helplessly along, dimly hoping it's only a dream, but unable to awaken myself and escape.

The road angles into a wasteland of hoary trunks and twisted wooden shards, pitched together in convulsed disarray, with knots of shoulder-high brush pressing in along both sides. Fans of mud and ash splay across the roadway beneath rilled cutbanks. In one place, the lower side has slumped away and left ten feet of culvert hanging in midair, spewing brown water over the naked bank and into a runnel thirty feet below.

A tall snag clawed with dead branches stands atop the hill. I decide to hike up toward it rather than walk farther along the road. At first, it's a relief to be in the brush, where I can touch something alive, and where my attention is focused on the next footstep rather than the surrounding view. But thirty yards into it, I realize that moving through a clearcut is unlike anything I've ever tried before. The ground is covered with a nearly impenetrable confusion of branches, roots, sticks, limbs, stumps, blocks, poles, and trunks, in every possible size, all gray and fibrous and rotting, thrown together in a chaotic mass and interwoven with a tangle of brittle bushes.

An astonishing amount of wood was left here to decay, including whole trees, hundreds of them in this one clearcut alone. Some flaw must have made them unusable even for pulp, but they were felled nonetheless, apparently so the others would be easier to drag out. Not a single living tree above sapling size stands in the thirty or forty acres around me.

I creep over the slippery trunks and crawl beneath them, slip and stumble across gridworks of slash, and worm through close-growing salmonberry, menziesia, and huckleberry. Even Shungnak struggles with her footing, but she gets around far better than I do, moving like a weasel through a maze of small holes and tunnels. I can tell where she is by the noise she makes in the brush, but only see her when she comes to my whistle. In some places I walk along huge, bridging trunks, but they're slick and perilous, and I risk falling onto a deadly skewer of wood below. I save myself from one misstep by grabbing the nearest branch, which turns out to be devil's club, festooned with spines that would do credit to any cactus. We also cross dozens of little washes that run over beds of coarse ash and gravel. There are no mossy banks, no spongy seeps, just water on bare earth. By the time we near the top I am strained, sweating, sore, frustrated, and exhausted. It has taken almost an hour to cross a few hundred yards of this crippled land.

I've heard no sound except my own unhappy voice since we entered the clearcut, but now a winter wren's song pours up from a nearby patch of young alders. I usually love to hear wrens, especially during the silence of winter. But in this topsy-turvy place the reedy, contorted phrases, rattling against the beaten hill, seem like angry words in some bewildering foreign tongue. I picture a small, brown-skinned man, shaking his fist at the sky from the edge of a bombed and cratered field.

A large stump raised six feet above the ground on buttressed roots offers a good lookout. The man who felled this tree cut two deep notches in its base, which I use to clamber on top. It's about five feet in diameter and nearly flat, except for a straight ridge across the center where the cutter left hinge wood to direct the tree's fall. The surface is soggy and checked, but still ridged with concentric growth rings. On hands and knees, nose almost touching the wood, using my knife blade as a pointer, I start to count. In a short while, I know the tree died in its four hundred and twenty-third year.

I stand to see the whole forest of stumps. It looks like an enormous graveyard, covered with weathered markers made from the remains of its own dead. Along the slope nearby is a straight line of four stumps lifted on convoluted roots, like severed hands still clasping a nearly vanished mother log. Many of the surrounding stumps are smaller than my platform, but others are as large or larger. A gathering of ancients once stood here. Now it reminds me of a prairie in the last century, strewn with the bleached bones of buffalo. Crowded around the clearcut's edges are tall trees that seem to press forward like curious, bewildered gawkers.

Two centuries ago, it would have taken the Native people who lived here several days to fell a tree like this one, and weeks or months to wedge it into planks. Earlier in this century, the hand-loggers could pull their huge crosscut saws through it in a couple of hours. But like the Native Americans before, they selected only the best trees and left the others. Now I gaze into a valley miles deep, laid bare to its high slopes, with only patches of living timber left between the clearcut swaths.

Where I stand now, a great tree once grew. The circles that mark the centuries of its life surround me, and I dream back through them. It's difficult to imagine the beginnings—perhaps a seed that fell from a flurry of crossbills like those I saw a while ago. More difficult still is the incomprehensible distance of time this tree crossed, as it grew from a limber switch on the forest floor to a tree perhaps 150 feet tall and weighing dozens of tons. Another way to measure the scope of its life is in terms of storms. Each year scores of them swept down this valley—thousands of boiling gales and blizzards in the tree's lifetime—and it withstood them all.

The man who walked up beside it some twenty years ago would have seemed no more significant than a puff of air on a summer afternoon.

Perhaps thin shafts of light shone down onto the forest floor that day, and danced on the velvet moss. I wonder what that man might have thought, as he looked into the tree's heights and prepared to bring it down. Perhaps he thought only about the job at hand, or his aching back, or how long it was until lunch. I would like to believe he gave some consideration to the tree itself, to its death and his responsibilities toward it, as he pulled the cord that set his chainsaw blaring.

The great, severed tree cut an arc across the sky and thundered down through its neighbors, sending a quake deep into the earth and a roar up against the valley walls. And while the tree was limbed and bucked, dozens of other men worked along the clearcut's advancing front, as a steady stream of trucks hauled the logs away.

A Koyukon man named Joe Stevens once took me with him to cut birch for a dog sled and snowshoes. Each time we found a tall, straight tree with clear bark, he made a vertical slice in the trunk and pulled out a thin strip of wood to check the straightness of its grain. When we finally came across a tree he wanted to cut, Joe said, "I don't care how smart a guy is, or how much he knows about birch. If he acts the wrong way—he treats his birch like it's nothing—after that he can walk right by a good tree and wouldn't see it." Later on, he showed me several giant, old birches with narrow scars on their trunks, where someone had checked the grain many years ago. In the same stand, he pointed out a stump that had been felled with an ax, and explained that Chief Abraham used to get birch here before the river made a new channel and left his fish camp on a dry slough.

Joe and I bucked the tree into logs and loaded them on a sled, then hauled them to the village and took them inside his house. It was important to peel the bark in a warm place, he said, because the tree still had life and awareness in it. Stripping the log outside would expose its nakedness to the winter cold and offend its spirit. The next day, he took the logs out and buried them under the snow, where they would be sheltered until he could split them into lumber. Later on, when Joe carved pieces of the birch to make snowshoe frames, I tried to help by putting the shavings in a fire. His urgent voice stopped me: "Old-timers say we shouldn't burn snowshoe shavings. We put those back in the woods, away from any trails, where nobody will bother them. If we do that, we'll be able to find good birch again next time."

The clearcut valley rumbled like an industrial city through a full decade of summers, as the island's living flesh was stripped away. Tugs pulled great rafts of logs from Deadfall Bay, through tide-slick channels toward the mill, where they were ground into pulp and slurried aboard ships bound for Japan. Within a few months, the tree that took four centuries to grow was transformed into newspapers, read by commuters on afternoon trains, and then tossed away.

I think of the men who worked here, walking down this hill at the day's end, heading home to their families in the camp beside Deadfall Bay. I could judge them harshly indeed, and think myself closer to the image of Joe Stevens; but that would be a mistake. The loggers were people just like me, not henchmen soldiers in a rebel army, their pockets filled with human souvenirs. They probably loved working in the woods and found their greatest pleasures in the outdoors. I once had a neighbor who was a logger all his life, worked in these very clearcuts, and lost most of his hearing to the chainsaw's roar. He was as fine a man as I could hope to meet. And he lived by the conscience of Western culture—that the forest is here for the taking, in whatever way humanity sees fit.

The decaying stump is now a witness stand, where I pass judgment on myself. I hold few convictions so deeply as my belief that a profound transgression was committed here, by devastating an entire forest rather than taking from it selectively and in moderation. Yet whatever judgment I might make against those who cut it down I must also make against myself. I belong to the same nation, speak the same language, vote in the same elections, share many of the same values, avail myself of the same technology, and owe much of my existence to the same vast system of global exchange. There is no refuge in blaming only the loggers or their industry or the government that consigned this forest to them. The entire society—one in which I take active membership—holds responsibility for laying this valley bare.

The most I can do is strive toward a different kind of conscience, listen to an older and more tested wisdom, participate minimally in a system that debases its own sustaining environment, work toward a different future, and hope that someday all will be pardoned.

A familiar voice speaks agreement. I squint up into the sleet as a black specter turns and soars above, head cocked to examine me. A crack of light shows through his opened beak; his throat fluffs out with each croak; downy feathers on his back lift in the wind; an ominous hiss arises from his indigo wings. Grandfather Raven surveys what remains of his creation, and I am the last human alive. I half expect him to spiral down, land beside me, and proclaim my fate. But he drifts away and disappears beyond the mountainside, still only keeping watch, patient, waiting.

I try to take encouragement from the ten-foot hemlock and spruce saplings scattered across the hillside. Interestingly, no tender young have taken root atop the flat stumps and mossless trunks. Some of the fast-growing alders are twenty feet tall, but in winter they add to the feeling of barrenness and death. Their thin, crooked branches scratch against the darkened clouds and rattle in the wind. The whole landscape is like a cooling corpse, with new life struggling up between its fingers. If I live a long time, I might see this hillside covered with the beginnings of a new forest. Left alone for a few centuries, the trees would form a high canopy with scattered openings. Protected from the deep snows of open country, deer would again survive the pinch of winter by retreating into the forest. The whole community of dispossessed animals would return: red squirrel, marten, great horned owl, hairy woodpecker, golden-crowned kinglet, pine siskin, blue grouse, and the seed-shedding crossbills. In streams cleared of sediment by moss-filtered runoff, swarms of salmon would spawn once more, hunted by brown bears who emerged from the cool woods.

There is comfort in knowing another giant tree could replace the one that stood here, even though it would take centuries of unfettered growth. I wish I could sink down into the earth and wait, listen for the bird voices to awaken me, rise from beneath the moss, and find myself sheltered by resplendent boughs. And in this world beyond imagination, such inordinate excesses toward nature will have become unthinkable.

Shungnak looks at me, whines, and wags her tail, asking if we can leave; so I climb down and struggle along behind her. She leads us up over the hilltop, unwilling to retrace the tangled route that got us here. A short while later we step from the last rakers of the brush onto the glorious openness of gravel roadway. This might be the only time I ever feel so pleased to be on a logging road in the middle of a clearcut. Our other luck is a temporary reprieve from the mixed rain and snow. The clouds brighten above a spectacular view of the island's outermost shore. I pull the binoculars from inside my jacket and vow to ignore the foreground.

Across the breach of Roller Bay, Ocean Point and Ragged Point stretch out beyond the flanks of Kluksa Mountain. For the past year, I've dreamed of riding into the bight between those forelands and anchoring the skiff behind a reef shown on navigation charts. Ragged Point is as plainly visible as the moon on a cloudless night and just as untouchable. I memorize every detail of the shore, reaching for whatever knowledge I can find. It's clear that the two promontories are totally exposed to the full weight of storm winds, thrashing seas, and whatever else threatens a small boat on this open coast.

The anchorage behind Ragged Point is thirty miles from home, in stages of increasingly exposed water and diminishing access to help or shelter. Sometimes I wonder what lunatic cravings incite my desire to visit such places. More than anything else, their remoteness is what possesses me, the thought of reaching a nearly inaccessible shore and experiencing the purity of its wildness. Right now the swells are so huge I can't imagine how a skiff could survive in any anchorage along that stretch of coast. My only chance to stand ashore at Ragged Point is to wait for calm summer weather.

Looking along the island's outer flank helps to take my mind off the devastation close at hand. On the coast from Ocean Point to Cape Deception, and from there to Tsandaku Point, the forest and shore remain as they were when the first square sail rose up from beneath the horizon. Sometimes I feel like a survivor from that age, a figure on a faded tintype, standing in a long-vanished, pristine world. I read my scrawled island notebooks as if they've been discovered in someone's attic, recollections of a lost way of life. It creates a strange feeling of self-envy and romance, and makes me live this miracle all the more intensely.

Kluksa Mountain climbs away to its vanishing point amid the clouds. Spatters of sleet flick against my face. As I stare out across the ocean, a deep yearning wells up inside, a sadness for what is lost, mixed with gratitude for the wildness that remains, for being alive to experience it, and for the blessed gift of eyes.

The shadowed forest lofts over us, surrounds and shields us, smoothes a way for us, and leads us gently back into itself. We hurry toward camp, amid the slow breathing out of dusk. Hard exercise drives away the chill and cleans out the residue from too much thinking. Shungnak paces beside me, ignoring the temptations of squirrel sounds and beckoning scents.

An hour later we reach camp. It feels cold and clammy inside the tent, but the little stove quickly changes that. I savor a hot cup of tea and share a piece of last fall's smoked salmon with Shungnak, then unwrap a slice of venison for tonight's dinner. While it cooks, I relax on my sleeping bag, thinking of Nita and Ethan at work in our warm kitchen, lights from the front window glowing out across the bay. Then I listen to the steady throb of surf that resonates through the trees, and the chatter of raindrops on the tent wall. My heart is torn between the island and home. Born into a culture that keeps the worlds of humanity and nature apart, I am always close to one love but longing for another.

The candle has burned down to a mound of hardened wax. As I stare into the flame, my thoughts sift back through the day. First to the mountainous surf, marching in from the Pacific to disgorge itself against the shore. And to the high pleasures of exploring a part of the island I've never seen before. Then the moss forest, nurturing itself on the remains of its own dead and fallen. All the past generations of trees are here, alive in the bodies of those now standing. And perhaps alive in some communality of spirit that stretches back to the forest's beginning and permeates all who come into it.

I think next of the clearcut and the gray, lichened stump, remnant of a great tree whose body was taken away and lost to whatever future generations might arise there. For thousands of years, the Native American people also cut trees from this forest, but whatever they used remained here. Generations of houses and canoes, ceremonial poles and paddles, spear shafts and lost arrows rotted back into the place they came from, just as Joe Stevens's sled and snowshoes and whittled shavings will do in my own lifetime. A tree used in that way is little different from one thrown down in a storm: its own land will have it back, spirit and body, still rooted within its place on earth.

And what of rootedness in death among humans? I was raised to believe that the souls of people who have lived well are given the reward of heaven, far removed from the place that nurtured them in life, distant even from the earth itself. And those who commit evil are threatened with the punishment of hell—to spend eternity deep inside the body of the earth.

When I asked Koyukon people about death, they said a person's spirit is reluctant to leave the company of friends and family, so for a time it lingers near them. The spirits of virtuous people eventually wander along an easy trail to the afterlife, in a good place on the Koyukon homeland. Those who have lived badly follow a long trail of hardship and suffering, but they finally arrive among the others. The dead sustain themselves as hunters and mingle through the spirit world of nature, eternally rooted to their place on earth.

The candle's wick topples and drowns. Perfect blackness releases me into the free and boundless night, to roam in dreams through an everlasting, untrammeled forest; a forest that gives me breath and shelters me; a spirit forest; a forest that envelops me with shining, consecrated webs and binds me here forever.

Jeff DeBonis

Thinking Globally

The environmental problems, frustrations, and issues facing us today on national forests are only a microcosm of the issues facing the entire nation, which again is a microcosm of world-wide issues. The absolute bottom line for all of these concerns is that our northern industrial societies are *not* sustainable, not by any measure of the word. Our population growth is not sustainable; our energy consumption is not sustainable; our agricultural practices are not sustainable; and our forestry practices (based on the flawed industrial, agricultural model) are not sustainable. The local, regional, national, and global struggles boil down to this: How do we become a sustainable society, a sustainable species?

After hearing about the tremendous global environmental issues that face us, many people have told me that the situation seems hopeless—the problems so big, the corporate multinationals so strong. And it is true that no individual can stop the destruction of the Amazon rain forest or clean up the Volga River in Russia (a river in which 50 percent of the flow is composed of sewage and petrochemicals). But we *can* have an influence locally. We, as individuals, can assess our areas of influence or impact, devise a strategy for action, and become part of the solution.

The Association of Forest Service Employees for Environmental Ethics (AFSEEE) has a large impact on the Forest Service. We are exercising a strategy to push the agency toward environmentally sound management. Each individual can do a similar thing. If you are a banker, a teacher, a resource manager, or a homemaker, you can have an impact on moving the world toward a sustainable society.

Together, our individual influences will synergize into a force that will cause a paradigm shift. Only then will we change the current course of planetary destruction. Knowing the global context in which we operate (although it's "depressing") will further motivate us with the urgency and energy needed to prod us into action locally. It will be these collective individual actions that will affect the paradigm shift.

It's time to challenge the paradigm by asking the right questions. Rather than asking: How much pollution can we dump into our biosphere before we all die of cancer?, let's ask the questions: How can we do *without* pesticides? How can we do *without* products that can't be made without causing toxic wastes? How can we do *without* products that cannot be recycled entirely?

Instead of wrestling with the question: How will we fill our *demand* for wood products in the U.S. *and* practice New Forestry, preserve some ancient forests and, perhaps, let the multinational timber companies fill the northern countries' demands by going to the Third World? *Instead,* we should be asking the question: How are we going to responsibly *control* the multinationals, *limit* demand, recycle, and do with *less?*

Foresters have long known about the grave threats that face the world's temperate, tropical, and boreal forests, about the threats to the biological and cultural diversity of forest dwellers. But our post-industrial society has yet to learn from the lessons of the past—from the questions concerned people asked then and ask now. Let's go even one step further than asking the right questions and receiving the grave answers: Let's *really learn* from the past, and from the present, from our ever dwindling prospects for future generations. Let's take action.

The time to change our paradigm is now. The time to get involved is now. The time to *live* your life in a fashion sustainable to the rest of the planet is now. We can wait no longer.

Edward Abbey was born in Home, Pennsylvania, in 1927. He is the author of several books, including *Desert Solitaire: A Season in the Wilderness* (Simon & Schuster, 1990), *Down the River (with Henry Thoreau & Other Friends)* (NAL-Dutton, 1982), and *Fire on the Mountain* (University of New Mexico Press, 1977). He died at his home in Oracle, Arizona, in 1989.

Jody Aliesan (Al-*ee*-es-ahn) was born in the midwest and lived in three corners of the continental U.S. before finding home in Puget Sound country in 1970. She has earned her living as an editor, press representative for an antiwar organization, researcher, co-director of a women's center, street singer, produce worker and packager at a food co-operative, environmental columnist, coordinator of a Braille project, substitute postmaster, agricultural laborer, office worker, and teacher. She is the author of five books of poetry, including *Grief Sweat* (Broken Moon Press, 1991), *Desire* (Empty Bowl, 1985), and *as if it will matter* (Seal Press, 1978). She thanks David Howard, who read the essay for factual accuracy, and Steve Koenig, who made possible a flight with Michael Stewartt and Lighthawk over what's left of the Olympic National Forest.

Catherine Caufield lives in San Francisco, California, where she works as a journalist. Her articles have appeared in many magazines and journals, including *New Scientist, The Guardian, New Statesman, The New Yorker,* and *The International Herald Tribune.* She is the author of *Multiple Exposures: Chronicles of the Radiation Age* (University of Chicago Press, 1990) and *In the Rainforest: Report from a Strange, Beautiful, Imperiled World* (University of Chicago Press, 1984).

John Daniel was born in South Carolina and grew up in Washington, D.C. He now lives in Portland, Oregon, where he works as the poetry editor for *Wilderness* magazine. He also occasionally teaches at the Northwest Writing Institute of Lewis & Clark College. In 1982 he received a Wallace Stegner Fellowship in Poetry at Stanford University. He then taught and lectured in creative writing and composition at Stanford for five years. His books include a collection of essays, *The Trail Home* (Pantheon Books, 1992), and a book of poems, *Common Ground* (Confluence Press, 1988).

Jeff DeBonis worked for the U.S. Forest Service for twelve years as a timber sale planner. He is the founder and currently serves as the executive director of the Association of Forest Service Employees for Environmental Ethics. (AFSEE can reached at P.O. Box 11615, Eugene, Oregon 97440.) He currently lives in Eugene, Oregon.

John Ellison lives in Seattle, Washington, where he is co-publisher, along with Lesley Link, of Broken Moon Press. He also serves as Broken Moon's poetry and non-fiction editor. Since 1986 he has also been a technical editor working in the microcomputer industry, and currently works on documentation related to multimedia software. Broken Moon Press publishes ten titles per year, including poetry, essays, fiction, and nonfiction. Several of Broken Moon Press's books and authors have won national design and literary awards, including the Governor's Writer's Award in Washington State, the American Book Award, the Harold Morton Landon Translation Award from the Academy of American Poets, the Bumbershoot/Weyerhaeuser Publication Award, and the Western States Book Award for Fiction.

Edward C. Fritz lives in Dallas, Texas, and works as the coordinator of the Forest Reform Network. He has won several conservation awards, including the Feinstone Award. He served as an attorney in the red-cockaded woodpecker endangered species case, and he is a proponent of citizen participation to strengthen democracy. He is the author of several books on forest issues, including *Clearcutting: A Crime Against Nature* (Eakin Press, 1989) and *Realms of Beauty: The Wilderness Areas of East Texas* (University of Texas Press, 1986).

Michael Frome lives in Bellingham, Washington, and has worked as a journalist, travel writer, activist, and educator. He is the Environmental Journalist-in-Residence at Huxley College of Environmental Studies, a division of Western Washington University. His writings have addressed a wide range of social topics, including pacifism, education, social justice, ethics, forestry, and freedom of expression. He is the author of several books on environmental issues, including *Conscience of a Conservationist* (University of Tennessee Press, 1989).

Reginald Gibbons is the editor of *TriQuarterly* magazine and teaches at Northwestern University and in the MFA program at Warren Wilson College. He is the author several books, including poems, *Maybe It Was So* (University of Chicago Press, 1991), which won the 1992 Carl Sandburg Award, and stories, *Five Pears or Peaches* (Broken Moon Press, 1991). He also edited *New Writing from Mexico: A TriQuarterly Collection of Newly Translated Prose and Poetry* (TriQuarterly Books, 1992).

Art Goodtimes is a performance poet and activist who lives in Norwood, Colorado. He has performed his works at Headwaters II at Western State College in Gunnison, Colorado, the First Inaugural Performing Arts Festival at the Denver Performing Arts Complex, and the Ah-Haa School of Book & Story Arts in Telluride, Colorado, where he teaches creative writing. He is a former editor and is currently a staff writer and columnist for the *Telluride Times-Journal.* He is a co-founder of the Sheep Mountain Alliance and the San Miguel Greens. He is the author of several books, including *Mushroom Cloud Redeye* (Western Eye Press, 1990), *Slow Rising Smoke* (Blackberry Books, 1987), and *Dancing on the Brink of the World* (Sleeping Gypsy Press, 1980).

Christopher Harris is a writer and photographer who lives with his family in Redmond, Washington. His poetry and essays have appeared in several periodicals, including *Small Moon, Renascence, Southern Literary Journal,* and the *New York Times.* Some of his photographs of clearcuts recently appeared in the magazine *Left Bank #2.* He is currently working on a photo essay of the homeless in Seattle, Washington.

Peter Levitt lives in the Santa Monica Mountains and is a poet, translator, essayist, meditator in the Zen tradition, and a member of the community at Sonoma Mountain Zen Center. He has received numerous honors and awards for his poetry, including a Lannan Foundation Literary Fellowship in 1989. He has taught poetry workshops privately and at UCLA Extension Writer's Program for over fifteen years. He is the author of several books, including *One Hundred Butterflies* (Broken Moon Press, 1992), and *Bright Root, Dark Root* (Broken Moon Press, 1991).

Peter Matthiessen was born in New York City in 1927. In 1950, he graduated from Yale University and the following year was one of the founders of *The Paris Review.* A widely acclaimed novelist, naturalist, and explorer, he has received numerous awards for his writing, both for his fiction and nonfiction. He has twice been a finalist for the National Book Award for his books *At Play in the Fields of the Lord* (Vintage Books, 1991) and *The Tree Where Man Was Born* (with Eliot Porter, NAL-Dutton, 1983). In 1978 he won the National Book Award for *The Snow Leopard* (Viking Penguin, 1987). Other books include *African Silences* (Random House, 1991), *Nine-Headed Dragon River: Zen Journals 1969–1982* (Shambhala Publications, 1987), and *The Cloud Forest: A Chronicle of South American Wilderness* (Viking Penguin, 1987).

Gregory McNamee lives in Tucson, Arizona, and works as a writer and editor. He is the book columnist for *Outside* magazine and a regular contributor to several periodicals. He is the author of several books, including *Christ on the Mount of Olives* (Broken Moon Press, 1991), *The Return of Richard Nixon* (Harbinger House, 1990), and *Inconstant History* (Broken Moon Press, 1990). He is also the co-editor, with James Hepworth, of *Resist Much, Obey Little: Some Notes on Edward Abbey* (Harbinger House, 1989), editor of *Living in Words: Interviews from* The Bloomsbury Review, *1981–1988* (Breitenbush Books, 1988), and translator of Sophokles's tragedy *Philoktetes* (Copper Canyon Press, 1987).

Tim McNulty is a poet, conservationist, and nature writer who lives with his family in the northern foothill country of Washington State's Olympic Peninsula. His poems have been published widely in the U.S. and Canada, and his nature writings have been translated into German and Japanese. His articles on natural history and conservation issues have appeared in numerous magazines and journals, and he remains active in Northwest environmental issues. He is the author of several books of poetry, including *In Blue Mountain Dusk* (Broken Moon Press, 1992), and he has written several books on natural history, including *Washington's Wild Rivers: The Unfinished Work* (with Pat O'Hara, Mountaineers, 1990). He has also written an award-winning series of books on national parks, co-authored with photographer Pat O'Hara.

W.S. Merwin was born in New York City in 1927 and has lived in several countries around the world, including Spain, England, Mexico, France, and Portugal. He currently lives and works in Hawaii. A distinguished poet, translator, and essayist who has been a frequent contributor to *The Nation,* he has received many honors for his writing through the years, including the Pulitzer Prize in 1970 for *The Carrier of Ladders* (Atheneum, 1970). In 1974 he was awarded The Fellowship of the Academy of American Poets, and in 1987, he received the Governor's Award for Literature of the State of Hawaii. He is the author of several collections of poetry and prose, including *Selected Poems* (Atheneum, 1988), *The Rain in the Trees* (Knopf, 1988), and *Selected Translations 1948–1968* (Atheneum, 1968), which won the P.E.N. Translation Prize in 1968.